Taking Flight

Christopher Watkins
Stephen Marenka

M&T Books
A Division of MIS:Press
A Subsidiary of Henry Holt and Company, Inc.
115 West 18th Street
New York, New York 10011

Library of Congress Cataloging-in-Publication Data

Watkins, Christopher.
    Taking flight: history, fundamentals, and applications of flight simulation / Christopher Watkins & Stephen Marenka.
        p. cm.
    Includes bibliographical references and index.
    ISBN 1–55851–384–1 : $29.95
        1. Flight simulators — History. I. Marenka, Stephen. II. Title.
    TL712.5.W38   1994
    629.132'52'0113—dc20   94–22464
                                                                          CIP

97   96   95   94   4 3 2 1

Publisher: Brenda McLaughlin
Development Editor: Laura Lewin
Technical Editor: Vincent Mallette
Copy Editor: Vicky Stevens
Production Editor: Eileen Mullin
Associate Production Editor: Cari Geffner

Table of Contents

Section III—The Fundamentals of Flight Simulators   75

Acknowledgments

The outline for this book was generated by Christopher D. Watkins and Stephen R. Marenka. The technical text was written by Christopher D. Watkins, and the writing of the general text was done primarily by Stephen R. Marenka. Vincent Mallette of the Georgia Institute of Technology made contribution to the human perception section of the book. The graphics engine and application software found with this book was written by Christopher D. Watkins. Vincent Mallette acted as technical/copy editor for the book.

All of the software in this book was written in C using Borland C++ version 3.1. The Borland C++ software was furnished by Borland International, 1800 Green Hills Road, Scotts Valley, CA 95066.

Thanks also to WATCOM of 415 Phillip Street, Ontario, Canada, N2L 3X2 for supplying the WATCOM compiler version 9.5.

Thanks go to Keith Blanton for his ideas about flight simulation systems, light points, and where to go and find information.

Thanks go to director Michael Sinclair of the Georgia Institute of Technology Multimedia Technology Laboratory for his help in obtaining information on simulation.

Thanks go to Paul Kingston, Peter Sherlock William Martin, and Schelly Weedman of IVEX Corporation for information and images regarding the IVEX Visual System for Flight Simulation. IVEX Corporation designs, manufactures and markets a series of high performance visual simulation systems for use in civil and military training markets. Their systems distinguish themselves from others in that the overall reality of the visual scene is greater. This "reality" is primarily achieved using fractal texturing methods and high polygon counts for detail. IVEX Corporation is located at 4355 International Blvd., Norcross, Georgia 30093.

Thanks go to director James D. Foley, Larry Hodges and Tom Meyer of the Georgia Institute of Technology College of Computing Graphics,

Visualization & Usability (GVU) Center for their information on virtual reality systems and simulation research.

Thanks go to Ken Welton and Michael Glaser of Lavista Systems, Inc., Tucker, Georgia for supplying equipment necessary for the completion of this book.

Thanks to Jordan Hargrave for supplying us the BGI graphics drivers found along with our software. The drivers are copyright Jordan Hargrave.

Thanks to Jack Brady of Southeastern Digital Images, Inc. and C/Food Software, Atlanta, for acting as a sounding board for ideas. *Buy his scanner drivers and film recorder drivers for the SGI* (subliminal message).

Thanks go to Jack Tumblin for his ideas about flight simulation systems and where to find information.

Thanks go to Ed Boothe who is a well-respected consultant to the airline industry regarding flight simulation and training systems for his ideas about flight simulation systems.

Thanks go to Stephen B. Coy for his help obtaining information on algorithms for polygon-generation and filling.

A special thanks goes to Christopher Laurel for his assistance with the 3-D 6-degrees-of-freedom fixed-point texture-mapping code, while in a time crunch…he develops real-time 3-D graphics for microcomputers.

Algorithm, Inc. of 3776 Lavista Road, Suite 100A, Atlanta, Georgia 30084 produces tools for ray tracing, volume rendering, 3-D modeling and VR, animation, image processing and interactive image warping and morphing. Contact us at the above address or call/fax (404) 634-0920 for more information regarding our products.

And special thanks again go to our parents, wives and friends for their patience with us during this project. It's nice to know that we actually have friends after it, well I guess it's nice to know that we have friends at all — te he he.

And once again, a most grand thanks to the Coca-Cola Company and to the Jolt Cola Company for providing cola and to Snapple for providing tea to keep us awake long enough to complete this project.

About the Authors

Christopher D. Watkins is founder and president of *Algorithm, Inc.*, an Atlanta-based scientific research and engineering company that produces software for medical imaging and visualization, photorealistic rendering, virtual reality, and animation. His latest focus is bringing large companies and individuals on-line to the Internet—look for *The Internet Edge* (Academic Press, 1994). He is an electrical engineer, an experienced programmer, and coauthor of *Photorealism and Ray Tracing in C* (M&T Books, 1992) and *Virtual Reality ExCursions* (Academic Press, 1994). He received his degrees from The Georgia Institute of Technology and is a member of the IEEE Computer Graphics Society and of the ACM/SIGGRAPH.

Stephen R. Marenka is an electrical engineer from the Georgia Institute of Technology, specializing in intelligent control, data reduction techniques, and human-computer interfaces for multiplatform computing (VAX/VMS, Unix, Macintosh, and PC systems). He is working on his MS in electrical engineering control systems. He is also a coauthor of *Virtual Reality ExCursions* (Academic Press, 1994) and *The Internet Edge* (Academic Press, 1994) and is a member of the IEEE Control Systems and Computer Societies and of the ACM/SIGGRAPH.

INTRODUCTION

Welcome to Taking Flight

The modern age of flight simulation is generally dated to the work of Edwin Link whose first patent was granted in 1930. In those days and continuing through World War II, flight simulators consisted of little more than a cockpit with a seat and a control stick. Movement of the control stick would produce corresponding movement in the orientation of the cockpit (for example, if you pulled back on the stick, the "nose" of the craft would raise somewhat). Most of us are more familiar with a different type of flight simulation—paper airplanes, the construction and flight of which provided many of us with an introduction to aerodynamics. Many airplane designs, subject to the quality of construction, had certain advantages over others. The need for a design to carry heavy cargo is a different goal than building for speed, maneuverability, or efficiency. In short, a Boeing 747 carries people better than an F-15 does, but performs somewhat poorer in a dogfight, and I'd prefer a biplane to either for dusting crops.

Flight simulators can vary from a simple paper airplane to the multi-million dollar computer controlled full-motion platform which, from the inside, cannot be distinguished from a real aircraft. So, the first section of the book explores the defining characteristics of a flight simulator. You might wonder why anyone would build a multi-million dollar flight simulator, or any flight simulator at all. Next, you'll learn about the origins of flight simulation. The first section, discusses some of the applications of flight simulation and covers some of related fields.

Perhaps the most difficult part of any flight simulation design is to accommodate the operators and participants. We humans are complex creatures with a marvelous array of environment sensors. Our eyes can keep track of several different things at varying distances and in three dimensions. Our hearing is acute and spatial. Our haptic system provides information about our orientation, velocity, acceleration, and temperature. Many of the more complex flight simulators must account for these differing information sources—if they fail, the result can be simulator sickness (similar to motion sickness). The second section provides a basic discussion of how the relevant human systems work, how they can be fooled, and how they play their part in the larger scene.

Real flight simulators must obey the laws of our universe. And, most flight simulators must mimic a real aircraft—at least enough to fool real pilots. The third section of this book discusses these aircraft and the basics of what makes them fly. You will develop some understanding of things such as turbines and control surfaces, and why such things are used.

In the fourth section of this book you will find a brief look at the future possibilities and the current research directions of flight and flight simulation. The related field of virtual reality has already had some impact; it is certain to have more.

The fifth and final section of this book is devoted to creating a software based flight simulator for an IBM-compatible PC computer. You'll step through the process of building a three-dimensional computer graphics library that handles texture mapping, polygon clipping, and other assorted computer graphics arcana. You'll need a database to handle objects from clouds to trees to mountains, so we'll also help with that. And finally, you'll learn how to do a nighttime simulation complete with a lighted runway, other lighted aircraft, stars, and other interesting nighttime events.

Throughout this book, you will find straightforward descriptions and some entertainment. You will also find everything required to understand flight simulation—including some mathematics. But don't worry; you don't need any math experience to get the most out of this book.

Let's fly.

Section I

In the Beginning

Flight simulation is widely implemented throughout the military and civilian aviation industry. Chapter 1 is an introduction to some of the important concepts found in this book. Chapter 2 recounts a brief history of flight to provide some perspective. Chapter 3 provides a brief history of the flight simulation industry and how it came to be. Chapter 4 discusses flight simulation, some of its motivations, and takes a brief look at some related applications.

CHAPTER

1

What is Flight Simulation?

Let's start with the term *simulation*. Webster defines simulation as

> "the imitative representation of the functioning of one system or process by means of the functioning of another.
>
> Examination of a problem often not subject to direct experimentation by means of a simulating device."

Computer-based simulations involve mathematical models of a system such as an aircraft flying through a storm. These models may be of arbitrary complexity and precision, varying from very simple models that execute quickly to very precise, computer-intensive models that may take a great deal of time to complete. For instance, a video game may display an airplane cartoon that can be controlled with a joy stick. The environment this airplane is flying through may not be modeled at all, except perhaps for gravity's effect on any projectiles. By contrast, an

3

engineering simulator may include all of the details necessary to determine the effects of wind, over time and in various strengths, as it blows around a wing and its wingtip.

Webster's definition for a *simulator* is

> "a device that enables the operator to reproduce or represent under test conditions phenomena likely to occur in actual performance."

Rolfe and Staples are authors of one of the premier books on flight simulation. Their definition for flight simulation follows:

> "The essential form of flight simulation is the creation of a dynamic representation of the behavior of an aircraft in a manner which allows the human operator to interact with the simulation as part of the simulation."

From this we may gather that a flight simulator involves a simulation of flight in an aircraft including the pilot. The focus of their book is what we call *flight simulators*. This book treats flight simulation and flight simulators somewhat differently. In general, flight simulation might *include humans*, while flight simulators are simulations of aircraft including interactive *manipulation by humans*. This subtle difference stems from the fact that in some instances, we are more concerned with how the aircraft is interacting with the environment than how the human and aircraft are interacting.

Why Simulate?

Actually, a number of motivations make simulation feasible, desirable, and even preferable. Many of these motivations are discussed in more detail in Chapter 4, which deals with flight simulation applications. However, in brief, flight simulation has a number of advantages, including cost, safety, availability, and even ecology. Flight simulators are much less expensive to operate than aircraft. They may be used to research and train for flight hazards in a completely safe environment. Simulators may be used at whatever time is convenient and may simulate any particular weather of interest—you need not wait for dusk to practice dusk flying, let alone snow for snow flying. Flight simulators do not require expensive and limited resources such as fuel to maintain them, they do not pollute the atmosphere, and they don't leave spent shell casings on the ground, thus helping to preserve the ecology.

The most important applications for flight simulation are training, research and design, and investigation. Training simulators allow pilots to rehearse all types of flight operations, and especially hazardous maneuvers. Before the common use of flight simulators, many aircraft accidents were caused by rehearsals for difficult, hazardous predicaments (seems almost silly). Simulations can be used to try out new ideas for aircraft inexpensively, thus allowing many different, even radical, designs to be attempted. Only the promising designs need ever be built, even to be flown in wind tunnels. Flight simulators are also becoming increasingly important in the investigation and determination of the causes of flight accidents.

Properties and Definitions

Flight and flight simulation have a number of terms, or jargon, associated with them unique to the field. Most of these will be explained where they are encountered. But following are a few that seem to be common enough that they should be presented here.

angle-of-attack—the angle of an aircraft wing with respect to the angle of the oncoming air flow.

camber—the convexity of the curve of an airfoil from the leading edge to the trailing edge (Webster). Especially, across the upper surface of the airfoil.

display—a device that communicates information.

force feedback—representations of the inertia or resistance objects have when they are moved or touched. The computer guides a machine to offer just the degree of resistance to motion or pressure a situation would offer in real life.

glider—a heavier-than-air craft without an engine.

haptic—relating to or based on the sense of touch, including tactile, texture, force-feedback, motion, and pressure.

ornithopter—an aircraft designed to derive its chief support and propulsion from flapping wings (Webster).

soaring—the act or sport of flying a heavier-than-air craft without power by utilizing ascending air currents (Webster).

stall—the condition of an airfoil or airplane operating so that there is a flow breakdown and loss of lift with a tendency to drop. Usually occasioned by a chaotic transition from streamline to turbulent flow.

tactile feedback—see *force feedback*.

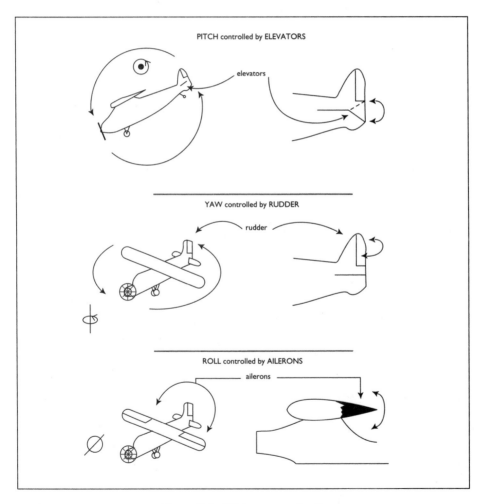

Figure 1.1 *Pitch, yaw, and roll.*

A Brief History of Flight

Throughout our history, humans have looked into the sky and been awed by the creatures we watched cavorting about, effortlessly, far above our heads. The theme of wings and flying made its debut in many of our earliest forms of expression—paintings, carvings, sculpture, and writing. The significance of flight is clear: to fly is to be above the daily woes and toil of humankind. To fly is to dominate, to conquer, to soar gracefully over mountain-obstacles with ease. To fly is to be a god.

Myths and Legends

One of the earliest recorded stories of humans in flight comes from the ancient Chinese *Annals of the Bamboo Books*, about 4,000 years ago. The Emperor Shun escaped captivity as a boy by "donning the work-clothes of a bird." Another time, he became a flying dragon. The young boy also escaped a burning granary by seizing two wide-brimmed reed hats and floating to the ground. Since such hats are typically three feet wide, and the young Emperor must have been small, Shun may have been the first parachutist.

The Chinese have many other legends about flight. Lei Kung, god of thunder and lightning, had the wings of a bat. Ki-kung-shi supposedly invented a flying chariot in the eighteenth century B.C., although most pictures depict him sailing along with no visible means of support and a smirk on his face. Sixteen hundred years later, Liu An created a levitation elixir. As he rose, he dropped the bottle of elixir, and all of the barnyard animals that drank of the spilled elixir floated after him.

Kai Kawus, an ancient king of Persia was said to have a flying chariot pulled by four hungry eagles that were chasing raw meat hung on spears just out of their reach. (Alexander the Great was also supposed to have had such a chariot pulled by winged griffins.) The halls of ancient Persia were also guarded by winged bulls.

The ancient Egyptian's first god is usually referred to as the *Benu bird*. Isis, the goddess mother, was often depicted with wings, and sometimes even as a bird. Her fame spread across the Greco-Roman empire. Amon-Ra, in goose form, laid the cosmic egg from which all life came.

Africa had a great warrior named Kibaga, who flew invisibly over his enemies and dropped rocks on them. Northern Europe had Wayland the Smith and his shirt of feathers. The Incan beliefs were dominated by sky gods. The Greek god Hermes, the messenger of the gods, was portrayed with wings on his shoes. The Greek goddess of victory, Nike, had large wings on her back. Christian angels have always been depicted with wings. All over the world, nearly every culture finds legends of flying gods and humans—and these legends are usually attached to that which the culture holds most dear.

Perhaps the best-known flying legend from western belief is the story of Daedalus and Icarus. Daedalus, "revered by the Greeks as the greatest of mortal craftsmen and inventors," created wings of wax and feathers so that he and his son, Icarus, could flee the Mediterranean island of Crete and the wrath of King Minos. (King Minos was upset that Daedalus aided Theseus in destroying the Minotaur.) Daedalus cautioned Icarus not to fly too close to the sun less the wax holding the wings together should melt. Once Icarus was airborne, he became caught up in the thrill of flight. When he flew too close to the sun, the wax melted, the wings came apart, and Icarus plunged into the sea. Daedalus maintained his composure and flew on to land (Sicily or mainland Italy, depending on the text). Interestingly, here is another myth that may hold a kernel of truth. Daedalus probably knew about seafaring sails and how they harness the wind. The updrafts near a steep cliff overlooking the sea can be very strong—Crete has just such cliffs. The principal parts of a glider, wood and light cloth, are the same now as they were in the Bronze Age, and equally available. Daedalus and his son may have been the first hang-gliders!

Certainly many other examples of myth and legend can be cited. The point, however, is that flight has always been associated with power and is to be revered. Scientists and engineers have long looked at ways to enable humans to fly. Let's take a look at some of the first recorded attempts, and successes, at human flight.

Figure 2.1—*The IVEX Corporation Simulator depicts a runway in the fog.*

The Early Science of Flight

Probably the first experiments with flight were done with kites. Like airplanes, kites are heavier than air and they rise from the ground into flight. Chinese kites have been around for many centuries. Mo To Tzu of China is generally credited with the invention of large kites around 400 B.C. His creations were constructed of light wood and flew tethered to the ground. In 1749 Scottish meteorologist Alexander Wilson, assisted by Thomas Melville, flew kites with attached thermometers to make measurements of atmospheric temperature distribution. Benjamin Franklin made his daring electricity experiments with a kite in 1752. It should be pointed out that tethered kites use quite different principles of flight than do free-flying objects.

Early Balloons and Airships

Balloons and airships were flown reliably well before other heavier-than-air craft. Roger Bacon (c. 1214–92), an English Franciscan monk, is one of the earliest recorded scientific sources on buoyant flight. He was familiar with Archimedes' law of buoyancy and made the suggestion that it could be applied to an airship. A balloon could float on the air, in much the same way as a ship floats on the sea, provided it was filled with a substance lighter than air. Unfortunately he had no idea that this "ethereal air" could be a substance as simple as heated air. Bacon also described a flying machine with "artificial wings made to beat the air," probably the first reference to an ornithopter. An ornithopter is a device meant to fly in the manner of a bird, by flapping wings, usually propelled by human power. (Humans have been obsessed with this idea throughout the history of flight, although no such systems have ever been made to carry a human being.)

da Vinci's Flying Machine Designs

Leonardo da Vinci (1452-1519), the famous renaissance Florentine, devoted over thirty-five thousand words and over five hundred sketches to flying machines, the nature of air, and the flight of birds. He provided some of the first sketches of helicopters and parachutes. He spent years of research working on ornithopters. Although he was well aware that the "sinews and muscles of a bird are incomparably more powerful than those of a man," he nonetheless believed that the goal of flight alone might be enough to rouse the extra strength in man needed to power ornithopters. It has been suggested that his passion for flight overrode the judgment he demonstrated in so many other branches of science. Leonardo's ornithopters were designed for pilots in a prone or upright position. The pilots flapped the wings, using both hands and feet in a pulley arrangement—clearly a more thoughtful approach than strapping the wings to the pilot's arms, the more conventional approach. It is unclear whether his beautiful illustrations were ever turned into models. It is even possible that a full-sized ornithopter was built. Leonardo also designed some gliders that could have flown during his time. Unfortunately, Leonardo's work was essentially unknown until the late 18th century, by which time much of his work had been duplicated.

Further Balloon Developments

In the late seventeenth century, Francesco Lana-Terzi, an Italian Jesuit priest and professor of mathematics and philosophy, suggested that a lighter-than-air gas was needed to lift a balloon; this was the way to achieve flight, rather than the human-powered flapping of an ornithopter. His thoughts were based on studies of the hot gases rising from volcanic eruptions. He reasoned that anything lighter than gas had to be no gas at all, that is, a vacuum, so Lana-Terzi designed an airship based on four evacuated spheres, each with a diameter of 6 meters (20 feet). A sail was added to the contraption to keep it on course. Vacuum pumps had been built in England and Germany before 1650 at the time of the Thirty Years War. However, Lana-Terzi soon realized that the extremely thin spheres could not withstand the external pressure. He was said to have believed that in any case God would not allow humans to fly because of the enormous possibility of destruction such power would bring. (Interesting thought, huh?)

Robert Hooke (1635–1703), one of Lana-Terzi's English contemporaries and master of design and experimentation, collaborated with Robert Boyle (1627–92) at Oxford University to develop what is commonly called *Boyle's Law*, an important law of gas (which is important in the study of fluid mechanics and aerodynamics). Hooke experimented with ornithopter models around 1655, but found them "difficult to keep aloft."

Italian Giovanni Borelli (1608–79) pronounced the scientific demise of ornithopters in 1679. He cited the physiological differences between humans and birds. In the *De Motu Animalium,* he stated that humans were incapable of supporting their own weight in air "without mechanical assistance."

The Paper Balloons

The year 1709 found the Brazilian Jesuit priest Father Laurenzo de Gusmaõ flying balloon models. His paper balloons carried a small basket in which burned a fire. When he demonstrated his flying balloon in the palace of the king of Portugal, he managed to catch the curtains afire. The same year he designed an airship named Passarola, which was to be propelled by two magnetic spheres (an idea which has yet to become popular).

Joseph Michel Montgolfier (1740–1810) was a student of mathematics, mechanics, and physics who lived in the small town of Annonay near Lyons, France. His brother, Jacques Étienne (1745–99), was an architect. They had inherited a paper factory from their father, and so were conversant with the technology required to create a paper balloon. They experimented with tethered and free-rising models created with a paper skin reinforced with linen. Their full-sized "aerostatic machine" used a linen balloon treated with a chemical to aid in flameproofing. The balloon had a diameter of 15 meters (49 feet), a height of 23 meters (75 feet), and weighed some 7565 N (1700 pounds). This balloon held 2200m^3 (78,000 ft^3) of straw-fired hot air. On September 19, 1783 the basket of the balloon was loaded with a ram, a duck, and a cock. The balloon rose freely into the air and floated for seven minutes as King Louis XVI and 130,000 spectators watched. Friends of the Montgolfier brothers, Pilâtre de Rozier and the Marquis d'Arlandes—an artillery major—became the first human aviators on November 21, 1783. The starting place was the castle La Muette near Versailles. They drifted 12 kilometers (7 miles) across Paris and landed safely after their 25-minute journey.

Hydrogen Gas Balloons

The Academy of Sciences in Paris had no wish to be outdone by inventors from the provinces. (It's interesting that the Wright brothers had similar problems and competition.) The light gas hydrogen was discovered in 1766 by Henry Cavendish of Cambridge, England; the possibility of ballooning without a dangerous open fire was at hand. J.A.C. Charles (1746–1823) was financed by the Academy to study the effect of temperature on the volume of a gas. Meanwhile, the Robert brothers succeeded in rubberizing silk, which kept light gas from leaking through the material. Charles and the Robert brothers collaborated to design and build a hydrogen-filled balloon that used a net to cover the balloon and affix it to the gondola. Their advanced design included a valve to release gas and sand ballast that could be dropped to lighten the load; these two features allowed them to ascend and descend at will. Ten days after the first manned flight of the Montgolfière, the Charlière flew over the Tuileries Gardens of Paris, ascending to an altitude of 3000 meters (9800 feet). While the Montgolfier brothers remained the darlings of the public, the Charles design became ever-increasingly popular. Charles used his balloon to explore properties of the atmosphere, such as temperature as a function of altitude. Exploration by balloon quickly became very popular. Over one hundred years passed from the introduction of ballooning to the days when the stalwart dirigibles plied the skyways, relying on their own steering and guidance, rather than the whims of the wind. The fundamentals required for understanding heavier-than-air flight existed in principle, but were not quantified until 1800, when Sir George Cayley laid the foundation for modern heavier-than-air craft.

The Beginnings of Heavier-Than-Air Craft

Sir George Cayley (1773–1857) began by discarding the idea of ornithopters as scientifically ridiculous. Cayley's prophetic vision described the first rigid airplane, the basic design of which remains unchanged even today. His aircraft designs featured for the first time, lifting surfaces that were separate from propulsion. He separated and quantified the forces of drag and lift, and described them using force diagrams. His designs included combined rudder and elevator control surfaces and his wings had camber. He even proposed the first rubber-band-driven propeller for his models. (In 1853 Cayley's toy helicopters rose 27 meters (90 feet) into the air!) Cayley's work covered many branches of science and all the branches of aerodynamics. His efforts ranged from aerodynamically stabilized projectiles, a hot-air engine, and studies of airfoil geometry to streamlining shapes to reduce drag. His studies included kites, airships, and control surfaces. There is little dispute that Cayley is the father of modern aviation.

Aircraft Development Abroad

The beginning of ballooning and Cayley's contributions all came at a time of great turmoil. The French revolution began in 1789, shortly after the first balloon flights. Napoleon became emperor in 1804 and began his conquest of Europe. The English made a final attempt to regain their lost colonies in 1814 and burned the White House. These troubled times did not deter would-be aviators, but many strange contraptions were the order of the day.

Some of the important ventures included the collaboration of Englishmen W. S. Henson (1805–88) and John Stringfellow (1799–1883), who in 1842 created a model monoplane driven by a one horsepower (745 W), 10-pound, steam engine. The model had a wingspan of 6 meters (20 feet) and weighed in at 25 pounds. Although the model never flew successfully, the design featured a very modern configuration, including a single wing, an undercarriage, and two propellers.

The first lighter-than-air steerable craft was built by Frenchman Henri Giffard. The balloon was ellipsoidal (like a blimp) and covered with netting (as in Charles' design). The net suspended a flat open platform beneath it. The platform held a 3 horsepower (2238 W) engine which drove a large propeller. The airship required perfectly still air, but could move at a speed of 8 kilometers/hour (5 miles/hour). On September 24, 1852, this craft rose over Paris and flew 25 kilometers (16 miles) at an altitude of 1500 meters (5000 feet). Although this machine could only be steered in calm air, it was the first human powered flight machine capable of being steered at all.

The first truly successful stable, flying airplane models were created by Alphonse Pénaud around 1871. Pénaud was unaware of Cayley's work and independently advanced many ideas on stability. His model was called a "planophone" and featured a small rear wing and a large forward wing sitting on top of a rubber-band-driven pusher propeller. His design featured both longitudinal and lateral stability. This model was very similar to many of our modern rubber-band-driven toy airplanes, except for the pusher propeller.

The public was becoming increasingly aware of aviation. The Aeronautical Society of Great Britain was founded in 1866. The first airshow ever, a static display, was held in 1868 at the Crystal Palace in London. Interestingly, the Crystal Palace was built for the 1851 Exhibition (which was organized by Prince Albert, the consort of Queen Victoria) which featured nothing related to flight in its science and machinery displays. John Stringfellow showed a triplane model at the 1868 airshow based on Cayley's ideas; this model would later influence Chanute and the Wright brothers.

The Englishmen Butler and Edwards patented plans for rocket-driven propellers in 1867. Their craft featured a delta wing, which is a large single triangle wing, much like the Space Shuttle—a design featured in many of the first rocket-powered aircraft of the mid-twentieth century. The Englishman Phillips patented airfoils that demonstrated that properly curved surfaces, surfaces with camber, showed greatly enhanced lifting capabilities.

Lilienthal's Flight Developments

Otto Lilienthal (1848–96) is truly one of the great pioneers of flight. He was born in the small town of Anklam in Pomerania (Germany). He grew up interested in flight; he built wings as a teenager and studied the flight of storks. He studied at what is now the Technical University of Berlin, after which, he founded a machine and boiler factory. His brother Gustav helped with many of his projects. Otto Lilienthal published a most famous book on bird flight in 1889, which was supplemented by a book on the biotechnology of flight by Gustav in 1925.

Lilienthal developed gliders, the forerunners of modern hang gliders. These gliders were created out of wood and canvas and featured a central frame for the pilot. Their wingspan covered 6.7 meters (22 feet) and they typically weighed about 45-pounds. Lilienthal was familiar with the work of other pioneers, which led to the adoption of camber (which provided fantastic lift) among other design ideas. About eight of these gliders were built and sold to aviators in countries as far as Russia and the United States. By 1895, Lilienthal had added biplanes to his glider production. Lilienthal made around 2,000 glider flights in five years. His designs accounted for stability in pitch, yaw, and unlike his predecessors, roll.

Lilienthal dreamed of soaring above his starting place on earth. The year 1876 saw the first four cycle internal combustion engine constructed by N. A. Otto. Gottlieb Daimler improved this machine a great deal by increasing its power-to-weight ratio. Lilienthal began to think about combining engines and wings. Unfortunately, Lilienthal fell from his monoplane glider on August 9, 1896 and died from the resulting injuries at 48 years old. A lot of speculation about the cause of this crash ensued; many believe that Lilienthal achieved soaring flight (as opposed to gliding) and momentarily lost his concentration, causing a stall. Lilienthal had no followers in his country; his brother did not succeed him, but rather emigrated to Australia, a disappointed man.

Fortunately, Lilienthal's student, Percy S. Pilcher (1866–99) of Scotland, did carry on with his work. Pilcher, a lecturer at the University of Glasgow, built a monoplane glider, called the Bat, in 1895. It demonstrated stability superior even to Lilienthal's gliders. His fourth and final glider, Hawk, featured an undercarriage to soften landings and further improve roll stability. He flew 250 meters (820 feet) across a valley in the Hawk. Unfortunately, Pilcher's career was cut short when his glider's tail broke and he crashed in September 1899.

Precursors of the Wright Brothers' Methods

Octave Chanute (1832–1910), a French railroad engineer who later emigrated to the United States, became entranced with aviation at the age of 60. Chanute collected works on aviation and published *Progress in Flying Machines* in 1894. (The Wright brothers read this text and befriended him.) An American follower of Lilienthal, A. M. Herring (1865–1926) joined Chanute as pilot and coworker. They owned and flew a Lilienthal glider, as well as gliders of their own design. Herring added a compressed-air engine and a propeller to this hang glider and made short flights. The Wright brothers were greatly influenced by Chanute's biplane and its resemblance can be seen in their first aircraft.

Samuel Pierpont Langley (1834–1906) was to become the Wright brother's chief rival. Langley graduated from high school in Roxbury, Massachusetts. He studied astronomy and engineering on his own at libraries in Boston. He became a professor of Physics in 1866 at the Western University of Pennsylvania, now the University of Pittsburgh. Langley made many significant contributions to astronomy including measurements of the spectral energy distribution of sunlight, the instrument used to make those measurements (the bolometer), and studies of solar and lunar spectra. Langley's accomplishments gave him the opportunity to become the head of the Smithsonian Institute in 1887. While at the Smithsonian Institute, Langley established the National Zoo and an astrophysical observatory.

Langley's fascination with flight dates to a lecture at the annual meeting of the American Association for the Advancement of Science in 1886. He built more than 100 rubber-band-powered models, but none met with his approval. He proceeded to build steam-powered models with wingspans up to 4.3 meters (14 feet). Two of his models flew up to 1.3 kilometers (4200 feet) in 1896. These accomplishments landed him a $50,000 grant from the War Department to develop a full-sized, manned aircraft. Langley's chief assistant and pilot, Charles M. Manley, was a gifted designer of gasoline engines. Manley developed a 52 horsepower (39 kilowatt) light radial (the cylinders projected radially in a star pattern) engine capable of spinning two propellers at 575 revolutions per minute. Langley's aircraft was of tandem wing design, with each wing having a span of 15 meters (50 feet). The craft was launched from the top of a houseboat on October 7, 1903 and promptly crashed into the water—Manley was unhurt. Langley's understanding of stability lagged behind the common knowledge of the time and Manley had no experience with gliders, let alone powered flight. The craft was launched again on December 8, again crashing, but this time breaking into pieces. Again, Manley was unhurt. Langley was attacked in Congress and in the media; the failure overshadowed his gifted career for the rest of his life.

Manley, however, continued designing engines that were especially noted for their low drag.

Langley supporters still claim that the launching mechanism was the heart of the problems with the aircraft. In 1914, a refurbished airplane based on Langley's plans with some wing enhancements and equipped with floats was flown successfully for 46 meters (150 feet). Glenn Curtiss (a man destined to make his mark in aviation history) was the pilot and designer of the new wings for the craft. In 1915 the Annual Report of the Smithsonian Institute contained the claim "that former secretary Langley had succeeded in building the first aeroplane capable of sustained free flight with a man." This dispute with the Wright brothers continued until 1948, when the Wright Flyer I was finally inducted into the Smithsonian Institute's museum (next to the Spirit of St. Louis which was already there).

The Wright Brothers at Kitty Hawk

Wilbur Wright (1867–1912) won the right to be the pilot of the first powered aircraft by the toss of a coin on December 14, 1903. It was a beautiful day in the sand dunes of Kill Devil Hills, about four miles south of Kitty Hawk, North Carolina. The wind was somewhat insufficient so the Wright Flyer I was set to start from the nine-degree slope of a dune. This aircraft had skids that were set on a yoke running along a single track. Five men from the local lifesaving station helped with the work and acted as independent witnesses. The craft was held still while its engine warmed up. When the craft was freed, it ran down the track and lifted off the yoke into the air. Unfortunately its nose turned up too quickly, causing it to stall. Its rough landing broke a skid and damaged a control surface, ending the attempts for the day.

The repairs were completed by December 17th. The wind—the original reason for choosing Kitty Hawk—was blowing at 27 miles per hour, so no slope was needed. Again, the witnesses were present. Many claims to powered flight had been made, but none proven, and the Wright brothers had no intention of being another such claim. Orville strategically positioned a camera for one of the witnesses, John T. Daniels, to take a picture of the craft in flight. Orville took the controls, and the craft ambled down the rail, finally launching into the air. The craft's marginal stability and Orville's lack of experience piloting such a craft (the price of being first) led to an erratic flight covering 120 feet in 12 seconds. Even this modest achievement put the Wright brothers well ahead of their competition. They were making 30-minute flights by 1905, yet the first flight accomplished in Europe was a one-minute flight by Henri Farman in November 1907.

One of the prime elements for success of the Wright brothers' craft was that their control system included all three axes of flight. Some of their techniques were based on a book called *L'Empire de l'Air* (The Empire of the Air), a collection of observations on flight published by L. P. Mouillard and passed to the Wright brothers by Chanute.

The Wright brothers continued with their work. In 1904, the Wright Flyer II made nearly 80 flights. By 1905, it was banking, turning, and flying in circles and figures of eight. Twice it flew more than 30 minutes. In 1908, the Wright brothers toured Europe, spurring on those who watched, especially the French. On October 4, 1909, Wilbur flew his plane, with a canoe attached, on a 21-mile circuit between Governor's Island in the New York harbor and Grant's tomb. That year the Army finally bought the Wright brothers' airplane.

The U.S. Government and Aviation

The United States government has supported aviation research nearly from its inception. Dirigibles and biplanes played very important roles in World War I. To preserve the U.S. interests, the National Advisory Committee for Aeronautics (NACA) was founded on March 3, 1915 by President Woodrow Wilson. NACA was populated by scientists and engineers whose purpose was to attempt to bring some order to the chaos that was the field of aviation and to advise the government. NACA suggested initiatives including that the government should itself build research laboratories to help keep the U.S. competitive in the field.

The United States entered World War I in 1917. It was decided that NACA's advice would be taken and that the first lab was to be built at

Langley Field, Virginia. The research results from the NACA labs was shared with industry in a process that still exists today. Aviation research was also conducted at many universities across the country under the auspices of NACA. The launch of Sputnik on October 4, 1957 resulted in NACA's responsibilities being extended and a new name, the National Aeronautics and Space Administration, NASA. Further, NASA became an independent civilian agency of the federal government. NASA's efforts have created aircraft that could fly nearly at the height of satellites, landed humans on the moon and brought them back, created the Space Shuttle, and begun the detailed exploration of our solar system and universe. As you will see, the U.S. government will play an equally important role in the development of flight simulation.

Today we board aircraft and fly around the world in a day (okay, a long, long, long day) and we hardly think about it. Ballooning has recently returned as a popular sport. And blimps now fly over many outdoor sports events. Space shuttle launches have become so regular that people expect them to fly without a hitch (each flight is a minor miracle in itself!). Humankind's fascination with flight has paid big dividends (including your television and computer). However, none of this would be possible, or nearly as safe, without the field of flight simulation.

Figure 2.2—*A runway shown by the IVEX Corporation Simulator.*

CHAPTER

3

A Brief History of Flight Simulators

The importance of flight simulation has been understood for as long as heavier-than-air craft have flown. Each new generation of aircraft introduced has features that differentiate it from previous generations and from all other aircraft. Simulators become steadily more important for first-time training and for retraining of entire flight crews. The following discussion provides a brief history of flight simulators from their earliest days until the present, with a brief glimpse of things to come. Part of the following discussion is adapted from *Flight Simulation* by Rolfe and Staples.

The First Simulators

In the days before manned, powered airplanes flew, people widely believed that these machines would be as stable and easy to handle as airships. It was thought that no previous experience or training would be required to pilot a powered airplane. These beliefs changed rapidly as people encountered the Wright Flyer I. This plane was unstable and required the constant attention of the pilot to make flight corrections. All of the immediate successors to the Wright brothers' aircraft had particular idiosyncrasies that made flying dangerous.

One of the first solutions for teaching prospective pilots involved an airplane safely attached to the ground. The Sander's Teacher is an example of this type of simulator. It was simply an airplane mounted on a universal joint that was linked to the ground. When the wind blew, the airplane "flew," which allowed students to learn the principles of flying an airplane without endangering themselves. This method, however, required the wind to blow vigorously.

A variation on the captive airplane theme was patented by Eardley Billing in England in 1910. Billing's simulator was a custom-built machine. The control stick operated control surfaces to maintain equilibrium. The rudder bar was connected to the base to allow the system to be turned into the wind.

A common theme used by a number of flight simulators of the day to avoid the wind requirement involved a system of pulleys and an instructor. The instructor operated some system of levers, which caused a disturbance in the trainer. The trainee then had to operate the controls to maintain equilibrium. It has been suggested that these systems probably provided no real training value, and in fact, may have proved detrimental to training because of the immediate response of the controls operated by the students.

World War I Flight Simulators

World War I was the first great catalyst for aviation. For the first time, there was a tremendous need to train a large number of people in a short amount of time. Unfortunately, the current state of flight simulator technology was not up to the task and had virtually no impact. The

English training system was developed by Smith-Barry and emphasized actual flying from the beginning of the program. France used the Blériot system, which used a number of planned stages including the use of the Penguin, a monoplane with part of its wings sawed off so that it could only fly in short hops at about 40 mph.

Psychologists were also employed to help choose and train better prospective pilots. Many flying aptitude tests were invented, most of which had little validity. The two most popular tests centered around reaction time and coordination. It was also widely believed that pilots could be trained to orient themselves spatially and training blindfolded could help adapt the pilot's system to flying at night or in poor visibility. Later, it was realized that orientation depends more on vision than any other sense.

By 1920, the mechanics of flight was understood well enough to develop a mathematical model. Unfortunately, there was no way to translate such a model into a simulation at that time. The evolution of automatic controls provided many improvements in flight simulators at that time. These flight simulators employed sensors, actuators, and computing mechanisms based on empirical data and the practical understanding of flight. They were based on three-axis motion platforms and performed actions based on the control stick and rudder controls. They also provided a way of introducing disturbances. The goal of these systems was to simulate the feel of the aircraft, but most did poorly because they had no dynamic simulation capabilities.

Lender and Heidelberg described such a simulator in their patents of 1917 and 1918. Their cockpit simulator rode on top of a three-axis motion platform, which was driven by compressed air. For the first time, the effects of changes in speed on the controls was included using the control stick and *pneumatic integration*, a mechanical system used to perform a numeric integration—advanced math—based on compressed air in much the same way hydraulics uses fluids. A visual projection display was outlined but only in a rudimentary form.

The Link Trainer Development

The Link Trainer was perhaps the most realistic feeling of the simulators of this time. Edwin Link was born into a family that built mechanical musical instruments. His father was founder of the Link Piano and Organ Company of Binghamton, New York. Edwin received his first patent for a pneumatic enhancement to the player piano's capabilities, air-driven switches that activated the piano keys according to a series of holes punched in a ribbon of paper.

The trainer was developed in the basement of the Link factory from 1927 to 1929. The pitch, roll, and yaw movements were similar to other contemporary designs except the actuators were pneumatic bellows. Link spent a great deal of time adjusting the performance of the simulator by trial and error. He filed for the patent in 1930 for "an efficient aeronautical training aid—a novel, profitable amusement device." The first trainer had no instruments and the simulated effects of the ailerons, elevators, and rudder were independent of other operations. Like other simulators of the time, it did not attempt to provide correct motion cues. Link had trouble convincing people that this device was a worthy investment, primarily because it did not serve a particular training need.

Many of Link's competitors stopped using full motion cockpits, since that by itself provided little value in training. For instance, the 1928 patent of Rougerie described a simple trainer, fixed to the ground, used to train students in flying by instrumentation. The student's instruments were connected to the instructor's controls. The instructor would then modify the student's instruments based on the student's reactions.

Simulated Instrument Panels

W.E.P. Johnson, an instructor at the Central Flying School, Wittering, was one of the pioneers of instrument flying in England. In 1931, he created an instrument flying simulator based on a discarded Avro 504 fuselage. Johnson began by implementing an airspeed indicator, turn indicator, and bank indicator—all directly operated by the control sticks and rudder bars of the student and instructor. Further enhancements included a throttle control that affected the airspeed indicator and integrating devices for the altitude and heading displays. Unfortunately, although the device seemed to meet all of its objectives, future development was not pursued primarily because Johnson "was too preoccupied with real flying."

Roeder described the first flight simulator that included all of the aspects of a true simulator, as opposed to the previous flight imitators. Roeder's patent describes a complete and detailed altitude control system for a simulator. His system was based on an elaborate state diagram that related all of the control inputs to display outputs. The computer was part mechanical and part hydraulic and could handle nonlinear relationships. His discussion included the difficulties of choosing initial conditions, introducing disturbances and instrumentation failures, and recording a student's performance. It was Roeder's opinion that a movable cabin could be useful for an airship or submarine simulator, but not for an airplane simulator.

The Link Trainers and World War II

The 1930s were a pivotal time in the real world and in the world of flight simulation. The Link Trainers added instruments as standard equipment. The Link schools began to teach blind flying—flying with instruments only. When the Army became responsible for carrying air mail, interest in blind flying skyrocketed (as did Link's sales). These Link trainers could be rotated a full 360 degrees, which allowed the use of magnetic compasses. Altitude was simulated with pressure in an air tank connected to a standard altimeter. Rudder and aileron interaction, including a stall feature, became part of the advanced simulators. A simple form of analog computer associated controls and instrument displays, although the aircraft dynamics were still based on empirical data. Perhaps one of the most useful additions to the trainer came in the form of a course plotter for the instructor. This device was self-propelled and steerable and marked the student's flight progress with an ink wheel on the instructor's map table. This allowed the instructor to monitor the student's progress and manually adjust the simulated radio beacons in the trainer. The first passenger airline trainer was sold to American Airlines in 1937. The many different versions of the Link Trainer were sold to countries all over the world, including England, France, the U.S.S.R., Japan, and Germany. Interestingly, at the start of

World War II, the German bomber pilots had at least 50 hours of blind-flying training in a Link Trainer.

World War II brought the need to train a large number of people relatively quickly, both in individual and team maneuvers. To further complicate matters, the numbers and types of military aircraft increased rapidly. Basic instrumentation training was made in a standard Link Trainer. Then specialized simulators, which reproduced the instrument layout and typical performance characteristics of a particular type of aircraft were used for further training. These systems had to account for variable pitch motors, retractable undercarriages, and higher speeds—all of which made the sound processing in the simulator much more important.

The Link Trainer Used in England

In 1939, the British requested Link to design a simulator to help train crews in celestial navigation. The crews ferrying aircraft from the U.S. to Britain and hopefully the night bombing crews could benefit from such a trainer. Edwin Link and P. Weems, the aerial navigation expert, designed a trainer suitable for an entire bomber crew to be housed in a 45-foot-high, silo-shaped building and called it the *Celestial Navigation Trainer*. This trainer featured a fully instrumented cockpit for the pilot. The bombardier's station provided an image of targets and other appropriate sights over which the trainer was flying. The navigator's station included all of the standard radio equipment, including an elaborate view of the stars that moved appropriately as the trainer flew which could be used to compute latitude and longitude. The first of these trainers was completed in 1941 and the Royal Air Force (RAF) placed an order for 60 more, only several of which were ever completed and installed. However, hundreds of these trainers were created and operated in the United States.

In England, training was not given a high priority for resources. Consequently, many RAF instructors improvised and created their own devices. Frequently, these simulators were little more than a fuselage section mounted on a crude motion platform. Such simulators could be used to let crews practice everything from dropping bombs (into sand beds underneath the craft) to malfunction and emergency drills, complete with parachutes and dinghies. Perhaps the best known of these simulators was the *Silloth Trainer*, which gave realistic responses based on the same player piano technology with which Link was familiar, pneumatics (the designer was from the pianola industry). Although many enhancements were designed, further development was abandoned after the war ended, as was all flight simulator work in England.

As an aside, a man named Fred Waller began experimenting with multiple-projector, multiple-screen display systems as a way of presenting a wider field of view than films. His goal was to fill as much of the participants' peripheral vision as was possible. Waller obtained an Air Force contract for a flight simulator that had five projectors, three on the bottom and two on top. The cameras were all mounted at slightly different angles and synchronized, as were the projectors. After World War II, Waller found a Hollywood producer named Mike Todd. Together, they created a three-projector system called *Cinerama*. Their first production was entitled *This is Cinerama* and it was a big hit.

The Electronic Simulator

The influence of World War II lasted well beyond the end of the war. World War II forced the development of a range of new technologies, many of which were enabling technologies for other fields. Finally, the technologies to transform flight imitators into flight simulators were at hand.

In the 1930s, Vannevar Bush encountered problems in computing and predicting electric power flow. The U.S. power system was becoming increasingly interconnected and distributed and control of this system was becoming vastly more complex. Bush designed and built a mechanical computer called the "differential analyzer," a room full of cogs and rods that could approximately solve particular differential equations numerically. Perhaps more importantly, Bush proved that such a system could be built.

The military needed to determine ballistics tables faster and more accurately. These tables were used by a gunner or bomber to determine the force and direction to apply to a long-range projectile to allow for missile weight, atmospheric conditions and phenomena. The Army also wanted to be able to calculate many of the solutions for a wide range of problems. The U.S. Army's Aberdeen Proving Ground was responsible for the work load. By 1944, they were receiving an average of six requests a day. A single, 60-second trajectory could be solved by hand in about 20 hours. A machine such as Bush's differential analyzer would cut that time to 15 minutes. A new development at the University of Pennsylvania promised to calculate a trajectory in 30 seconds, faster than real time. The Electronic Numerical Integrator and Computer (ENIAC) was commissioned to do the job. The designers also pointed out that the ENIAC could solve other types of problems as well.

A More Refined Flight Simulator

On the flight simulator front, an electronic simulator that solved the equations of motion for an aircraft was developed in England in 1941 by Telecommunications Research Establishment (TRE), a firm famous for its radar work. The simulator was part of the training system for their aerial interception radar system. This system was based on the work of F.C. Williams, who would be one of the pioneers of digital computers.

Also in 1941, U.S. Navy Commander Luis de Florez visited England and wrote the "Report on British Synthetic Training," which was influential in establishing the Special Devices Division of the Bureau of Aeronautics. This later became the Naval Training Systems Center. A Silloth Trainer was also brought to the U.S.; however, the difficulties in maintaining the system rendered it unusable. A fully electric version was designed by Bell Telephone Laboratories under the auspices of the Navy. In 1943, an operational flight trainer for the PBM-3 aircraft was completed. It included a fully instrumented cockpit, complete controls, and auxiliary equipment. This system used an electronic computer to solve the equations of motion.

Dehmel, who was instrumental in developing the PBM-3 at Bell Labs, continued to develop his ideas independently of Bell working with Curtiss-Wright. Curtiss-Wright proceeded to develop and produce an AT-6 simulator and went on to develop other simulators. This competition eventually forced Link to develop electronic simulators, after the war. Link was also one of the last manufacturers to abandon the use of motion platforms and finally switched to fixed-based simulators.

The Whirlwind Simulator

In 1944, Jay W. Forrester at MIT's Servomechanisms Lab led a project to build an "airplane stability control analyzer." The project's goal was to use the same electronic, digital technology that created the ENIAC to build a generalized flight trainer. A member of the team, Robert R. Everett, promised that "putting wind tunnel data into the trainer would cause it to fly like an airplane not yet built." The project was dubbed *Whirlwind*. It was finished for testing in 1949 and it was completely operational in 1951, just in time for the U.S. Navy's funding to run out. The new funding would have to come from the Air Force, which was interested in the system for air defense purposes.

The researchers who built Whirlwind learned some entirely unexpected things. In late 1948 and early 1949, while playing with the oscilloscopes that were used to display system information, they noticed that certain computer instructions would cause certain patterns on the oscilloscope displays. They even managed to create a game including a dot, called the "ball," which could be made to fall through a "hole" in the "floor" by adjusting some of the input variables. The dynamics of a real ball could be reproduced using just the pure math. They had developed the first interactive computer display, as well as the first computer game.

One of the early Whirlwind testing programs displayed the states of the system's memory devices on the oscilloscope as a series of dots. The researchers wanted to know which dot represented which particular memory tube. So, they built a "light gun" from a tube and a light-sensitive detector. When it was hooked up to the system and pointed at the oscilloscope, it could identify the associated vacuum tube. This was the first lightpen and the first interactive graphics tool.

Finally an Aircraft Developer Gets a Simulator

In 1948, Curtiss-Wright installed for Pan American Airways the first full aircraft simulator owned by an airline. The Boeing 377 Stratocruiser simulator duplicated the behavior and appearance of the aircraft. The trainer was especially useful for procedures such as emergencies, involving the whole crew. Whole practice flight routes could be flown using the same navigational aids encountered in the real world. This simulator was praised for its high degree of procedural realism. However, the lack of motion gave the aircraft an unnatural feel and even introduced some control problems.

The Beginnings of the Modern Simulator

The 1950s found the simulator manufacturers with the means to simulate aircraft parameters that were largely unmeasured by aircraft manufacturers. This left the simulator manufacturers with empirical data, trial and error, and pilot responses. Analog computers played an increasing role in the systems until reliability actually began to decrease because of the number of interacting systems. About this time, the second generation of digital computers became available and a sudden shift from analog to digital computers took place in the flight simulator industry.

In 1950, the U.S. Navy began funding another effort at the University of Pennsylvania with the ENIAC developers. Their job was to develop a real-time simulation system to model aerodynamics. The project was called the *Universal Digital Operational Flight Trainer* (UDOFT) and it was successful in this quest even as Whirlwind was not. It also demonstrated the feasibility of digital simulation.

The 1960s saw the commercial development of a flight simulation computer when Link released the Mark I. The system allowed the pilot to manipulate the controls, which responded according to the rules of aerodynamics. The simulator included landscape seen through the cockpit window, wind, and engine noise. The pilot's instruments and the force feedback on the controls all responded accordingly.

The late 1950s and early 1960s saw the re-emergence of motion platforms. The more complex systems could reproduce accelerations in six degrees of freedom (two degrees of freedom in the direction of roll, two for pitch, and two for yaw—see Figure 1.1). Visual systems also became increasingly standard and featured a number of different methods for handling scene generation.

Figure 3.1—*Another runway as shown by the IVEX Corporation Simulator.*

The first computer image generation systems for simulation were produced by the U.S. General Electric Company for the space program. Ivan Sutherland, inventor of the head-mounted display, teamed up with David Evans in 1968 to form Evans and Sutherland. They developed electronic scene generators for flight simulators using digital computers.

The earlier systems of constructing scale models for scenes used paint, foam, and glue. Any three-dimensional object can be recreated on a computer with points and lines; the object is said to be *digitized*. The view of the object may be transformed with a series of calculations. It has long been known that the closer to reality the simulation is, the more use it is. The problem with this is that "realism" involves a great number of calculations. These calculations have to be done quickly enough that the scene can be rendered before it is already out of date. Every computer has a limit on what complexity can be achieved in what time. If the rendering is too slow, no amount of detail will make the system appear real. In fact, it can cause the operator to experience "simulator sickness," a feeling very much akin to motion sickness, which is described elsewhere.

Figure 3.2—*Fractal mountains created by the IVEX Corporation Simulator.*

Virtual Simulators

Essentially modern flight simulators are refinements of existing methods. They may incorporate the latest graphics tricks or central processor, but in effect, little has changed in the construction of a flight simulator. The amount of computer power now available, however, has opened up new alternatives to traditional flight cockpit design, information display and presentation, and training techniques. The world of virtual environments (virtual reality) has been slowly intruding into flight simulation. Although the truth of the matter is that in many ways virtual-environments research is still in its infancy, we have finally reached the point that usable devices are available.

Military Experimentation

The U.S. military began experimenting with head-mounted displays (HMDs) in 1979. The idea was to reduce expense and the size of the system by projecting the whole display directly into the pilot's eyes. One of the first of these systems was produced by McDonnell Douglas and was called VITAL. It used an electromechanical head tracker to determine head orientation and gaze. It had two monochromatic cathode ray tubes (CRTs) mounted in the helmet next to the pilot's ears. The CRTs projected the image onto beam splitters in front of the pilot's eyes. VITAL allowed the user to view and manipulate the mechanical controls in the cockpit while simultaneously viewing the world painted by the computers on the CRTs. Problems with the bulky helmet and the unnaturalness of looking through beam splitters limited its acceptance.

In the 1970s, for the first time, the capabilities of advanced fighter aircraft began to exceed that of the humans who flew them. The F-15 had nine buttons on the control stick, seven more on the throttle, and a bewildering array of gauges, switches, and dials. Worse, in the midst of the stress and confusion of battle, perhaps even as they begin to black out from the high-G turns, pilots must choose the correct sequence of manipulations.

 NOTE Pilot jargon: 1 gravity or G is earth's normal gravity. At 2 G's you would weigh twice your normal weight. At 10 G's you would weigh ten times your normal weight—it's sort of hard to move and the blood rushes out of your extremities, including your head.

Thomas Furness III had a background in creating visual displays for the military dating back to 1966. He had some ideas on how to manage the deluge of information provided to pilots. He succeeded in securing funding for a prototype system to be developed at Wright-Patterson Air Force Base in Ohio. The Visually Coupled Airborne Systems Simulator (VCASS) was demonstrated in 1982. Test pilots wore the Darth Vader helmet and sat in a cockpit mockup.

VCASS included a Polhemus tracking sensor to determine position, orientation, and gaze direction in six degrees of freedom. It had one-inch-diameter CRTs that accepted images with 2,000 scan lines, four times what a television uses. It totally immersed the pilot in its symbolic world, a world which was created to streamline the information to be presented to the pilot. The world was symbolic for the same reasons we use a map and not a photograph to determine where we are going.

The Air Force saw promise in VCASS and funded its second phase, called *Super Cockpit*. Thompson, in an Air & Space article, described what the future Super Cockpit pilot might see:

> When he climbed into his F-16SC, the young fighter jock of 1998 simply plugged in his helmet and flipped down his visor to activate his Super Cockpit system. The virtual world he saw exactly mimicked the world outside. Salient terrain features were outlined and rendered in three dimensions by two tiny cathode ray tubes focused at his personal viewing distance. Using voice commands, the pilot told the associate to start the engine and run through the checklist ...
>
> Once he was airborne, solid clouds obscured everything outside the canopy. But inside the helmet, the pilot "saw" the horizon and terrain clearly, as if it were a clear day. His compass heading was displayed as a large band of numbers on the horizon line, his projected flight path a shimmering highway leading out toward infinity.
>
> A faint whine above and behind him told the pilot even before the associate announced it that his "enemy" ... was closing in ...

Furness found a new way to combat the information overload that advanced fighter pilots face. He manufactured a symbolic virtual world that presents the important information from the fighter's instruments and sensors while filtering out the irrelevant. He incorporated voice and sound cues to simplify the many tasks the pilot has to perform. Radar and sensors become the pilot's eyes and ears; his words command his fighter to perform.

Summary

Flight simulation has progressed in many of the same ways as heavier-than-air flight, and over much of the same time period. More features and more realism have been progressively added to flight simulators. Modern simulators can offer truly incredible realism both from a procedural and from a flight perspective. A true explosion is occurring in the numbers and types of flight simulators due to be used for training in the near future.

CHAPTER
4

Applications and Uses

This chapter explains the application of flight simulators. The discussion begins by covering their most important advantages. You will learn about some of the typical applications of flight simulators including research and design, training and education, and entertainment. Finally, the chapter discusses some applications that are related to flight simulation—applications which readily share technology.

The Advantages of Flight Simulators

Flight simulators have advantages over other common simulator applications. The most significant advantages are cost, safety, availability, and ecology.

Cost

Flight simulators can consume a large portion of a budget. Modern aircraft capital, operating, and maintenance costs are quite high. Further, an aircraft devoted to training generally cannot support its original mission. For example, an aircraft used for take-off and landing practice (touch-and-gos) isn't terribly useful for transporting people long distances; and most governments do not support training missions in combat zones. Also, keep in mind that simulators typically cost between 30% and 65% of the craft simulated. Operating costs are close to 8% and life-cycle costs are near 65%. An effectively used simulator can be amortized in as little as two years, if it's used 80–90% of the time. Moreover, a flight simulator can "crash," "burn," and "lose engines" without incurring any aircraft repair or replacement, not to mention human costs.[1]

 These statistics apply to classical flight simulators; virtual environment based simulators are often much less expensive.

Researching and engineering flight simulators allow the designers to test and refine principles before employing significant resources; this is especially true of full computer simulations. Many new and even radical designs can be tested rapidly and more thoroughly than ever before. Design cycles can be shortened, system design and maintenance documentation can be maintained automatically, and more design and test iterations can be performed.

Safety

Flight-related accidents have occurred throughout history (see Chapter 3 for examples). Training in a flight simulator is inherently safer and more reliable than training in a real aircraft. Risky maneuvers and emergencies can be rehearsed and practiced in complete safety. Strangely, before the adoption of flight simulators, in many cases more aircraft were lost to *training* for a particular emergency than were lost to the emergency itself. The best documented of these cases was emergency handling of asymmetrical aircraft after an engine failure. Tests and studies for a variety of enhancements, new designs, and the verification of aircraft design limitations can be performed without risk to aircrew or aircraft.

The military supports many high-speed, single-seat aircraft. Pilots must train for such craft in either a two-seat aircraft or with flight simulators. The specially developed two-seat aircraft are far more costly than the original and have different handling characteristics by virtue of the difference in design. Flight simulators provide an attractive alternative that is equally valid, allows a superior allocation of resources, and is totally safe.[2]

Availability

Aircraft resources can also be measured in terms of availability. High-ticket or new aircraft may simply be unavailable for any purposes, especially training. This point can best be exemplified by spacecraft pilots: how many practice runs does a pilot get to land a real space shuttle (a huge glider with no power)? Further, reliance on the weather for training or testing is no longer required. Trainers can conduct day, dusk, and night flying in a variety of weather and visibility situations at any convenient time in a simulator. Additionally, pilots can rehearse missions that involve flying over enemy positions and practice precision strikes with a variety of aircraft, without angering a potential adversary or ally and without tipping your hand.

Ecology

Military, space, and other high performance aircraft use a great deal of nonrenewable resources for fuel and construction. These aircraft also produce pollution. Military aircraft often leave a litter of spent shell casings and other paraphernalia in their wake. Noise is another form of pollution, found especially near airbases and along heavily traveled air corridors. Supersonic aircraft are major noise polluters, and primarily for this reason have been limited in their roles of civilian transport. Pollution and environmental concerns have been on the rise since the

1970s. Flight simulators provide a very real means of minimizing environmental disturbances and conserving precious resources.

Typical Applications of Flight Simulation

The applications for flight simulation generally fall into the categories of training and education, research and engineering, and entertainment. Entertainment is the only one of these fields that does not require real aircraft to complement the services flight simulators provide.

Training and Education

Modern air and spacecraft are highly complex vehicles, requiring specialized knowledge, skills, and reflexes to operate properly. Flight simulators provide an important ingredient in developing, maintaining, and assessing both civilian and military flight crews.

Both civilian and military aviation use flight simulators extensively for further training. Simulators are commonly used for conversion training and to meet recurrent and upgrade requirements and qualifications. *Conversion training* refers to training an aircrew on an aircraft with which they are not familiar. Aircrews must meet certain levels of flight and emergency preparedness training to maintain their flight status. Simulators are often used to develop and validate aircrew proficiencies. Flight simulators can also prepare and test candidates for new positions or ratings, and to provide advanced training such as air-to-air refueling.

The U.S. military has perhaps the greatest acceptance of flight simulators. This is partially due to the deeper and broader training and higher level of maintenance required of military aircrews. The military also uses flight simulation from the very introduction to flight received by aircrew candidates. The civilian sector relies on smaller and less expensive aircraft for basic flight training, so flight simulation is not as thoroughly entrenched.

Simulators, although less costly to operate than an aircraft, remain a significant expenditure of resources. However, they are excellent tools for applications requiring a high success rate in the operating layout, functionality, and behavior of an aircraft, and where the tasks to be learned test the operator's development and proficiency.

Design, Research, and Engineering

Modern aircraft design and development have become very complex. Aircraft need to be more fuel efficient, fly faster, carry a larger payload, land on and take off from shorter runways, require fewer flight crew to do more, simplify maintenance, and increase reliability (to name a few goals), all while reducing costs and design cycle time. In short, designers have to do much more, more reliably, and in a shorter time than ever before. Flight simulation is expected to fulfill an ever-increasing role in this process. An excellent example is the new Boeing 777, which was completely designed and simulated on computers. Part of this plan is intended to provide a completely paperless maintenance system. Future enhancements to this process may allow maintenance technicians access to the design notes of the aircraft, and indeed all of the information used to design and supervise the construction of a particular aircraft.

Research simulators have quite different requirements than training systems. Typical training simulators are designed to support the education and assessment of flight crews on real aircraft. They need to provide only a generally representative flight model which may be tuned for computational efficiency (the "quick and dirty" approach) in an effort to provide real-time responses. The user interface must be complete, accurate, responsive, and flexible. Training systems provide the instructor and perhaps the student with situational analysis. These systems may include built-in instructional features to help the student.

Research simulators can help determine design limitations and analyze and validate alternative designs. These simulators typically require very precise, mathematically complete flight models, which might require too many complex calculations to provide real-time response.

The user interface might be one of many designs and may not even resemble any aircraft. Data analysis is typically performed after the simulation is complete.

Modern in-flight simulators have been used since the 1950s. Cornell Aeronautical Laboratory (later CALSPAN) pioneered work on variable-stability aircraft. The advantages of using an in-flight simulator include the obvious: the aircrew is operating in a natural environment, displays and controls need not be simulated, and the pilot receives the proper motion stimuli. The electrical feedback control system for the aircraft can be modified and monitored for later analysis. Such systems are required to provide empirical data on the behavior of flying systems.

Ground-based simulators run the gamut from relatively simple computer-based systems designed to provide a proof of principle, to full-sized simulators used to devise and practice docking and orbital maneuvering of spacecraft not yet invented. The whole U.S. space effort has been heavily dependent on flight simulation.

Entertainment

Flight simulators have long been associated with entertainment. Link's 1930 patent described the simulator as an amusement device among other things. Simulators used by entertainment have quite different requirements than those used for training or engineering. For example, the accuracy of the flight model and the handling characteristics of the craft need not concern the entertainment simulator designer. In fact, the accurate layout of a cockpit or the precise amount of haze and visibility are often sacrificed to produce a very responsive simulator that merely approximates aircraft flying. These simulators are not judged by their accuracy, but rather by their playability and the amount of revenue they can generate. Nonetheless, these are the types of simulators the public is most often familiar with, and the technology needed to mass produce these simulators often reduces the cost of other types of simulators, making them more accessible.

Related Fields

A number of related fields have benefited from the technology created by the quest for a better flight simulator. Some of the more important of these fields include simulation, scientific visualization, virtual environments, and military warfare simulations. All of these fields are subjects of intense research at this time; each specialty providing new technology for other fields. The following sections provide a definition and brief discussion of each of these fields.

Simulation, Modeling, and Scientific Visualization

The general field of simulation has been around since the advent of computers. The goal of general simulation is the same as for flight simulation—to imitate the functions of one system on another (usually a computer) in order to study, experiment, and perhaps interact. The 1950s found aircraft designers crunching numbers on mainframes to produce graphical output, a process called *modeling*—this was not an interactive process. Keep in mind that the Digital Equipment Corporation (DEC) PDP-1, the first minicomputer, was introduced about this time, costing merely hundreds of thousands of dollars (as opposed to millions) and at only the size of a large refrigerator instead of a large room. J.C.R. Licklider of the Massachusetts Institute of Technology (MIT) began the spearhead toward interactive (as opposed to batch) computing. Scientific Visualization is the latest outgrowth of this line of technology.

Scientific visualization is the marriage of simulation, modeling, and interactive computing. Near real-time simulations provide graphics from simple line plots to three-dimensional animated surface plots. Often the perspective of the viewer, as well as many other display variables, may be changed interactively as the simulation proceeds.

Many other related fields help fuel the rapid developments now progressing in this family of fields. Graphics, photorealistic ray tracing and radiosity, and animation (more details later) affect the quality and speed of the displays. New computer architectures are being designed and implemented to enable higher-quality simulations with more realistic, more responsive displays.

Virtual Environments (Reality)

A technology that is just becoming practical is often known to the public as *virtual reality* (VR). Alternative names include virtual environments (popular among researchers) and *artificial reality* (a particular category). This field extends widely but is generally associated with *head-mounted displays* (HMDs) and gloves. HMDs cover your eyes with small computer monitors on which the computer projects a computer world or a melding of a computer world with the physical world. As you turn your head, the display changes in much the same way it does when you turn your head in the real world. HMDs also often include stereo or three-dimensional sound cues that are modeled on the way we hear. The gloves enable you to interact with objects in the virtual environment. Gloves may provide *tactile* or *force-feedback* when you collide with objects in the virtual environment—that is, if you push an object, you can feel it push back.

Modern virtual environments research is generally dated to 1965, when Ivan Sutherland (the future co-founder of the flight simulator company Evans and Sutherland) published a paper entitled "The Ultimate Display." His challenge and his vision contributed substantially to the state of the computer world today. Only now do we have computers powerful enough to create virtual environments that can be of use. Today's virtual environments include such diverse categories as architectural walkthroughs and computer-aided design, augmentation and decision support, telecommunications and human-computer interfaces, scientific research, and entertainment.

Architectural walkthroughs are static virtual environments, usually consisting of the designs for a proposed construction project. These range in size from reorganizing or building a new kitchen to rebuilding large areas of Berlin and making large scale changes to the Port of Seattle. Once you don the gear and enter the virtual environment, you can "walk" or "fly" through the designs, deciding what you like and what you don't. Ideally you could spend a day in this world, doing all the things you would normally do, and verifying the design. *Computer-aided design* is related to architectural walkthroughs, but may not be necessarily related to architectural projects. A typical example might allow you to sit in your tractor, look around, and ensure that things are placed to give the operator the greatest possible view of the surrounding areas (for safety verification). The equipment used to fix the Hubble Space Telescope was all created in a virtual environment that allowed many design fixes to be made before expensive models had to be created. Additionally, the engineers had a baseline to determine how they should verify a physical model of the repairs.

Virtual environments allow stock brokers to fly over fields of rapidly changing data in order to spot trends and support their decisions. Future field technicians may wear a small set of spectacles allowing all of their manuals, and indeed all of the design notes and designers' thoughts, to be spread out conveniently in virtual space while they perform maintenance in the field.

Human-computer interfaces are perhaps where virtual environments could potentially shine the most. For example, chemists searching for new compounds can don gloves and goggles and manipulate simulated molecules. Operators whose equipment works in a place hazardous for humans (inside a nuclear reactor) or far away (on the moon, in space, or out in the boondocks) may don their gear and operate that equipment safely from home. *Telediagnosis* is a recently popular idea that allows people in rural or remote areas to be seen by a doctor who is physically far away but, via computer, can look over a patient and prescribe treatment for local medical people to perform. This is an excellent way to access specialists. Scientific researchers are creating complex simulations, and then standing in the midst of them while the simulations run and evolve.

Training is another important area for virtual environments. Medical researchers are practicing eye surgery complete with instruments, texture, and sounds. Medical students can fly through the stomach to gain a new perspective on things. Baseball pitchers,

Olympic and professional athletes, and beginning skiers can enter virtual environments geared to help them train and increase their abilities more efficiently.

Then there's entertainment: virtual environment games are the current rage, including Dactyl Nightmare, where different contestants fight each other in mock combat while avoiding an unfriendly Pterodactyl, and BattleMech, where contestants sit in simulated high-tech vehicles and fight battles with others. In the meantime, Carnegie Mellon is building a networked virtual art museum that will provide a multi-cultural forum for a variety of exhibits.

Virtual environments research is just starting to make a substantial impact on other fields. While a number of substantial obstacles remain before virtual environments become widespread, it looks to be a very promising field. In case you were wondering, chapter 11 describes how virtual environments research has affected flight simulation. Another excellent place to learn more about virtual environments is *Virtual Reality Excursions* by C. Watkins and S. Marenka (Academic Press Professional, 1994).

Military Warfare and SIMNET

Modern warfare is perhaps the most complex activity performed by humans. Mistakes not only cost lives, but can endanger a culture's or nation's very way of life. Consequently, the U.S. military heavily supports training in a variety of manners. Large-scale exercises such as the Army's National Training Center and the Air Force's Red Flag provide valuable opportunities for complete teams from air defense forces to attack aircraft and bombers to compete in mock combat. At some point, everything needs to be hooked together to see if, indeed, everyone can even talk to each other. (This is not as simple as you might think in battle.) However, the cost of such exercises is high and safety constraints must be followed.

Enter SIMNET, a network of relatively inexpensive simulators that allow soldiers in vehicle simulators all over the world to fight mock battles without regard to cost, safety, environmental impact, geographic boundaries, or the constraints of time. Simulators exist for vehicles ranging from the M1 Abrams main battle tank to the A-10 close combat air support fighter to AH-64 Apache attack helicopters. These simulators are not the full-blown training simulators designed to fool even the most discriminating. For instance, the M1 simulator frame is constructed out of fiberglass and all of the non-combat gauges are dummies. However, all of the viewports show scenes of battle. Sounds range from the rumbling of your tank's engine to the blast of its muzzle, as well as those around you. These simulators are real enough that sweat drips from your body as you maneuver and fire on the battlefield. It is not uncommon for your tank crew mates to swear as things unfold. In short, a terrific emotional impact is achieved without full-blown realism.

This kind of training is more similar to the large-scale exercises than to the single-person or crew simulator. Unlike a more traditional simulator, no reset button exists if you make a mistake. Instructors aren't looking over your shoulder and no controllers or umpires exist. You must consider logistics throughout. If you're low on fuel or projectiles, how and where do you rendezvous with a supply truck? You can drive or fly off in the wrong direction. Casualties and kill removal happen in real time—when your displays die you are dead. Commanders must modify their battle plans to accommodate the vagaries of a particular battle. Another benefit comes after the battle: de-briefing and reviews can be performed in the same manner that they would be after real battles. Absolutely no alternative exists to real empirical trial-and-error experience, but SIMNET provides a forum to gain this experience in a manner that is cost effective enough to allow its regular use, while completely safe and valid.

Summary

A wide variety of applications related to flight simulation exist. All of these fields share new technologies to some extent, although they all have a different focus on what is important. The technology used for flight simulation can affect such diverse fields as medicine and

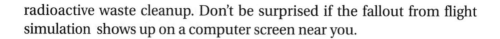

radioactive waste cleanup. Don't be surprised if the fallout from flight simulation shows up on a computer screen near you.

Notes

[1] Rolfe, J. M. and K. J. Staples. *Flight Simulation.* Cambridge: Cambridge University Press, 1986, p. 234–5.

[2] *Ibid.,* p. 235.

Section II

Concerning the Operators of Flight Simulators

Human beings are tremendously versatile creatures. Humans have adapted to live all over the world in a wide variety of climates from the snowbound north to the hot jungles of the equator. We've even made brief forays outside the relative safety of our own planet. Flight simulation makes use of one of our greatest strengths—our ability to imagine. We can believe so much with so little data. Who'd believe that people sitting in a small room could think they were really flying through the clouds with the birds?

CHAPTER

5

Sight and the Human Eye

The eye, whilst it makes us see and perceive all other things, takes no notice of itself.

—John Locke, *Essay Concerning Human Understanding*

The human eye is arguably the most flexible and advanced viewing system on the planet. A hawk could read a newspaper headline at a quarter mile—if it could read. The harbor seal has greater dark sensitivity; certain fish can distinguish finer shades of color, and cats can perceive very fine motions. But only the human eye can resolve a penny at 215 feet, see 10 million colors, register a single photon, pick out the Andromeda Galaxy two million light years away, and spy a fly washing its nasty little head.

Animals are separated from plants by the presence of eyes and by their motility. Indeed, the very origin of eyes is thought to lie in the demands of motility: early swimming life forms developed visual pads to

enable them to swim toward the light and away from shadows (as hovering predators were visually blocking the light). This theory also explains the crossover of visual fields in the two sides of the brain: the theory being that to swim *toward* the light you wiggle your fin on the *opposite* side of your body.

The Human Eye

The human eye peers out on the world from a bony socket, riding on a cushion of fat. Six muscles hold the eyeball in a sling which allows it to rotate in whatever direction it wishes. The eye also contains the only true pulley in the human body. Figure 5.1 shows the human eye. The white outer layer of the eye is called the *sclera*; it is the tough, opaque tissue that holds everything together. The sclera surrounds a transparent tissue called the *cornea* which allows light to pass further into the eye. Directly beneath the cornea is the *iris*, the colored part of the eye. The many different flecks of color on the iris are more distinctive than fingerprints. In fact, these patterns can be used to allow computers to recognize you and verify your identity. The iris has circular and radial muscles that control the expansion and contraction of the *pupil,* which is the dark hole in the center of the iris and of the eye. Bright lights and close focusing cause the iris to contract, while dim light and far focusing causes the iris to expand, allowing more light to enter the eye. Interestingly, emotions also affect the pupil; an unpleasant sight can make the pupil contract (to shut out the pain?). The pupil expands when we sense danger or excitement.

N O T E To take a closer look at your own pupil, get a large piece of aluminum foil and make a pinhole in it. View the sky (not the sun!) through the pinhole. It's your pupil that you are seeing! Try drenching the other eye with strong light from the sky while the first eye looks through the pinhole. You will see the pinhole patch expand and contract in sympathy with your illuminated pupil. Also, note the short but apparent time delay.

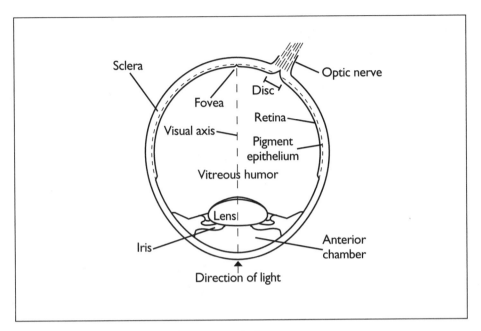

Figure 5.1 *The human eye.*

Directly behind the pupil is the *lens*, which deforms, changing shape to focus the image on the *retina*, at the back of the eyeball. The lens of a camera changes focus by moving back and forth; the lens of the eye works by changing shape—thickening and rounding to focus near images, and flattening to focus far images. With age, the geometry of the eye changes, the lens thickens, and nearly all people need reading glasses by age forty.

Filling the region between the lens and the cornea is a fluid called *aqueous humor*, which supplies nutrients to the lens and the cornea. The interior of the eyeball is also filled with another fluid called *vitreous humor*. At the back of the eye is the *retina*, the region where light is converted to nerve impulses. This is not a passive process; light is absorbed by light-sensitive chemicals such as *rhodopsin*. Carrots and other vegetables containing vitamin A help replenish these chemicals, and thus help us see.

Cells in the Human Eye

Two types of light-sensitive cells, named for their shapes are *rods* and *cones.* They handle the details of converting light into an image. Figure 5.2 shows rods and cones. If you look up at a star-filled sky, you may notice that there appear to be more stars at the edge of your vision than wherever you are currently looking. The 125 million rod cells responsible for dim, gray-scale vision are scattered about the retina, but are concentrated at the periphery. Another interesting property of the rods is that they respond much slower than their cone cousins. Notice how slowly you adapt to seeing in a dark theater, but how relatively quickly your eyes re-adapt to the bright light of day. This is perhaps because when rods function in low-light conditions (where there is less chemical energy), they must work on a slower time frame allowing a longer period of exposure, much as is required for low-light photography. But once adapted, the rods are quicker to detect fleeting movement out of the "corner" of your eye—perhaps a system developed to help you notice your fleeing dinner (prey), an attacking mountain lion (predator), or an unhappy neighbor.

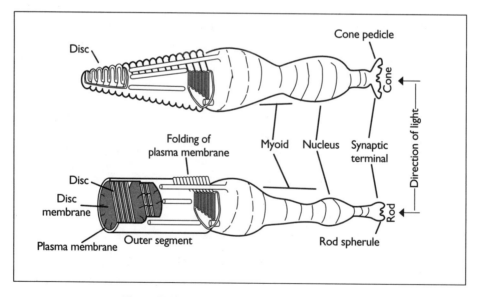

Figure 5.2 *Rods and cones in the human eye.*

Seeing Colors

The 7 million cone cells are predominantly located in the center of the retina, which is an area called the *macula lutea*. For hundreds of years, scientists have believed that there must be three types of color receptors in the eye to account for our color vision. However, objective evidence of this has only very recently been offered. Although the three types of cones are referred to as red, green, and blue, they don't all peak at those colors and they overlap in their responses, especially the red and green. This overlap is important because it enables us to distinguish related colors; the brain measures the ratios of the excitations of these different cones. This is a powerful strategy for identifying colors, but it has an interesting side effect. Certain look-alike colors may be built of different spectral components (a fact known back in Newton's time). While a *spectrophotometer* can tell the difference, the human eye cannot. These colors are called *metamers*. Without metamers we could not have color matching—that is color printing, photography, and television would not exist as we know it, and Barney dolls would look different from Barney rugs because the shades of purple wouldn't match exactly.

As it turns out, the three-gun video system is an efficient way of driving the color system of humans. Red, green, and blue (say, 650, 520, and 436 nanometers respectively) are chosen as the primary colors because they make up a triangle that encloses most of the colors on a standard horseshoe-shaped chromaticity diagram. You will notice that certain colors, called *selvage colors*, cannot be reproduced using this technique. In fairness, I would have to admit that these selvage colors do include many of the most vivid and pure spectral colors[1]; however, these colors cannot be fully reproduced by present-day printing or video techniques. Therefore, the failure is not a fatal criticism of the 3-primary color system.

Seeing Sharpness in Images

In the middle of the retina, at the center of the macula lutea, is a pin-hole-sized area called the *fovea*, which contains roughly 4000 cones and no rods. Almost every cone in the fovea has its own nerve fiber, which gives this area the highest *bandwidth* (the largest communications channel) available, directly to the brain. The rest of the cells on the retina must share time on a nerve fiber, so that they can't produce as sharp an image. When a sharp image is needed, the fovea is called into play. Try looking at one thing, such as one letter on this page, directly and fixedly for any time at all. It is quite hard; the eye keeps dodging around looking for new things to resolve. The fovea is a very small focal area, and the eye has to keep moving to present it with new data.

Intuitively, you might think that with your eyes darting around and your head moving, you'd see a picture that never holds still much like an amateur-made camcorder video. The eye has no shutter and no scanning raster (as does a camera). When we walk down the street, the buildings seem quite stationary. We do not perceive them as a bundle of streaks on our retina, which in fact they are.[2] Simply, the eye is not like a camera, neither still nor video, but rather an image-processing system backed up by the greatest image processor of them all, the human brain.

Millions of years ago, all the creatures that saw their landscape as no more than a blur, died. Think of it as evolution in action. Those creatures that lived had to develop a system to stabilize the scenery. The human brain came up with a wonderfully flexible system, one that is not hampered by any adherence to *Euclidean geometry*. Indeed, parallel lines can and do frequently converge on the retina.

Why don't you take a look at your retina? In a darkened room, wave a glowing penlight back and forth in the corner of your open eye. Keep the light over at the side and don't look at it directly. (Blue cellophane over the bulb might also help.) With each wave of the light, you should see a momentary flash of a scarred and alien vista: your retina is covered with a thicket of nerves and blood vessels. The light-sensitive cells on the retinas of vertebrates are beneath, overlain by their own life-support system. Our clear view of the world is another example of the magic of the brain's processing system.

Perhaps the most important part of the retina contains no rods and no cones. It is an area called the *blind spot*, and this is where the one million nerve fibers hook up to form the *optical nerve*, which is the pathway to the brain. Interestingly, no one seems to have noticed the blind spot until Edmé Mariotte spotted it in 1660. Mariotte was well versed in the anatomy of the eye, and he deliberately set out "to make therefore the Rayes of an Object to fall upon the Optick Nerve of my Eye, and to find the consequence thereof...."[3] The consequence thereof was that the Object disappeared, when the other eye was closed.

Figure 5.3 *Cross and Circle.*

Look at Figure 5.3 while covering your left eye (cover it, don't just close it). Now look at the cross with your right eye. Move the page closer, then farther away. At some distance the circle will disappear and be replaced by white. If the background were checkered, the circle would be replaced by the same pattern. The reason the surface area corresponding to the blind spot can look black or white or colored or striped or checkered or slanted is that it *cannot* appear to be a hole or gap in the surface. To see a hole or gap requires stimulus information, and that is just what the blind spot cannot provide. *Filling in* is a misnomer, therefore, since there never was a phenomenal hole in the world to be filled in.[4] This blind spot can actually cover an area the size of 75 to 100 full moons,[5] however, little, preyed-upon animals like mice have tiny blind spots the better no doubt to see lurking predators.

Sending Images to the Brain

From the back of the eye, the optical nerves traverse to a meeting place in front of the pituitary gland, which is called the *optic chiasm*. Here, those optic nerve strands that carry signals from the right side of each visual field split to the left hemisphere of the visual processing center of the brain. Those strands carrying left side signals head for the right hemisphere. The optic nerve dumps out deep inside the brain. Oddly, the information stream is next sent all the way to the rear of the brain, the area farthest from the eyes, called the *striate cortex*. The striate cortex then passes the data along to the inferior temporal cortex and the posterior parietal cortex for advanced processing. In these areas objects are broken up into different attributes. Edges are analyzed independently of overall shape, and spots of color are handled separately from areas of widespread color—all this constitutes the *object pathway*. Position, with respect to visual landmarks, is assessed separately in its own *spatial pathway*. The brain works massively in parallel. Individual neurons flag certain object properties and no others. The tremendous efficiency of the brain allows us to recognize a pattern from almost no information. The flip side to this strange attribute processing is that we are vulnerable to a wide variety of optical illusions.[6]

Optical Illusions

Optical illusion is a rich field of study—one that any flight simulation designer must understand, in order to exploit what is desired and avoid possible pitfalls. Despite the fact that Aristotle described the "waterfall" illusion in the fourth century[7] (where after a few minutes of watching a waterfall, the scenery around you appears to move up), people still generally have the attitude that "seeing is believing" and can be reluctant to admit that their eyesight can play tricks on them.[8] Illusions that fool most of us might not even be perceived by other people. For instance, geometrical illusions are not normally perceived by people who live in "nonorthogonal" or "colorless" worlds. The Zulus live in round huts, which have round doors; they plow their fields in curves and they don't even have a word for "square" in their language.[9] The Jalé tribe of New Guinea describe things only in terms of lightness and darkness—they have no specific words for color.[10] Cultural background and previous visual experience can greatly affect the perception of illusions that are the basis of computer graphics today, which must be considered as part of flight simulation design.

Stereo Vision—Seeing in Three Dimensions

Three-dimensional computer graphics makes use of illusions to fool our eyes into believing that some objects on a computer monitor are closer than they appear, and some objects are farther. These illusions work only because humans, among other animals, have two eyes whose visual fields overlap significantly. Further, we have developed *binocular vision*—this is the ability to locate objects in three dimensions (out to about 100 feet, sometimes farther). Although it is apparent to us today that these separate visual channels can be fed different perspectives artificially to mimic the sensation of seeing in three dimensions, this experiment seems not to have been attempted until 1832 when Sir Charles Wheatstone invented the *stereoscope*, a device featuring two lensed, eye pieces used to focus the user's eyes on an image producing a three-dimensional view. The stereoscope reached its height during the 1860's but virtually disappeared by the turn of the century.

Holograms, head-mounted displays (more about which later), and blindingly fast computers have revived an interest in three-dimensional displays, although most of us still stare at flat, two-dimensional displays. Experiments have shown that babies will reach for a *stereo* picture of a rattle many months before they will recognize the rattle in a flat photo. Pre-literate people also fail to respond to flat photos.[11]

Something that should be kept in mind, both in flight simulation design, and in all vehicle design, is that stress impairs our binocular vision. A case in point is the naval battle of Jutland. The British rangefinders, which aimed the big battleship guns, were mechanical contraptions that matched two images with the turn of a crank. In contrast, the Germans had state-of-the-art Zeiss rangefinders which were based on an optical enhancement of the gunner's stereo vision. When the big shells began to fall, the Germans lost their stereo perception and were helpless. The British were just as terrified, but their horribly antiquated coincidence rangefinders scored hit after hit.

Three-Dimensional Video Hardware

Essentially, there are three major ways to break down flight simulation three-dimensional video hardware. The cheapest method makes use of a computer monitor and nifty three-dimensionally projected graphics. The most expensive of flight simulators generally uses this approach, but uses several monitors to simulate different windows built into a cockpit. Fred Waller was perhaps the first to make use of synchronized projectors for flight simulation during World War II; his system was like an extremely wide screen movie (five projectors: two on top, three across the middle). Perhaps the newest entry into flight simulation is the head-mounted display. The first head-mounted display was developed by Ivan Sutherland at M.I.T. and then at the University of Utah in the late 1960s. Today even the fastest computers, specially designed for the purpose, are barely adequate to build virtual environments of reasonable use. Their first application to flight simulation was in the early 1970s by the U.S. Air Force, but none of these systems proved viable. It took the VCASS and SuperCockpit programs of the early 1980s to show the worth of head-mounted displays—but these systems were designed as a new kind of human interface to a flight system, not as a training aid! Nonetheless, head-mounted displays and other tools from the virtual environments or *virtual reality* field are increasingly being used in related areas.

Summary

As you have seen, a flight simulation designer has a number of things to consider to properly handle vision. Stereo or three-dimensional vision is very complex and subject to a great many optical illusions; many of these illusions can be used to great effect by the designer. While vision is perhaps the most demanding of our senses, the other senses are also very important, especially if you want the participant to believe your simulation. After all, big shells falling around you wouldn't be as terrifying without sound as they are with full living stereo.

Notes

[1] Rossotti, Hazel. Colour: *Why the World Isn't Grey.* Princeton, NJ: Princeton University Press, 1983, p. 154.

[2] Johansson, Gunnary. "Visual Motion Perception." *Scientific American.* June 1975, pp. 76 ff.

Sound and the Human Ear

In 1923, sound made its debut in the movies in New York City. *The Jazz Singer,* released in 1927, ushered in "talkies" for good. Two years later, most theaters had added sound systems. Sound provides a natural complement to sight. Most humans use a mix of gesture and speech, and sight and hearing, to communicate.

Doors slamming, feet pattering, and dogs barking all communicate subtle clues as to our surrounding environment; we know about many things going on around us, many of which we cannot see. Likewise, the sound of engines, controls, other flight personnel, and even weather plays an important part in flight simulation. The sound of the tires touching pavement communicates as much information as its feeling. Computer games that simulate combat provide a constant din of weapons fire and explosions to make them more realistic. How many video games have you ever played without sound? Did you enjoy them as much without it? (If you did, then the sounds probably weren't integrated well into the game).

Our two ears give most of us *binaural hearing*—we hear in stereo. Stereo hearing helps us to figure out from which direction a sound is coming. Perhaps the most important aspect of this ability is known as the *cocktail party effect*. With stereo hearing, we can tune in on a particular conversation in a crowded room, filtering out all the other competing conversations. However, give us the highest fidelity monaural (mono) recording of that same party, and we would be helpless to repeat this process. Well-made binaural recordings, delivered to our ears by headphones, and surround sound systems enable us to recover much of this ability. One of the latest developments is *three-dimensional sound reproduction*, which can fully duplicate this effect.

Perhaps we should explore more about what sound is and how the human ear works, before further explaining the types of sound reproduction and their implications. Later in this chapter you'll learn what kind of equipment exists and what it can do.

A sound, such as the rustle of a corn chip bag, is actually comprised of lots of air molecules bumping around. When the bag is crumpled, it forces some of the air molecules away from it—this is called a *shell of compression*. As this shell, or group, of molecules moves, it bumps into other molecules in one direction, creating another shell. In the shell's wake is a small band of air with fewer than the average number of molecules, called *rarefied air*. Since this area has fewer air molecules, other air molecules try to rush into this region. Essentially, the crumpling bag creates waves of air around it, much like a stone dropped into a pond, except that the sound expands in three dimensions.

Sound Waves

These waves of air, or *sound waves*, move about 1100 feet per second through air and even faster through liquids and solids. Eventually they find a human ear. As far as the human ear is concerned, sound has two important physical attributes: *frequency* and *amplitude*. Frequency, or pitch, describes the number of compression shells (or vibrations) that are observed at a given point in space per unit time. The standard unit of measure for frequency is *hertz* (hz), which is the number of cycles (or vibrations) that occur per second. Human hearing typically ranges from 20 hz, lower than a string base, to 20,000 hz, higher than a flute.

Amplitude refers to the volume of sound. The standard unit of measure for amplitude is *decibels* (dB), which is a logarithmic scale. Zero dB is the quietest sound a human can hear. The ticking of a watch is about 20 dB. Whispering in a quiet library is about 30 dB (or ten times louder than the watch). The hum of a refrigerator is about 50 dB (or one thousand times louder than a watch). Jet engines and metal bands tip the scale at 140 dB—the point where pain and permanent hearing damage occur.

To see a simple illustration of frequency and amplitude, get a jump rope and tie it to a chair or door knob. Shake the rope up and down so that you make an alternating hill or valley with the rope. This is called a fundamental frequency. The height of the hill (or depth of the valley) is called the amplitude, or intensity. Shake the rope at twice the speed you were shaking it. Now you should see a sine wave—one peak and one valley, alternating back and forth. This is called the first harmonic; the frequency is twice as high, and unless you are shaking harder, the intensity should be the same. Shaking three times faster than the original frequency gives you two peaks or two valleys separated by one peak or one valley. This is called the second harmonic. Shaking the rope harder increases the size of the peaks and valleys, but not their number. Shaking the rope less vigorously decreases the heights and depths of the hills and valleys, but again does not affect their number. I think you've got the point—now give your arm a well-deserved rest.

Another aspect of sound, often called *sound quality*, or *timbre*, is also important. It is the manner in which different sounds intermingle. As sounds of different frequency and their harmonics combine, the sound appears to change. A piano, violin, and flute may all produce the same note, but each instrument contributes different overtones to add a different quality to the music. This is how we recognize the different instruments.

Parts of the Ear

Eventually the sound waves reach a human ear. The outer ear is skin-covered cartilage. It acts primarily as a sound funnel, although the different folds contribute some signal processing. The ear flap is also called the auricle. It opens onto a downward curving tube, the auditory canal. The canal is roughly an inch long, and ends at the eardrum. The outer ear also buffers the middle and inner ear from the environment, which is where ear hair and earwax enter the equation. Wax is secreted by glands inside the ear to help keep foreign material out. The outer ear is also where frequencies resonate.

The *eardrum* is a membrane covered with skin on the outside and a mucous lining on the inner side. This membrane measures a third of an inch in diameter and 1/50th of an inch thick (paper thin). The eardrum displaces air as sounds pound on it from the outside. Beyond the eardrum lies the middle ear and the three smallest bones in the body: the malleus (hammer), the incus (anvil), and the stapes (stirrup), each named for its shape. Figure 6.1 shows these three bones. They act as a chain of levers that transmit and transform energy across the air-filled middle ear to the inner ear, matching the impedance of the outer world to our specialized, liquid organ, bringing the sounds of the dry land to the sea where we evolved. The middle ear absorbs sound and lowers its amplitude while increasing its intensity and maintaining its frequency. Everything moves with the beat of the eardrum.

The stapes attaches to the inner ear's oval window, which is one of two small openings between the middle and inner ear. The other is round (called the *round window*) and compensates for the vibrations of the oval window. In order for the eardrum to vibrate properly, air pressure on both sides of the eardrum must be the same. The one-and-a-half-inch long *Eustachian tube* connects the middle ear and the pharynx to balance the air pressure. This accounts for the "popping" we often hear when we yawn or swallow and the Eustachian tube does its job.

The inner ear is an irregularly shaped cavity in the bone of the skull behind the eye socket. This cavity consists of bone and membrane channels, the bone encasing each fluid-filled membrane. At this point, sound is converted to pressure waves moving in liquid. Just inside the oval window is the *vestibule*, where a pea-sized, snail-shell spiral, called the *cochlea*, is located. It contains a duct winding from the oval window back to the round window. Along the spiral is tissue containing the *basilar membrane*, home to the 25,000 auditory receptor hair cells that are known as the *organ of Corti*. The pressure waves in the cochlea gently bend these hairs, sending small electrical signals along the auditory nerve to the brain. Hair cells near the oval window are best at discriminating high sounds—hair cells farthest are better at low sounds.

The inner ear is an irregularly shaped cavity in the bone of the skull behind the eye socket. This cavity consists of bone and membrane channels, the bone encasing each fluid-filled membrane. At this point, sound is converted to pressure waves moving in liquid. Just inside the oval window is the *vestibule*, where a pea-sized, snail-shell spiral, called the *cochlea*, is located. It contains a duct winding from the oval window back to the round window. Along the spiral is tissue containing the *basilar membrane*, home to the 25,000 auditory receptor hair cells that are known as the *organ of Corti*. The pressure waves in the cochlea gently bend these hairs, sending small electrical signals along the auditory nerve to the brain. Hair cells near the oval window are best at discriminating high sounds—hair cells farthest are better at low sounds.

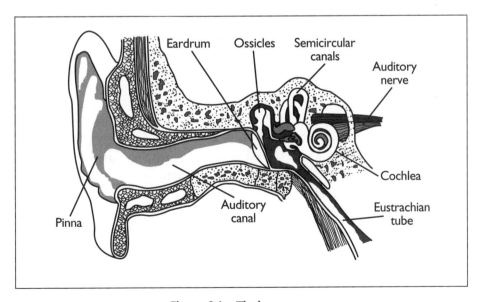

Figure 6.1—*The human ear.*

Very loud noises (and some diseases) can break hair cells; once broken they are dead forever. While the noise of a restaurant or traffic (70 dB) is generally considered safe, a loud lawn mower or chainsaw (90–100 dB) can cause some hearing loss. Walkman headphones can reach 100 dB and rock concerts over 120 dB, which can cause permanent hearing loss. Deterioration of hearing is not necessarily due to age. The Mabaan people who live in the Sudan often have sensitive hearing even when they are old because their world is a quiet one. The human body is a remarkably quiet platform on which to mount the exquisitely sensitive human ear. Consider this: 100,000 people at a football stadium, and just before the national anthem is played... you can hear a pin drop. Imagine by contrast 100,000 autos idling.

Auditory Illusions

The flight simulator designer must be aware of the limitations and strengths of human hearing to use sound effectively in a simulation. Our two ears provide stereo hearing in much the same way that our two eyes provide us with stereo vision. We can resolve sounds like clicks to within 4 degrees azimuth under ideal conditions.[12] Have a blindfolded person sit in a chair. Walk around the person while clicking two spoons together. Ask the subject to say when you are directly behind, judging just by the sound. Most people estimate correctly to within 10 degrees.

On the downside, we are limited to locating sounds in the horizontal plane (we can't distinguish up from down) and we have trouble with pure tones.

Humans localize sounds, using a variety of techniques that are dependent on the sound's duration and spectrum (or the different components that make up sound). The simplest technique we use for locating sounds is taking note of which ear hears the sound the loudest. A more subtle trick is based on the relative arrival time of a sound. Perhaps the most subtle technique is the phase difference between the different ears of the same incoming sound, which can be used to detect as little as one hundred-thousandth of a second difference. Try the clicking spoon experiment again, but this time have the subject place a cardboard tube tightly over one ear (the core from a roll of paper towels does fine). This time, click the spoons several feet off to one side and see if they are judged to be behind. The ear and brain have equalized the *path length*, which now includes the channel through the tube.

Musical illusions can teach us how human hearing works and how we can fool it. This is nearly as important as the visual equivalents, such as perspective. A very simple musical illusion was popularized by Bell Labs. In this experiment, musical tone rises in pitch in 12 steps, and then pauses. After the pause, the tone drops a whole octave, but hardly anyone notices.[13] Such strangeness can be found throughout human hearing.

If you ever have the opportunity to visit a high-quality anechoic (echo free) chamber, you can test out the sensitivity of your hearing system. The room is lined above, below, and around with incredibly efficient sound absorbers. It is so efficient, in fact, that generally people outside will monitor your reactions inside the room. Some people freak out when they can hardly hear the sound of their own voice. But if you keep your sanity, after a couple of minutes, you hear a very faint hiss. Opinion is divided on whether this is the sound of air molecules bombarding your eardrum (calculations show we should be 3 dB shy of having the sensitivity for that), or the sound of turbulence in your blood flow. In any case, you are definitely hearing noise in your auditory sensory channel. And maybe it *is* the air; calculations to the contrary—it's known that the ear can detect a sound which moves the eardrum less than the diameter of a hydrogen atom!

Hearing Hardware

Sound systems found in flight simulators range with the quality of the simulator. The quality of sound directly affects the operator's belief in the simulation. These days, stereo systems provide sound from practically all directions. Surround sound and home theater systems are becoming less expensive and more popular. These systems are based on sound generation techniques now mature in the film industry. However, none of this was good enough for Scott Fisher and the NASA Ames Human Factors Lab's virtual environments test bed (virtual environments is a field also known as *virtual reality* and represents a large portion of the future of flight simulators).

Fisher wanted a system that could reproduce sound accurately enough to allow one to determine its direction. Dr. Elizabeth Wenzel, Dr. Frederick Wightman of the University of Wisconsin, and Scott Foster of Crystal River Engineering devised just such a system. The device is called a *Convolvotron* and works by mathematically modeling a specific human's signal processing function. The model is called the *Head Related Transfer Function*, and it accounts for how our ears transform the sound signal as it is passing through the air near our head. An average person can generally pick out several conversations in a large crowd and can tell the direction from which a conversation is coming. The Convolvotron adds this ability to the NASA system. The operator can hear up to four different conversations or radio tunes simultaneously without the conversations or tunes becoming entangled. The NASA system also eventually included a voice recognition system to combine voice commands and three-dimensional sound cues to aid in the navigation of data space (and perhaps eventually astronauts building a space station in outer space). The Convolvotron suffers from the same problem as the head-mounted display and the gloved-based input device— all of them require calibration on a person-by-person basis.

Perhaps even a better system could come from recent developments in the medical field, the *cochlear implant*. People with sensorineural deafness have problems with their cochlea. A new electronic implant can transmit impulses from a microphone directly to the auditory nerve, in effect bypassing the middle and outer ear altogether. At this point of development, conversation cannot be distinguished by the system, but the volume and rhythm of sound appear to be preserved. Improvements in multiband implants and breakthroughs in the encoding process that the brain uses for signal transmission promise even better sound quality for the hearing-impaired. Interceptions from the nerve channels cause a seeming babel of signals, neither truly analog nor digital as we know it.

Summary

Clearly, sound contributes a great deal to the effectiveness of a simulation, since we humans value it to such a great degree. Now that we've explored the senses of sight and hearing, we're going to look at perhaps the most complex and least understood of the human senses: the haptics system.

Haptics and Creating the Illusion

The senses of touch, pressure, temperature, and pain are often referred to as the *cutaneous senses* (from *cutin*, the Latin word for *skin*). As humans, our boundary and primary interface with the world is our skin—our largest organ at two meters and massing 2.8 kilos. Embedded in our skin are millions of information receptors. Some of these receptors are very specialized, such as those responsible for our taste sensitivity, and hair cells that can feel the slightest breeze. Other receptors, commonly called *free nerve endings*, are less sensitive and generally react slowly to pressure and touch. This proprioceptive system also adapts dynamically to changes in our surroundings that are constant over a long time. This is why a cat can sit on your lap for a long time without continuously exciting your pressure-detection system. Another good example is texture: place your hand on a slick surface; after experiencing a short transient you can't tell what type of surface your hand is

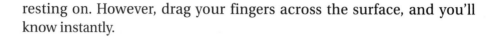

resting on. However, drag your fingers across the surface, and you'll know instantly.

The Effect of Gravity on the Ear

Human beings generally walk upright on two legs. Having evolved in a gravity well, we prefer to orient ourselves with respect to that field—with our feet "down" and our heads "up." Our balance systems expect a gravity field. When astronauts ply the starways, they often get *space sickness*, a form of motion sickness that occurs in the absence of gravity, since they are unable to tell which way is "up." Interestingly, gymnasts, who make more precise use of gravity, are more susceptible to space sickness. While gravity pulls us to the center of the earth, our sense of balance enables us to resist falling under gravity to some degree.

This ability does not depend on sight or sound, although the heart of the system lies within our inner ear. Part of the cochlear duct is made up of three fluid-filled bony loops called the *semicircular canals.* In the *ampula*, the bulbous end of each canal, are hair cells. The three canals are set perpendicular to each other, one each in the three planes of space about your head. Each canal is most sensitive to changes of direction in one of those planes when your head moves up and down, tilts side to side, or twists left and right. Movement in one of these directions (or combination of directions) sets the fluid in the canals moving; this fluid bends the hair cells. The bending hairs transmit signals to the brain. A short lag between a new motion and that motion registering with the brain will usually occur. If you twirl around really fast and then stop suddenly, the fluid is still rushing around inside your head, telling your brain that you are still spinning. This is why you feel dizzy when you stop.

Two other organs of balance may also be found in the inner ear, sacs known as the *saccule* and the *utricle.* Like the canals, these sacs are fluid-filled and employ hair cells, although the tips of the hair cells are enclosed in a gelatinous material. This membrane contains small calcium carbonate crystals called *otoliths* (or *ear stones*). These little stones act like small gravity magnets; they can detect the direction and strength of gravity. Where the semicircular canals provide angular (rotational) acceleration data to the brain, the otoliths and their neighbor hair cells cooperate to provide linear (planar) acceleration data—so your brain knows if you bend over or stand up straight, and which direction is "up."

In addition to our inner ear, certain receptors in our body measure things such as joint angles, position in space, and muscle tension. Some of these receptors help us to balance when we are at rest, others when we are in motion. Our ability to know where all our limbs are in space, without thinking about it, is called the *kinesthetic sense.*

Creating the Illusion

An individual sense cannot truly be treated in isolation. Overlaps and redundancy in data from different sources produce and discard hypotheses about the current state of our environment. The human brain can take small amounts of data and create a detailed database on the surrounding environment, including what kind of changes are taking place and what kind of changes are likely to take place. This database is fed with information from all the senses. We've talked about some of these senses, such as the eyes, ears, and touch, which apply directly to flight simulation; others, including smell and taste apply in more subtle ways (for example, the smell of machine oil). Research about our senses leads us to ask other questions such as: can humans orient themselves to a magnetic field as do birds? Do we use the sense of smell to recognize each other or to choose a mate? Some of these things may be important to tomorrow's designers. Also, different senses have different priorities, which vary depending on the stimulus. While you generally might not be aware of many smells, the sudden scent of baking bread can conjure up a memory from childhood. If you view a straight rod through a curvy lens, you will think the rod is curvy—this is true even if you can handle the rod! Rapidly spinning ballerinas and ice skaters compensate for the ills of their balance system by spinning their heads faster than their body, then locking their eyes on certain still objects. The seemingly still eye image, with some training, can carry more weight with the brain's processing system than the inner ear.

Visual stimuli generally outweigh other information—a fact simulation designers must not forget—but all the information supplied on overlapping areas must agree, or motion sickness (simulation sickness in our case) can occur.

Simulator Sickness

Flight simulators have a long history of a problem called *simulator sickness.* Operators, and even passengers, of all types of simulations have experienced motion sickness-like symptoms—sometimes lasting or re-occurring several hours after the exposure. The severe cases are enough to cause operator performance problems or even safety hazards. Common symptoms include eye strain, headache, nausea, vertigo, and general discomfort; aftereffects include sudden disorientation and flashbacks.

 N O T E A trivial case of simulator sickness is not a fault of the simulation at all, but rather one effect of an excellent simulation—when the "real" event is enough to make you sick. An example of this is a 10-G turn (a very real possibility in a modern jet), which causes you to black out.

Although the causes of simulator sickness appear to vary, sensory conflict appears to be a major contributor (e.g., the haptic system sensing motion different from what the eyes see). Transport delays and uncoordinated simulator displays (especially visual and haptic), perhaps due to breakdowns in the realism of the simulation, are often related to simulator sickness. In fact, visual delay by itself is enough to cause sickness, which means it can affect simulators who have no motion base.

Many aspects of these senses—touch, force, texture, pressure, temperature, pain, motion, and balance—are overlapping. They may be referred to collectively as the *haptic system.* This interconnected system provides much of our knowledge about our surroundings. For this reason, the more complete flight simulators include some sort of force-feedback to the controls of the craft. The better ones also include some sort of motion display. These are the two primary requirements of the haptic system with respect to flight simulation. The controls should move appropriately and "push back" appropriately, if they are going to be useful. When the controls are activated, not only should all the controls display the changes in acceleration, velocity, and orientation, but the pilot should be able to feel those changes. Indeed, one of the largest problems with flight simulation arises when different senses report different information.

Summary

At this point, the causes of simulator sickness are still being researched and debated. One result of simulator sickness is many participants must limit their exposure to the systems. Faster and higher-quality hardware and software will help the matter some, but until everything is figured out, the problem will persist. All this pessimism doesn't mean flight simulators cannot and should not be used, on the contrary, they have already proved their usefulness.

We've attempted to present the basics of how humans work and how they can be fooled, at least with respect to flight simulation. Now that you've got a grasp of the operator's strengths and limitations, to further understand flight simulation we must delve into the fundamentals of flight itself and the contraptions humans use to soar like the birds.

Section III

The Fundamentals of Flight Simulators

The chapters in this section are devoted to describing the fundamentals of flight. To have any valid simulation, we must understand how aircraft fly in the real world, so to this end we address Chapters 8 through 10. Chapter 8 covers fluid mechanics, the body of science governing how objects move through fluids (which includes aircraft moving through air). Chapter 9 builds directly on Chapter 8 by discussing the field of Aerodynamics, the field of science which explains how aircraft fly and what makes them efficient (or inefficient) in flight. Chapter 10 explains about the common propulsion systems found in modern aircraft. Chapter 11 describes virtual environments, the gear that goes with them, and their impact on flight simulation. Chapter 12 deals with many of the issues facing flight simulation today including Cockpit Resource Management (CRM) and Line Oriented Flight Training (LOFT).

An Introduction to Fluid Mechanics

The field of fluid mechanics is the heart and soul of aerodynamics. Fluid mechanics is the study of the motion of bodies as they move through fluids. Before we delve into lifting bodies, we must first understand how fluids such as air behave near and around surfaces such as wings. (Both liquids and gases are classed as fluids). Fluid mechanics is a mature field in its own right. It is also being used in studies of the origin of the universe, the behavior of stars and galaxies, the surface of the sun, the earth's liquid core, ocean currents, and weather. It was also used, with success, to predict traffic flow for the 1984 summer Olympics in Los Angeles, California. The following treatment of fluid mechanics is quite brief and includes no calculus descriptions, although some mathematical equations are presented.

Properties and Definitions

Matter is generally considered to exist in three phases: solid, liquid, and gas. Solid matter is different than the other phases because it offers resistance to any change in shape. If you bend a fork a wee bit, it will return to its original shape. If you bend it further, it may hold its new shape. If you bend it enough, it will break. Liquids and gases, in contrast, offer no resistance to change in shape; indeed, shape is not a quality typically used to describe either liquids or gases. Many of the important properties for describing a craft moving through either a liquid or a gas are the same. Consequently, liquids and gases may be considered together as fluids. The general application of fluid mechanics applies equally well to a submarine or an airplane.

Properties of Fluids

Since any gas or liquid can be considered a fluid, the properties of fluids vary enormously. However, once a few basic properties are understood and measured, we no longer need to consider the particular fluid for most of our analysis. Let's discuss some of the properties of fluids we need to know.

Density

Density describes how closely packed and heavy the molecules of a substance are. Solids usually have the most tightly packed molecules, so solids are commonly the densest form of matter. Gases have the loosest packing of molecules, so are said to be least dense. For example, a 50-gallon fishtank full of concrete would weigh over half a ton; 50 gallons of air weigh about half a pound. Density is a measurement of mass per unit volume, typically kg/m^3.

Incompressible Substances

A substance is *incompressible* if the volume of the substance does not change when pressure—force per unit area—is applied to it. Gases are considered readily compressible. Dense substances, such as solids and most liquids, are considered incompressible. For instance, if you squeeze on a plastic bottle, the stuff inside squirts out. If you squeeze anything hard enough, it will compress, even steel.

Viscosity

Viscosity is a measure of the internal friction of a fluid. Fluids with a high viscosity are generally slow moving and "sticky" such as oil and honey. However, fluids such as water and even air also exhibit the property of viscosity. The *dynamic viscosity* is a particular measure of force divided by velocity, typically $(Ns)/m^2$. *Kinematic viscosity* is the ratio of dynamic viscosity to density.

Pressure

Pressure is a measure of force over some unit area. One of the interesting properties of pressure is that it may be measured without regard to the orientation of the measuring device. The most direct example of pressure might be the atmosphere of our planet. The pressure constantly pushes in on our bodies, typically at one *atm* (atmosphere) or about 14.7 *psia* (pounds per square inch, absolute—measured from the zero of a vacuum, no pressure). Pressure may also be given in Pascals (Pa—1 N/m^2) or *psig* (pounds per square inch, gauge—measured from atmospheric pressure).

Fluid Statics (fluids at rest)

The word *statics* refers to the study of a particle or body that is at rest (*equilibrium*). It is derived from a Greek word meaning "to make something stand". *Fluid statics* is the branch of fluid mechanics that describes fluids and their behavior at equilibrium. Examples of fluids at equilibrium abound. Imagine an untouched glass of water; the glass-like surface of an inland lake, untouched by wind or bathers; or the dead-calm air of a Southern summer, when no wind reaches your brow. Fluid statics helps us understand precisely how a balloon (helium or hot air) can hang suspended in air and how a steel ship can float supported only by water.

The ancient Greek scientist Archimedes (287?-212 B.C.) developed much of the foundation for fluid statics. His principle of *buoyancy* describes how an object immersed in a fluid experiences an upward lifting force equal to the weight of the fluid displaced. This upward force explains why a huge ship made of steel can float on the surface of the ocean. Hot-air and light-gas balloons rise for the same reason—hot air (and light gases) are lighter (less dense) than ambient air at the same pressure.

The Hydrostatic Equation

Archimedes was also the first to explain that in the presence of gravity "each part of a fluid is always pressed by the whole weight of the column perpendicularly above it, unless this fluid is enclosed in someplace or is compressed by something else." When expressed mathematically,

$$p_1 - p_2 = wh$$

it is referred to as the *hydrostatic equation*, the fundamental equation of hydrostatics—a field specializing in the effect of gravity on liquids in equilibrium.

 N O T E This version of the equation is applicable only for incompressible liquids. For this case, only weight in the vertical direction (*gravity*) and pressure are important.

The increase in pressure with depth depends only on the density of the liquid. In a lake, pressure increases linearly with depth from atmospheric pressure (1 atm or 14.7 psia) at the surface. For example, 10 meters (m) below the surface the pressure is 2 atm and 20 m below the surface the pressure has reached 3 atm. You now have enough information to understand Pascal's paradox. The mathematician and philosopher Blaise Pascal (1623-62) observed that for a lake or river with a dam at one end, the pressure at the base of the dam depends only on the depth of the water! It does not matter how big the lake is, only how deep. If there were two giant dams back-to-back, with a film of water a quarter-inch thick between them, each would experience as much force as if they held a thousand-mile sea!

Compressible Media

Unlike water, air is a *compressible medium*, meaning that air at ground level is denser and therefore heavier than air at the tops of mountains. Pascal verified this in 1648 on a mountain, and in a nearby valley, near Clermont, France. For this reason, pressure gauges—*barometers*—are an effective means of measuring altitude. (There is an old joke about the three physics students who were given barometers and asked to measure the height of a building. The "A" student applied Pascal's principle to readings at top and bottom of the building; the "C" student dropped the barometer from the roof and measured how long it took to fall; the "F" student approached the building super and said, "I have a fine barometer here—I'll give it to you if you'll tell me how tall your building is.") Indeed, barometric altimeters are standard equipment on aircraft, although modern altimeters are based on electromechanical devices. Interestingly, even though air is a compressible medium and its density and temperature vary with altitude (for low speed aerodynamics at relatively low altitudes) we may consider the atmosphere to be *isothermal*— of constant temperature. And we may ignore the compressibility of air. This will make our lives easier, and conveniently explains why the early pioneers of flight were so successful despite making such assumptions. Now that we've considered fluids that aren't going anywhere, let's set them in motion and see what happens.

Fluid Kinematics (fluids in motion)

Observing fluids in motion is one of the earliest experiences of the human race. We watch clouds and ocean waves and feel the wind and rain on our bodies. We navigate the flowing water and airways of our planet in various crafts—from canoes to hang gliders. Egyptian, Greek, and Roman records describe the founding of *hydraulics*, the first branch of modern fluid mechanics. The early studies of fluid flow included rivers, open channels, and closed channels such as pipes. *Empirical processes* (trial and error) led to the construction of waterwheels, wind mills, aqueducts, irrigation canals, and water clocks. Modern fluid mechanics is based on *equations of motion*—mathematical descriptions of fluid behavior. The fluid mechanics branch related to the behaviors of fluid in motion is called *kinematics*—a word derived from the Greek word for motion.

A Description of Flow

For our discussion of kinematics, we will use the continuum description of flow. Each element (or discrete piece) of the fluid may be traced in time and space, but is in no other way different from any other element of the flow—the flow is considered to be uniform, and fluid doesn't appear or disappear from the system. For example, air is composed of mostly nitrogen and oxygen with a lot of other substances found in varying but small (or *trace*) amounts. We won't distinguish nitrogen elements from oxygen or argon elements; we consider all of them air and leave it at that. In fact, once certain properties of the fluid are known, no other information need be considered for our purposes (unless the fluid is flammable and we strike a match). As to how we can trace one element of flow, simply consider a bit of cork or a leaf on the surface of a river (which is mainly how this whole field got started).

One of the most common illustrations of kinematics involves *streamlines*. A streamline is "a curve that is at all times and at all locations tangent to the velocity vector"[2] of the fluid flow. For a simpler illustration, consider smoke filaments released in the uniform flow of a wind tunnel (see Figure 8.1). The patterns that the smoke filaments make are streamlines—they show the direction and velocity the air is flowing.

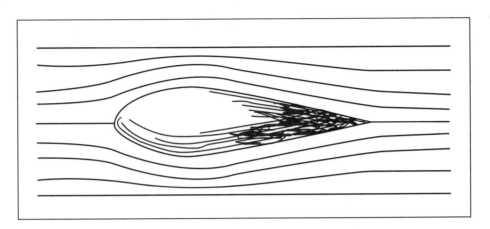

Figure 8.1 *Streamlines of smoke in a wind tunnel (flow is from left to right).*

Steady flow is the happy and convenient situation where on average the flow exhibits little variation. It is typified by an aircraft at cruising speed or water coming out of a faucet once it has been turned on. Each photograph of the streamlines would look practically the same as the last. For steady flow, element paths and streamlines are identical. Unsteady flow involves the ever-changing streamlines found when an aircraft is taking off or landing or when a faucet is first turned on and gurgling up to speed.

Conservation of Mass and Energy

In the following discussion, we will assume that our fluid is incompressible. This is not an unreasonable assumption because air can be considered incompressible for aircraft flying less than one-third the speed of sound (350 km/hr—220 mph). This is the case for arrows in flight, golf balls, and small aircraft. Water is much more incompressible than air, which means the same equations will also apply to fish, dolphins, and submarines.

We cannot escape the laws of nature and the *conservation of mass* and *energy*. Mass and energy may not simply appear and disappear. The forms of matter may change, but they must always sum to the same fixed total. When we consider high-speed and *supersonic flows*, *thermodynamics* and heat energy will also have to enter our equations.

Conservation of Mass

For the case of fluid with constant density, the conservation of mass equates to the conservation of volume. Consider steady flow (in an incompressible medium); since all streamlines point in the direction of the flow, mass cannot cross streamlines. We can select any group of streamlines from the flow; this group will have some cross-section A_1. If we follow these streamlines downstream, we can select another cross-section of the same group A_2. Since this is a steady, incompressible flow, we can treat these streamlines as if they were in an isolated conduit, separate from the rest of the flow. The steady flow from cross section A_1 to cross section A_2, is fixed at the discharge rate, Q (volume per unit time). We define the average flow speed for each cross section to be u. With these definitions we can compute the discharge rate with

$$Q = u_1 A_1 = u_2 A_2$$

We can immediately see something that we can confirm with intuition—the discharge rate is inversely proportional to the area of the flow. Cars shoot through the narrow gap around a traffic wreck, although many cars are backed up before the accident and moving slowly to get there (they are in a larger cross section). For an illustration consider Figure 8.2.

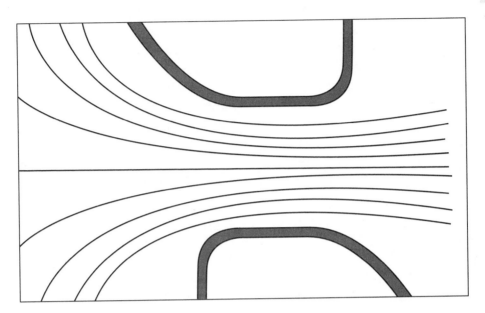

Figure 8.2 *Streamlines of smoke through a nozzle in a wind tunnel (flow is from left to right).*

Conservation of Energy

Now that we've got the conservation of mass, we need to add the *conservation of energy* to our equations. We will use the concept of an ideal fluid to explain the conservation of energy. Our conservation of mass fluid would be an ideal fluid if we specified that the fluid had no internal friction, that is, no viscosity.

An ideal fluid has a *constant density* (volume) and no viscosity. We have an innate idea of viscosity: motor oil is more viscous than water, both of which are more viscous than air. While neglecting viscosity appears drastic, in reality viscosity plays only a small part in most of our fluid dynamics problems. Fear not, we shall consider it later.

Potential energy is the energy stored in mass due to its position, z, above some arbitrary baseline, z_o, in the earth's gravity. For example, water stored in a water tower has a higher potential energy than water at ground level; this is our explanation for why water runs downhill (to a lower energy potential). When mass moves from one height to another (moving with or against gravity), the potential energy must change; these changes are by conversion to or from *kinetic* energy. We must also consider the internal pressure, p, acting on the mass. The sum of these three components must remain constant. For an ideal, incompressible (ρ = constant) fluid in a steady flow

$$p_1/\rho + gz_1 + (1/2)u_1^2 = p_2/\rho + gz_2 + (1/2)u_2^2 = const.$$

where g is the constant of gravitation for earth. This equation is generally referred to as *Bernoulli's equation* (although it does not appear in his famous works[3]); it is one of the most important equations in fluid mechanics because it is applicable to such a wide variety of phenomena. The subscripts again indicate different locations on the same streamline.

We find for air (due to its relatively low specific weight), and water traveling at a constant height z, that gravity becomes negligible. So we casually rid ourselves of the gravity term, which leaves us (with some manipulation)

$$p_1 + (1/2)\rho u_1^2 = p_2 + (1/2)\rho u_2^2 = p_o$$

or in general

$$p + (1/2)\rho u^2 = p_o$$

Consider Figure 8.3. As the fluid approaches the body, it splits, some fluid goes to one side of the body while the remainder goes to the other side. A point exists on the body that is between these streams, the *stagnation point*—at this point the fluid's velocity is zero. The pressure at this point is known as the *stagnation pressure, p_O*. The term p is known as the *static pressure*, which is the pressure of the upstream, as yet undisturbed, fluid. The velocity-dependent term $((1/2)\rho u^2)$ is called the *dynamic pressure*.

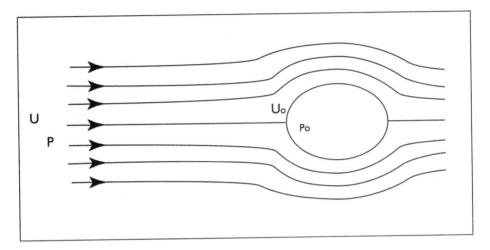

Figure 8.3 *Ideal fluid flow around a body.*

Measuring Flow

In theory, we could drill a hole in the leading edge of an airplane wing and use this to measure the stagnation pressure (at the leading edge, the flow stops). However, Henri de Pitot (1695-1771) thought of a better way. He dipped a tube into the water near his boat and by estimating its depth, he determined the approximate flow speed. Using this system, he also measured the speed of the boat and anticipated the use of this same system to measure air speed. An enhancement of Pitot's tube, known as a *Pitot-static* tube with an attached *differential manometer* (great name, see Figure 8.4), can be calibrated to measure air speed directly. A well-designed Pitot tube is insensitive to the angle of attack (angle with respect to the wind) of an aircraft, a very useful feature. Most modern aircraft use an electromechanical device that is based on the deflection of a membrane.

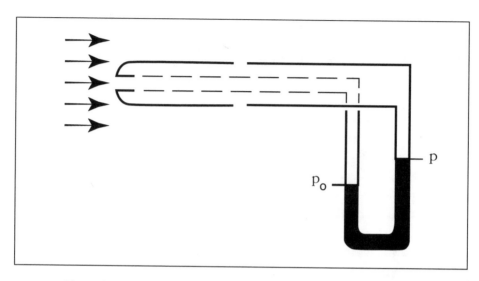

Figure 8.4 *Pitot-static tube with an attached differential manometer*

Now that we can compute both the stagnation and static pressures, the difference yields the dynamic pressure. We can derive our velocity from Bernoulli's equation (or from above).

$$u = [(p_0 - p)(2/\rho)]^{1/2}$$

While ideal-fluid laws cover a wide variety of fluid phenomena, as you will soon learn, eventually the *internal friction* of the fluid must be considered. (I told you we'd get to it.)

Viscosity—The Internal Friction of Fluids

Viscosity is a measure of the internal friction of a fluid, a property for which we actually have some intuitive feel. As stated earlier in this chapter, oil is stickier and slower moving than water—both are more viscous than air. For engineering however, we need a more quantitative description of viscosity. A common way to study the behavior of fluids requires two concentric cylinders with a fluid-filled gap that is much smaller than the radius of either cylinder. If one cylinder is held fixed while the other is turned at a known rate, the torque (turning moment) may be measured directly. Once the *torque* is known, viscosity can be calculated in a straightforward manner. This method also agrees with our intuition—the torque required to turn such a cylinder with an air-filled gap would be less than for the same system with an oil-filled gap (oil having the higher viscosity).

Consider two parallel plates, one held stationary, separated by a fluid-filled gap (such as shown in Figure 8.5). The upper plate moves with a constant velocity, *U*, by some force, *F*. You will observe in real applications that the fluid directly adjacent to either surface attempts to adhere to it. The fluid can no longer be considered ideal; the fluid sticks to both surfaces and the fluid's internal friction dominates the flow speed. For example, consider withdrawing a knife from a jar of honey: the outer coat of honey oozes back into the jar fairly readily while the honey next to the knife hardly appears to move. If you watch the side of a ship, the water closest to the ship is dragged along with it.

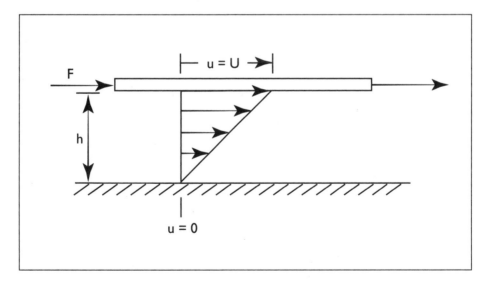

Figure 8.5 *Flow between parallel plates with the lower plate held stationary.*

From Figure 8.5 we can also introduce the concept of velocity pro-files. The horizontal lines represent the local velocity (flow speed) of the fluid (the longer the line, the faster the fluid is moving) with the station-ary base plate as the origin. This velocity profile is *linear*, that is, the increase of the velocity follows a straight line. Interestingly, this linear relationship governs narrow gap flows for fluids as diverse as oil, water, and air. The relationship is given by

$$u = U \bullet (y/h)$$

Notice that by setting $y = 0$ you get $u = 0$, which is the condition of veloc-ity zero at the base plate. For $y = h$, it gives $u = U$, which is the condition of velocity U at the upper plate.

Try thinking of the fluid as layers of fluid, stacked one on top of another, each layer exhibiting friction between the others. Take a phone book and lay it on a flat surface. Bend the book along an axis parallel to the spine. Notice the friction acting between the pages. This model of fluid interaction dominated by viscosity based on separate layers (*lami-nae* in Latin) is called *laminar flow*. The internal forces resisting the motion of the upper plate is defined as shearing force or shearing stress. This force is analogous to overcoming friction between two solid objects (such as shoving a brick across a desk). The shearing force τ is propor-tional to U/h and is given by the force required to maintain the flow F divided by the area of the surface in contact with the fluid, A ($\tau = F/A$). Additionally, it should be readily apparent that as the velocity, U, of the upper plate (see Figure 8.5) is changed, the slope of the velocity profile will change (for a larger U the slope will be smaller—further to the right). This proportionality constant was defined by Newton as the *dynamic viscosity*, μ. Newton's law of shear is given by

$$\tau = F/A = \mu \bullet (U/h)$$

This relation conveys that the shear force increases with increasing vis-cosity for a constant velocity. And additionally, with fixed viscosity, the shear force increases with increased velocity.

Dynamic viscosity, μ, divided by density provides us with another useful measure of the properties of fluids called kinematic viscosity. For incompressible fluids, density and temperature are both constant, which implies that *kinematic viscosity*, and thus the dynamic viscosity, is also a constant.

If we relax our constant temperature constraint, we find that as temperature increases, the viscosity of liquids decreases, while the viscosity of gases increases (over most temperature and pressure ranges). This seemingly contradictory behavior can be explained at the molecular level, although we will not discuss this further here.

Turbulent Flow and the Boundary Layer

Up to this point, we have considered only *inviscid* (or ideal) and *viscous* (or laminar) types of flow. The most common type of flow is called *turbulent*. At higher speeds the orderly layers of laminar flow give way to seemingly random swirling patterns. The shear rates of turbulent flow are much higher than that of laminar flow, with a correspondingly higher loss of energy. At this point, we must compute shear rates empirically because we still do not fully understand these flows. Turbulent flows can be found all around us. Leonardo da Vinci observed the *vortices* created by boulders in a river and turbulence in breaking waves. Consider leaves or snowflakes swirling in the wind, the flames of a fire, or the surface of the sun; all of these are different aspects of turbulent flow.

Theories in Flow

Gotthilf Heinrich Ludwig Hagen (1797-1884), a German hydraulic engineer, performed the first systematic study of turbulent flow. In his studies of laminar flow, he noticed that under certain conditions, such as water at higher temperature (and subsequently, lower viscosity), the

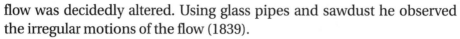

flow was decidedly altered. Using glass pipes and sawdust he observed the irregular motions of the flow (1839).

Concurrently, but separately, Jean Louis Poiseuille (1799-1869), a French physician, was studying flow in small pipes with applications to experimental physiology (such as blood flow). Poiseuille's experiments led to the exact mathematical derivation of viscous flow in pipes. The distribution of velocity as a function of pipe radius was found to be *parabolic* with a velocity of zero near the walls and a maximum velocity at the center of the pipe.

Osborne Reynolds (1842-1912) published in 1883 the definitive work on laminar and turbulent modes of flow as well as the transition between them. Reynolds used a glass pipe that took its flow from a reservoir. The apparatus was carefully designed so as not to disturb the flow as it moved from the reservoir to the pipe. The center of the streamline was marked with dye. Laminar flow would proceed part of the way down the pipe. Then, the flow would become wavy (the transition), then suddenly the dye would be spread from one side of the pipe to the other (turbulent flow). The velocity profile for turbulent flow seemed to be the same all across the pipe except right at the edges, where it went to zero.

Ludwig Prandtl (1875-1953), a German engineer, gave a presentation at the Third International Congress of Mathematicians in 1904 that can be counted as the beginning of modern fluid mechanics. He described a deceptively simple system for combining the turbulent and *inviscid* (free fluid) flow models; two very different branches of fluid mechanics. Essentially, fluid flow must be considered in two distinctive parts. Most flow can be considered inviscid. For flow in a narrow band near any fixed boundary, viscosity must be considered.

Consider Figure 8.6. Air flow is laminar as it first encounters the plate. Notice the distinctively laminar velocity profile (on the left). Then flow enters the transition region, finally becoming turbulent. Notice the turbulent velocity profile (on the right). This picture does not show any of the flow above δ, the boundary layer, because all such flow may be considered inviscid, as if the surface was not even there.

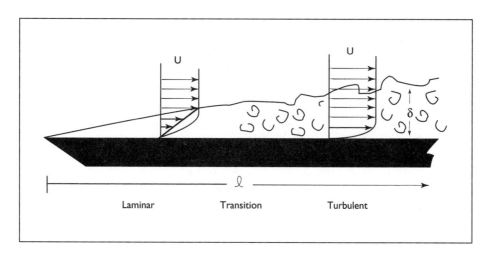

Figure 8.6 *The boundary layer of a flat plate exposed to a uniform flow of speed U (flow is left to right).*

The turbulent boundary layer is one of the most important fields of research in aerodynamics at this time. That ever present hissing noise you encounter on airplanes is the turbulent boundary layer creating irregular pressure pulses which beat on the cabin. The boundary layer around boats, bird wings, and even earth's atmosphere is turbulent. While turbulence is all around us, we still have no closed mathematical solutions, only empirical rules-of-thumb, unlike the case of laminar flow. Another thing to consider: one of the greatest differences between turbulent and laminar flow for our purposes, is that the skin friction is much higher for turbulent flow. Even an aircraft with low aerodynamic drag has a large surface area, and skin friction applies to all of it. For this reason, research into how to sustain laminar flow (hold off the transition) is also quite active.

Summary

Whew! if you made it this far you've got some small background in fluid mechanics—enough to continue on into aerodynamics, anyway. As you will see, aerodynamics builds on the inviscid and turbulent flow models we have just developed. Perhaps it should also be re-iterated that a great deal of calculus is required to go much farther with fluid dynamics (indeed, vector calculus was first created to deal with fluid flow). However a number of references are available that provide far more detail than found here while still keeping out of calculus' way. For those of you gung ho enough to tackle the calculus, some references are also included for you—enjoy!

Notes

[1] Wegener, Peter P. *What Makes Airplanes Fly?* New York: Springer-Verlag, 1991, p. 44.

[2] *Ibid.*, p. 59.

[3] Binder, R. C. *Fluid Mechanics*. 3rd ed. New York: Prentice-Hall, 1955., p. 64.

An Introduction to Terms and Concepts

At this point, you should have enough background in fluid mechanics to understand many of the subtleties found in the following discussion of *aerodynamics*. Again, much of the discussion of aerodynamics is applicable to movement in any fluid, not just air. This chapter covers the basics of aerodynamic drag and lift—two of the primary forces affecting flight. You'll notice in Figure 9.1 that drag is a force impeding progress through the air and lift is the force keeping us in the air.

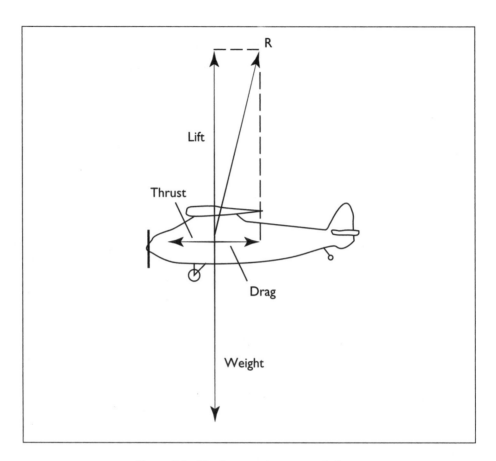

Figure 9.1 *The forces acting on an airplane.*

Since much of aerodynamic testing is done in wind tunnels, on less-than-life-size models, there must be a way to apply these small-scale tests to the creation of real aircraft. The most common similarity parameter is called the *Reynolds number* which is basically the ratio of *inertial forces* to *viscous forces* acting on a fluid. It is calculated as follows:

$$Re = (Ul\rho)/\mu = (Ul/v)$$

where U is the flow rate, l is the ratio of the length of the model to real scale (1:10), and v is *kinematic viscosity* (ρ/μ). In flows with high Reynolds numbers, fluid inertia is the dominant force; in low-Reynolds-number flows, viscous effects predominate. It is still a mystery how gnats manage to fly in what is for them a fluid as viscous as honey.

Aerodynamic Drag

When you swim, put your hand outside of a moving car, ride a motorcycle, or lean against a gale force or hurricane wind, you encounter a force pushing against you, resisting your motion—a force called *aerodynamic resistance* or *drag*. Indeed, any object moving through a fluid is impeded by this drag. From Figure 9.1 you can see that drag is balanced by another force, *thrust*. The larger the drag, the greater the thrust we must provide to move through a fluid. Worse, to increase the thrust, we may have to add to the weight and size of our craft, which may well increase the drag and increase the building expense. These concerns must be addressed during the aircraft design and development process. They directly impact the simulation of flight.

Fluid Dynamics and Drag

Let's delve into drag from our modern fluid-dynamics point of view. Recall from our discussion of the conservation of mass and energy in Chapter 8, our definition for dynamic pressure

$$q = (1/2)\rho U^2$$

where U is velocity and ρ is a fluid compressibility term (constant for incompressible fluids). We will define S to represent the surface area exposed to the impeding drag force, D. The drag coefficient can then be defined as

$$c_D = D / (qS)$$

By manipulating this equation

$$D = c_D Sq = c_D S(1/2)\rho U^2$$

This expression is related to one found in Newton's work in the late seventeenth century. Newton's law of force (force (F) equals mass (m) times acceleration (a)) can be written

$$F = ma = m(du/dt) = d(mu)/dt$$

where *mu* (mass times velocity) is momentum. In short, *drag* may be defined as the change over time (d/dt) of the momentum of the fluid due to the body in the fluid (our airplane in air). (Okay, in Chapter 8 I fibbed, that was calculus; I'll try not to let it happen again!)

Consider the previous equation—drag is proportional to the square of the velocity, irrespective of the type of fluid. Since the surface area, *S*, of our aircraft remains constant (we hope), *doubling* the speed of our aircraft *quadruples* its drag! This alone is a good reason for reducing aerodynamic drag in vehicles ranging from cars to airplanes, more drag requiring more power, and a bigger engine, to achieve the same performance.

Fluid and Object Shapes

From our intuition, we expect long slender objects to pass easier through fluid (have less drag) than blunt objects. The coefficient of drag for more aerodynamic bodies is less than for blunter bodies. Some objects and their coefficients of friction are considered in Figure 9.2.

Let us consider *blunt bodies* (blimps and traditional kites would be good aircraft examples). Blunt bodies have a streamline pattern which varies little with changes in speed. Consider Figure 9.3, the flow about a disk. At the top and bottom edges of the disk, the flow departs from following the shape of the disk. This is called *flow separation*. Notice the turbulent flow at the back of the disk. *Surface friction* will play a minor role, while the *parabolic drag law* will apply directly.

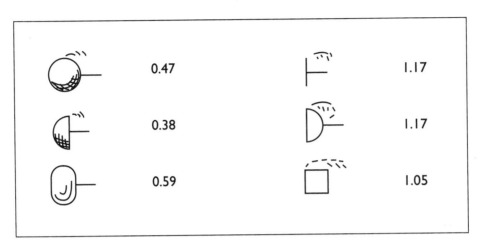

Figure 9.2 *Typical coefficients of drag for blunt bodies.*

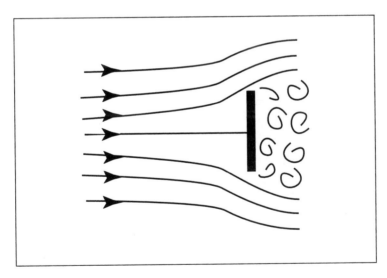

Figure 9.3 *Flow about a disk.*

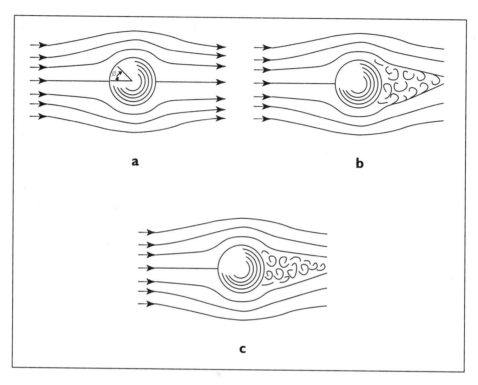

Figure 9.4 *Flow about a sphere.*

Figure 9.4a shows the ideal flow about a sphere. Since this is ideal flow, flow separation does not occur. When we determine the pressure at the front (the *stagnation point/pressure*) it equals the pressure at the back of the sphere (where the flow joins). Since there is no friction in ideal flow, drag forces sum to zero—no drag! This paradox confounded many researchers for a long time. While determining drag for the general case of blunt bodies, friction need not be considered. However, the sphere is a special case. Figure 9b shows real flow with a *laminar fluid boundary*, notice the flow separation. For this case there is no appreciable back pressure and drag is normal. Figure 9c shows real fluid flow about a sphere for the turbulent flow case. Friction at the *turbulent boundary layer* keeps the flow attached to the sphere longer. This in turn increases the back pressure (helping to move the sphere through the flow) and thereby reduces the overall drag. Indeed, for blunt objects, the higher friction of turbulent flow is more than compensated for by the increased back pressure and lower coefficient of drag. That is why golf balls have dimples—to force an earlier transition to turbulent flow, enabling the dimpled ball to fly farther.

Surface Friction

Up to this point, we have neglected *surface friction* in our calculations of drag; however, when we consider long, slender bodies streamlined to reduce drag, such an assumption is no longer valid. In Figure 9.5, the top view presents ideal flow about a streamlined body such as a fish or wing. The bottom view presents real flow including a boundary layer about the same object. Although the boundary layer is small, it still displaces the streamlines around it for a certain distance called the *displacement thickness*. The displacement thickness, which can be calculated from boundary-layer theory—a topic we will not pursue further—is some fraction of the boundary layer (which extends to the *free stream*). This displacement causes the geometry of the streamlines to change, which causes a change in the pressure field, effectively increasing the drag due to increased surface friction.

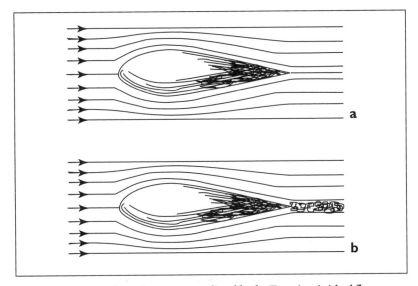

Figure 9.5 *Flow about a streamlined body. Top view is ideal flow.*
Bottom view is real flow, including a boundary layer.

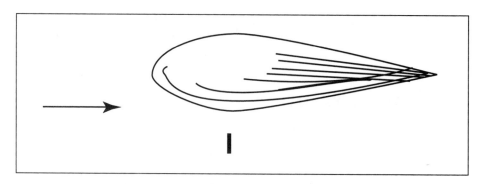

Figure 9.6 *A streamlined body and a disk with identical drag.*

Deriving a coefficient of surface friction is similar to deriving the drag coefficient. Surface friction is significantly higher for turbulent flow (on the order of $Re^{-1/5}$) than for *laminar flow* (on the order of $Re^{-1/2}$). *Laminar boundary layers*, however, have yet to be maintained over an entire surface in a practical manner. So for now, we have little choice but to work with turbulent flows and their much higher *surface-friction drag*.

The boundary layer further influences the streamlines by inducing flow separation. When the flow breaks away from the body's surface, *back flow* may appear, *vortices* are formed, and the pressure on back surfaces drops, increasing the drag. We now have the tools to explore this phenomenon further. From *Bernoulli's equation*, we learned that constricting the flow reduces pressure in the constricted region and increases *flow velocity*. Conversely, as the flow area increases, the pressure increases and the flow velocity decreases. All real objects have finite length and at some point have a maximum width, beyond which the flow has more area and consequently higher pressure. In short, for streamlined bodies, such as *airfoils*, the boundary layers must negotiate increasing regions of pressure as they reach the end of the body. Boundary layers *decrease* in thickness for regions of high pressure and *increase* in thickness for regions of low pressure. This means that at the rear of the airfoil, the pressure is decreasing and the boundary layer is thickening.

At some point, the flow velocity reaches zero. This may be on the surface of the body or beyond it. The surface friction goes to zero and the flow may even reverse—that is, flow backwards. At some point, flow separation will occur. Interestingly, the higher surface friction actually abets the role of turbulent flow in preventing flow separation longer than laminar flow, thus yielding an overall lower drag. Once flow separation occurs, it is often best to chop off the body at that point and have a flat base trailing the rear of the object; this is why many objects such as boats and cars have flat rear ends (peruse Figure 9.2 again).

Aerodynamic Lift

We have reached the heart and soul of heavier-than-air flight—aerodynamic lift. Recall Figure 9.1. *Lift* is the force that keeps our airplane in the air. The simplest and perhaps oldest man-made lifting device is the kite. The force you feel holding the kite string is the kite's *lifting force*. The kite is quite similar to the flat disk shown in Figure 9.3. The lift force is at right angles to the wind direction. At the center of the face of the kite the pressure reaches the *stagnation pressure, p_o*. During the last century, box versions of the kite were used much as tethered balloons were used to raise men above the battlefield for observation.

Kites are essentially blunt bodies; by contrast, modern flying machines generate lift in a manner similar to birds, based on slender wings. Indeed, birds were the first models for heavier-than-air, man-made craft. Consider Figure 9.5; three wings of different design with very different lifting properties, even though all of them have the same angle of attack. The wings in 9.5b and 9.5c have *camber*, meaning that the upper wing section is curved. If we divide the lift by the drag we get the *lift-over-drag ratio* (tricky name), a measure of wing efficiency. The lift-over-drag ratio for modern aircraft is typically close to 20.

Since we are primarily interested in how a lifting wing works, consider an infinitely extended wing to simplify matters such as flow about a fuselage and around the wing tips (simplification by ignoring). Since you now have a grasp on the subject of aerodynamic drag, we will again consider *inviscid flow* and ignore friction (and therefore drag).

The surface of the top of the wing is larger than the surface of the bottom of the wing, owing to the camber or arched shape of the airfoil. The flow must separate to pass around the wing, and so must rejoin after passing the wing. In fact, if you calculate what the flow should look like, it would look something like Figure 9.7a. Now we apply Bernoulli's equation—no lift or drag. This is much like the mystifying case of the sphere; we know there's lift because wings and birds fly.

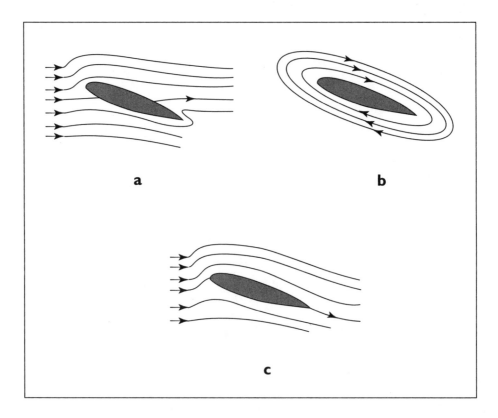

Figure 9.7 *Ideal flow about a wing. a) calculated basic flow,*
b) circulatory flow, c) the sum of a and b.

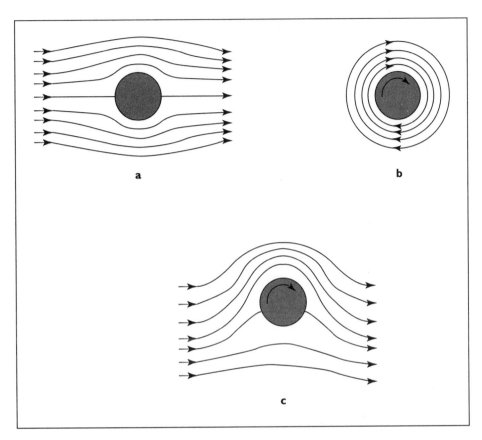

Figure 9.8 *Ideal flow about a cylinder. a) calculated basic flow,*
b) circulatory flow, c) the sum of a and b.

The Mangus Effect

An English doctor of law named Frank Lanchester (1863–1946) suggested that a *vortex* acting on the wing could be the cause of lift. Lanchester's idea was based on the *Magnus effect,* named after Heinrich Magnus (1802-70), a German physicist and chemist. Figure 9.8a shows the streamline patterns of a cylinder immersed in *ideal flow.* Recall that the pressure is identical in the back and front of the sphere which indicates no drag. Consider a cylinder immersed in *concentric streamlines*

(Figure 9.8b). Superimpose the two and add them together; the results are shown in Figure 9.8c. According to Bernoulli's equation and the conservation of volume in incompressible flow, we have low pressure on top and high pressure beneath the cylinder—a net force acting at right angles to the flow.

The force due to the Magnus effect has long been known to artillerists. A projectile shot from a smooth barrel suffers from erratic and unstable flight. If the barrel is rifled, that is, has helical indentations along the inside, the projectile comes out spinning, and is stabilized in much the same way as a *gyroscope*. This spinning produces a force acting on the projectile perpendicular to flight, causing a deviation in its flight path. This deviation may be calculated based on range and speed using empirical methods on a proving ground (firing range). A sliced tennis ball or a hooked golf ball also exhibits the Magnus effect, as does a baseball pitcher's intentional curve ball.

Lanchester's postulation essentially applied the Magnus effect to an airfoil. In short, one adds the original ideal cross flow to a *concentric circular flow*. This process is shown in Figure 9.7, with 9.7c being the result—lift.

Research Leading to Kutta's Condition

Wilhelm M. Kutta (1867–1944) became interested in Otto Lilienthal's glider flights. In 1902, Kutta published his thoughts on flight. Kutta's research was carried out independently, but in parallel with Lanchester's. Kutta wrote a doctoral dissertation on wing theory in 1910.

Kutta's work was followed, again independently, by Nikolai E. Joukowski (1874–1921) at the University of Moscow. Joukowski built a wind tunnel at the University to carry out his experiments. His first paper was published in 1906 in Russian; a translation in French soon followed.

Kutta and Joukowski, unlike Lanchester, provided mathematically based descriptions of their theories of flight. They quantified the vortex circling the wing (see Figure 9.7b). By choosing the strength of the circulation the *rear stagnation point* (where the under- and over-flows rejoin) can be chosen to be on the top, or even underneath, the wing. Kutta was the first to propose a solution to choose the flow speed that corrected some unrealistic mathematical predictions. His requirement, now called *Kutta's condition*, stipulated that the strength of the circulatory flow must be chosen such that smooth flow is ensured at the trailing edge of the airfoil. Interestingly, these theories of flight are equally applicable in other fluids.

Vortices in Air Flow

How does this vortex start? The air flow above the wing is moving slower than the air flow under the wing. A *shear force* develops where these two flows meet which results in the faster flow "curling up" to form an *eddy* (see Figure 9.9a). This eddy is called a *starting vortex*. It is shed after flow has become reasonably uniform across the airfoil, at a rate high enough to sustain some lift. Once the starting vortex has been shed, the circulatory wing vortex has begun. The starting vortex and the wing vortex must rotate in opposite directions to satisfy our conservation laws.

What happens to the vortex as the airfoil comes to a stop? When the airfoil ceases its motion, the circulatory vortex is shed in much the same way as the starting vortex; it is simply left behind.

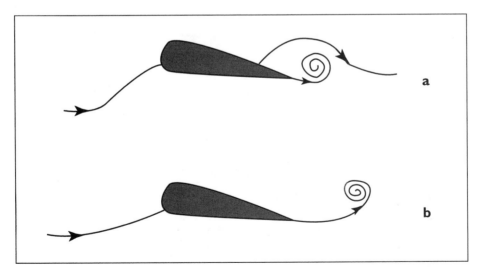

Figure 9.9 *The starting vortex. a) its formation, b) as it is shed.*

Lift and Control Surfaces

Lift as a function of *angle of attack* is nearly linear over its range—that is, the higher the angle of attack, the greater the lift. Past a sufficiently high angle of attack, however, the lift suddenly levels off then rapidly decreases, which leads to a *stall*. A stall occurs when there is a separation of flow across the top of the wing; see Figure 9.10. If the *lift force* drops below the aircraft weight, the aircraft begins to lose altitude.

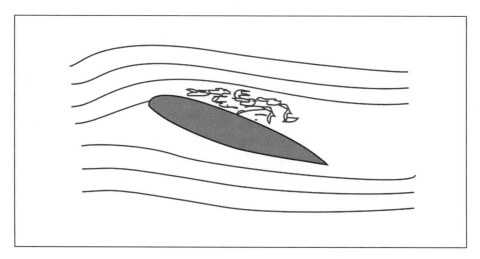

Figure 9.10 *Flow about a stalled wing.*

Pilots have detailed instructions about the maximum angle of attack for a given airplane to avoid a stall. They have sensors that warn them of an impending stall. Skillful pilots can even fly out of a stall. But how do we as designers safely provide the extra lift required for landings and takeoffs on short runways (emergencies, after all, do happen). One of the earliest solutions to this problem was the biplane, which featured two airfoils, one above the other. Biplanes remained the rage until wood and cloth gave way to metal; there was no easy way to build a long, smooth airfoil with wood and cloth. Biplanes suffered from a relatively high drag because the flow of the different wings interacted. Many other wing and fuselage arrangements are in use; however the most common way to increase lift is to take advantage of the way lift works—the pressure difference between the upper and lower part of the wing. A lift increase can be achieved by increasing the surface area and the camber of the wing. Figure 9.11 shows typical extensions. The leading-edge flap, or *slat*, and the trailing-edge flap, usually referred to as a *flap*, are added. Flaps increase the lift, while slats can increase the stall angle or change the angle of attack of maximum lift, depending on the design. Interestingly, the spaces between these movable sections and the main wing actually enhance flow attachment by allowing the higher pressure air from the lower surface to rise and mix with the low pressure, upper-surface air.

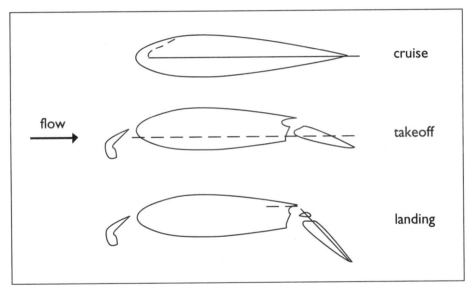

Figure 9.11 *Slats (leading edge) and flaps (trailing edge).*

Summary

Here ends our brief discussion of aerodynamics. You now have some background to help you understand the discussion of flight models and such found in Section V. True flight simulation requires mastery of calculus as well as a background in a number of interdisciplinary skills including fluid mechanics, aerodynamics, and power systems.

Flight Propulsion Systems

Most modern flight is made by powered, heavier-than-air craft. The propulsion systems used for these craft determine many of their flight characteristics. Propulsion systems ranging from rubber-band-powered propellers to rocket engines provide the force called thrust (see Figure 9.1). Newton defined *force* as the rate of change of momentum (mass times velocity) with respect to time. All propulsion systems impart momentum to the oncoming air (for air-bound vehicles). The way this is accomplished defines the primary differences between propulsion systems. Typical aircraft propulsion systems include propellers, jet turbines, and rocket engines. All of these systems employ Newton's third law to provide thrust; that is every action (force) produces an equal and opposite reaction (force). A force generated to change the momentum of the air produces an equal and opposite force, called *thrust*, which propels the aircraft forward.

Use of Propellers

Propellers are driven by an engine that effectively imparts kinetic energy (half of the mass times the square of velocity) to the oncoming air, speeding its journey. Until nearly the end of World War II, gasoline powered piston engines—often referred to as *internal-combustion engines*—were the only type of engine powering heavier-than-air craft. These engines are based on the same principles as car engines. In fact, the Wright brothers considered using a car engine of their time but those engines were far too heavy, so they built a custom, lighter one. In any case, a mixture of gasoline and air is forced into a cylinder, then ignited. The resulting explosion forces a piston within the cylinder away from the explosion. The piston, in turn, turns a crankshaft, which delivers power to the propeller. These engines generate anything from the 9 kW (12 horsepower) of the Wright Flyer to over 1500 kW (2000 horsepower). The most powerful of these featured the cylinders in a radial pattern around the propeller and achieved speeds of over 800 km/h (500 mph)—close to the cruising speed of modern jet airliners. The most efficient of these engines generated about 0.9 horsepower per pound.

A propeller works on the same principle as an airfoil (wing). As the propeller moves through the air, there is greater air pressure on the back surface than on the front surface. When the propeller is turning at constant revolutions per minute (rpm), or constant *angular velocity*, the linear speed of the propeller blade increases with its distance from the propeller's axis. To optimize the propeller's thrust (or *lift*) and account for these speed differences, the blades of a propeller are twisted to change the local angle of attack at each location. This is how propellers acquired their strange shape. Even stranger-shaped propellers can be found in modern times; they are called *turboprops* and can be incredibly efficient. Turboprops were invented to counteract or lessen the severity of the major failings of propellers. Because propellers derive their thrust from the same principles as wings, they encounter the same types of drag problems. Wing tip vortices (the strangeness of air flow around wing tips) contribute to drag and the propeller constantly interacts with its own wake, creating uneven lift distribution, yet propellers remain among the most economical propulsion systems. Turboprop airplanes are the marriage of gas turbines and newly designed propellers. While they typically produce on the order of 2000 horsepower, they do so at 2.5 horsepower per pound.

Use of Turbines

Gas turbines, the forerunner of today's jet turbines, were first used by coal and natural gas plants to generate electricity. Much of the technology to create jet turbines came from other industries and was quite mature before its introduction into airplanes. Jet turbines made their debut near the end of World War II, first by the Germans, then independently by the English. Although this propulsion system was clearly superior, it had little effect on the outcome of the war.

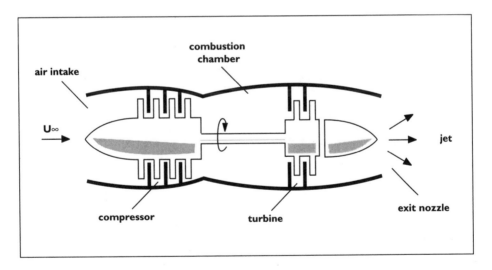

Figure 10.1 *A simplified turbojet engine.*

The Modern Engine

Let's take a tour through a simplified modern turbojet engine (see Figure 10.1). Large fans on the front of the engine suck air into the engine. These are *turbofans*, a common enhancement. An axial compressor (the most common type) increases the air pressure supplied to the combustion chamber using short propeller-like blades, called *vanes*, some of which are rotating around the shaft; others called *stators* are attached to the outer wall and remain stationary. Several stages of these turning and fixed vanes are used to increase the pressure gradually. This compressed air is mixed with liquid fuel and ignited in the combustion chamber. The intense heat and gases produced by the explosion contribute to and expand the volume of air. The turbine is also composed of fixed and static vanes, but these blades grow steadily longer to help expand the hot gases and air. The turbine also uses some of this energy to power the engine and other airplane systems. The greatly accelerated air is exhausted through the rear of the engine. Notice that this system imparts both mass and velocity to the airstream. The primary components of drag for jet engines are the drag of the outer covering and the *ram effect*—the stoppage of air as it enters the engine. The turbojet is very efficient and economical and may be largely responsible for the widespread popularity of modern air travel.

Rocket Engines

Rocket engines carry all of their own supplies and thus do not require an airstream to provide oxygen. This feature alone is what makes them suitable for use in space. (This was not understood at first; as late as the 1920s the *New York Times* said that people who believed in flight in outer space were "ignorant of that knowledge which is daily ladled out in our high schools.") The first rockets to be combined with airplanes were created by the Germans during World War II, the V-1 "buzz bomb" is the best known example. In 1947, Captain Charles E. "Chuck" Yeager flew a rocket-powered airplane to break the sound barrier in level flight for the first time. Rockets are generally powered by either liquid or solid propellant. Liquid fuel rockets generally contain two tanks, one filled with fuel such as alcohol, and one filled with an oxidizer such as liquid oxygen. These liquids are pumped to a combustion chamber where they mix and ignite. The beauty of this system is that the speed and mixture of the fuels can be computer controlled. The difficulties lie in working with the liquid fuel and oxidizer, which are often highly corrosive, flammable, and like liquid oxygen, may need to be kept at very low temperatures. *Solid propellant rockets* consist of simply a solid propellant with a star-shaped or circular channel cut through the middle. An igniter lights the fuel that burns along the surface of the channel; the channel effectively is the combustion chamber. Unlike liquid fuel rockets, solid fuel rockets burn at a constant rate until all the fuel is gone—once ignited, they can't be stopped (the "burning bars" used by thieves to penetrate bank vaults are essentially sticks of solid rocket fuel). On the plus side, solid propellants are generally very stable and somewhat hard to ignite, which makes them safer and easier to handle. Rocket engines provide thrust by discharging hot gases at high speed. The exhaust nozzle's shape is very important because it must produce a jet at supersonic speeds, which means it must account for the non-linear compressibility of gases among other esoteric problems.

Virtual Flight

A number of chapters is this text have mentioned or discussed virtual environments or virtual simulators to some extent. This chapter discusses virtual simulators, virtual flight, and their potential impact on flight simulation, especially for the areas of design and training.

Virtual Simulators

The U.S. government has backed flight simulation from its inception. This is also true of the field called *virtual environments* (*virtual reality*). VCASS and the SuperCockpit projects (see Chapter 3) were aimed at creating a new user interface between the pilot and an aircraft; however, such an interface lends itself readily to simulation. After all, if the pilot's normal view of the aircraft is provided by a computer, how will the pilot differentiate between a simulated and a real computer signal. In any case, the SuperCockpit has not found its way into any fighters as of yet, although the technology required to prototype it has had more success and finds itself creating virtual environments. In some respects, flight simulators can be considered virtual environments (VEs) already. In fact, drawing the line between them can be quite tricky, but let's take a shot at it.

At this point, you are probably familiar with a typical flight simulator, so let's walk through a typical VE setup. The pilot dons a special bug-eyed helmet, typically called a *head-mounted display* (HMD). The bug eyes house miniature *liquid crystal displays* (LCDs) or *cathode ray tubes* (CRTs) that are essentially computer monitors designed to present stereoscopic images of the computer-generated world around you. The helmet also includes sensing equipment to provide the computer with the orientation and position of your head. It is not uncommon for a stereo or three-dimensional sound system and perhaps even a gaze tracker to be built into the helmet. With all this information, the computer can determine what the operator is supposed to be looking at and provide an appropriate, constantly changing display, both visually and auditorily, in real time.

The pilot also pulls on some special gloves. These gloves can determine the operator's hand orientation, position, and how curved the fingers are; this also provides a mechanism for the pilots to see their hands in VE land. The pilot might be sitting in a simple mockup (*really* simple, some video games are more visually convincing). This mockup includes a control stick, foot pedals, maybe some other important, dummy controls, and perhaps a motion platform. The visual aspects of the mockup would not be important since all of the visual stimuli are computer-generated and displayed directly to the helmet.

Perhaps the interface for the visual stimuli constitutes a good distinction between flight simulators and VEs. Indeed, both systems use computers extensively for terrain and scene generation, collision detection, and to drive the controls and displays. In virtual systems, the whole visual scene is generated, cockpit and all. For flight simulators detailed hardware mockups are created, complete with accurate controls. So, you ask, what would you use a virtual simulator for?

Virtual Research and Design

Virtual environments began their association with flight as a research vehicle for new forms of flight control interfaces. The goal of such research was to reduce the information flood inundating the pilot by restructuring the information flow and hiding irrelevant information. VEs now provide an important research and design platform for new aircraft, for enhancements to existing aircraft, for designing new flight simulators, and as a supplement to existing flight simulators. VEs can contribute to interfaces, design from within, and rapid prototyping; in addition, they provide exceptional flexibility.

Flight cockpits are more complex than ever. Computers abound to help automate tasks, but in doing so, they often provide more information to the already overloaded pilot. The skies are steadily increasing in traffic. Different people, often remotely located, need to coordinate their activities more than ever, with deadly results the potential penalty for any mistake. VEs are already contributing as experiments in new ways to present relevant information quickly and cleanly to the pilot, while hiding unneeded information. VEs seem to provide a more natural computer-human interface than any yet devised. VEs can also be used to study existing interfacing issues with the added benefit that experimental changes to its presentations are quite easy to implement.

Computer-aided design has taken a new twist. Experiments with designing real environments from within virtual environments are now commonplace. For instance, a virtual environment operator might try moving the controls to new locations while inside the VE environment. This approach bypasses the arcane process of describing changes to a programmer, who must make the changes, which then must be verified. Skip the programmer, move the controls yourself.

VEs can totally redefine the field of rapid prototyping. A new aircraft can be constructed and tested without building any physical mockups. The Boeing Company, working with the University of Washington's Human Interface Technology Lab, created a new generation of computer-aided design tools to develop large aircraft. Indeed, the new 777 was designed and built without the creation of a full-scale physical mockup. While VE tools were used only for experimental and limited purposes, the engineers found them very useful for looking around inside a problem—literally. They expect to make more use of VEs as the technology matures and computers get faster.

Flexibility is the hallmark of VEs. Changes in everything from the layout of a console to the physics underlying flight can be made and tested in software. Whole families of aircraft can be simulated with the same equipment. Typical flight simulators generally apply to one particular aircraft. VEs are already beginning to make significant contributions to design by letting designers and critics experience potential designs first hand, before resources are committed to construction. An important benefit of this approach is superb communication—it is hard to misunderstand a design you can walk around inside and experience in three dimensions.

Virtual Training

The U.S. Federal Aviation Administration (FAA) is increasingly being pressured to increase minimal acceptable training requirements for commuter carriers due to the recent rash of accidents. Meanwhile the FAA is also attempting to broaden the definition of what is required for flight simulation certification to include alternative, and in many cases less expensive, training methods. Virtual simulators fall into this category. They have a significant cost advantage over many other forms of training, along with the flexibility to mimic a number of types of aircraft with minimal changes in equipment. Flexibility is again a key advantage of virtual simulators—software changes are almost by definition easier to make than hardware changes.

Summary

Before you get too attached to the notion of virtual simulators, keep in mind that only the high-end virtual systems provide scenes that are much more than cartoons. Computers are just getting fast enough to make VEs practical for use. Simulator sickness is also a consideration for virtual systems, just as in flight simulators, but in many instances less understood and even more prevalent. Be that as it may, these cartoons are convincing enough to make you instinctively avoid obstacles. And VEs enjoy all of the benefits that flight simulators have over other methods of design and training.

CHAPTER
12

Cockpit/Crew Resource Management

This chapter is largely adapted from the text *Cockpit Resource Management* edited by Wiener, Kanki, and Helmreich, especially the essays by Helmreich on Cockpit Resource Management (CRM) and Butler on CRM LOFT.

The first airplanes depended on highly skilled and naturally talented athlete-pilots, capable of flying potentially unstable airplanes in a wide variety of conditions much of which was not well understood. Pilots are still often viewed as brave, white-scarf clad solitary figures. Observers, navigators, copilots, and bombardiers are all examples of crew members added to reduce the workload of the primary pilot, now called *captain*. Secondary pilots often perform roles that reduce them to the status of a redundant pilot, instead of full-fledged team members in their own right.

Turbojet airliners were introduced in the 1950s, heralding a new era of reliable air transportation. More recently, "glass cockpits" have been introduced to automate many of the tasks formerly performed by pilots in their head. Yet, seven out of every ten aircraft accidents worldwide between the years of 1959 and 1989, that led to unrepairable aircraft, were the result of flight crew actions. This is according to an analysis by the Boeing Aircraft Company, which agrees with the National Association of Space and Aeronautics (NASA) and the National Transportation Safety Board (NTSB) findings. The causes of these accidents are often termed "pilot error," but in fact are generally deficiencies in flight team communications and coordination rather than "stick-and-rudder" proficiency failures. Still, each aircrew member's proficiencies are often evaluated separately instead of as a member of the team, and even then the tests are geared toward human-computer interaction, not interpersonal communications, which is where a large part of the problem seems to be.

Investigations such as those conducted by the NTSB include some of the following chilling instances in the failure of team coordination during critical moments:

- A crew, distracted by the failure of a landing gear indicator (a 59¢ light bulb), failed to notice that the automatic pilot was not engaged. The aircraft descended into a swamp.

- A copilot, concerned that the take-off thrust was improperly set during a snowstorm departure, failed to get the attention of the pilot. The aircraft stalled and crashed into the Potomac River.

- A crew failed to review instrument landing charts, ignored their navigational position with respect to the airport, and disregarded repeated warnings from the Ground Proximity Warning System before plunging into a mountain below the minimum descent altitude.

- A crew distracted by non-operational communications failed to complete checklists and crashed on take-off because the flaps were not extended.

- A breakdown in communications between the pilot, copilot, and Air Traffic Control regarding the status of aircraft fuel resulted in the complete exhaustion of fuel and a subsequent crash.

- An aircraft crashed on take-off because of icing on the wings after the crew had inquired about de-icing facilities. Pilot passengers had also communicated their concerns about the need for de-icing to the flight attendant who failed to convey those concerns to the pilot because of a company policy.

Crew Resource Management

The study of human error in aviation accidents has been formally pursued since World War II. Yet until the 1970s, most of these studies focused on factors surrounding single operators and their interactions with machines. Researchers at NASA Ames Research Center and other institutions throughout the world began to explore the broader scope of human interaction issues. John Lauber, psychologist and member of the NTSB, began using the term Cockpit Resource Management (CRM) to describe "using all available sources—information, equipment, and people—to achieve safe and effective flight operations." The acronym CRM is now often defined as Crew Resource Management to reflect inclusion of the whole crew, not just the flight deck officers.

CRM is responsible for optimizing interpersonal as well as human-machine communications and task planning. This includes such topics as leadership, team formation and maintenance, problem solving, decision making, situational awareness, workload management, and task delegation. Elwyn Edwards proposed that resources be categorized as SHEL—**S**oftware, including documents and manuals; **H**ardware, including physical resources; **E**nvironment, all resources external to the context in which the system operates; and **L**iveware, including the human crew, maintenance, and air traffic controllers. Human interpersonal communications must include building and maintaining an effective team on the flightdeck—an environment where junior officers are willing to contribute in critical situations. The inter-operation of the crew is more important than the abilities of any one of its members. Researchers must find a way for training and proficiency tests to somehow reflect this new outlook.

CRM Line Operational Flight Simulations (LOFT)

Full flight simulations are known as Line Operational Flight Simulations (LOFT). LOFT is a systematic training method intended to simulate actual flight conditions and the flight crew's handling thereof. LOFT and its relationship to CRM is defined in the FAA's Advisory Circular on Line Operational Simulations (LOS; Federal Aviation Administration, 1990). CRM LOFT simulates real and practical situations that require the crew to demonstrate good teamwork and decision-making skills for an effective resolution. To meet this challenge, the FAA's CRM advisory circular (FAA, 1989; in preparation) identifies three components of CRM training: awareness training, practice and feedback, and continuing operational reinforcement. Additionally, the organization must demonstrate an active commitment to provide training and verification in an environment that utilizes CRM concepts on a daily basis. Management support is essential in order to embrace this new method of training and operations.

LOFT scenarios must be designed to include CRM issues at the heart of the mission. Some CRM issues that might be included as part of such a scenario include:

- Problems with several satisfactory answers, none of which is obviously correct and including both some good and some bad alternative decisions. The problems should be framed to encourage crew members to propose various actions to allow the decision-making and conflict-resolution processes to be adequately studied.

- Workload should be high enough to require distribution of tasks and communication, but should also include relatively low workload rest periods.

- Some problems should allow time for discussion and review of alternatives before a decision need be reached.

- Scenarios should encourage active participation by all crew members, fostering an environment where free and open communications is permitted.

- Air Traffic Control and environmental factors should be included that require the crew to plan actions ahead of time.

Let's tour a sample CRM LOFT scenario.

Pre-Flight Activities

Full-mission LOFT simulations should include all the appropriate pre-flight documentation, following as closely as possible the normal organization's pre-flight and dispatch processes. Weather, weight and balance, and other documents should be identical to those normally provided for a mission. Adequate time should be given for normal pre-flight setup and checklists to be performed. Simulation should maintain realism in all reasonable manners.

LOFT Facilitator Pre-Flight Briefing

At all times during the mission, the LOFT facilitator should be as unobtrusive as possible, acting more as a communicator, observer, and moderator rather than as an instructor. The LOFT facilitator is available to the crew only as a stand-in for the Air Traffic Controller, Maintenance, or other resource, not as an instructor. The flight crew must understand that the cabin crew may and should be used as a resource. In addition to setting the stage for the LOFT mission, this briefing should serve as an opportunity for the crew to "reverse brief" the mission. The crew should be able to indicate what types of behaviors affect CRM performance;

this will help the facilitator determine the crew's level of understanding experience with regard to CRM.

The LOFT Mission

The LOFT mission should be conducted as a normal mission. At no point should a crew member ask for information from the LOFT facilitator, except when the facilitator is acting as someone else, nor indeed should the crew break from normal mission activities. Critiques and reviews may be saved for after the mission. Additional workload and stress requiring enhanced teamwork may be added by varying environmental factors as well as the simulated aircraft's performance.

Post-Flight LOFT Debriefing

The debriefing after the mission is of great importance to the reinforcement and improvement of CRM skills. The LOFT facilitator should encourage the crew to debrief themselves, again acting more as a moderator than as an instructor. The crew should review, critique, and discuss the mission. The LOFT facilitator and video tape should be considered resources in their exploration of the mission. In the best case, these crew-led debriefings will begin to occur naturally after every normal mission, enhancing CRM skills, pointing out areas requiring further work, and showing the strength of teamwork.

CRM LOFT has become part of the modern arsenal of training methods aimed at preventing all accidents. It addresses many of the concerns that earlier methods of training ignored, especially emphasizing the areas of interpersonal communications and crew teamwork. CRM is a relatively new concept and is just beginning to be truly implemented within many airline organizations. CRM LOFT and similar programs are the primary means of training and evaluating flight crews and their skill in CRM. Hopefully, this will serve to reduce substantially the number of accidents resulting from crew actions.

Section IV

The Future of Flight Simulators

The field of flight simulation is undergoing drastic change. New technologies are invalidating tried-and-true approaches to flight design, training, and simulation. In addition, training itself is undergoing sweeping changes. This section will discuss many of the coming reforms and their implications.

Where is Flight Simulation Headed?

Flight simulation is being affected simultaneously from a number of directions. New technology and new techniques are rapidly changing the roles flight crew members are required to play. Innovations in human-machine interfaces and new understanding of human abilities are steadily reshaping cockpits. At the same time, we must face the end of the cold war and the subsequent cutbacks to the military's funding of research and development. And let's face it, in recent times the airline industry has not been showing exactly stellar performance.

Training Trends

Crew Resource Management (CRM) and the Advanced Qualification Program (AQP) are important watchwords in today's flight industry. CRM is a training and operations technique that emphasizes interpersonal communications and teamwork between flight crew members. Further, CRM followers should make use of all of the resources at their disposal—including physical hardware, documentation, and human resources from the cabin crew to maintenance to Air Traffic Control—in order to make decisions, plan tasks and workload, and solve problems. Individuals are de-emphasized while teamwork is strongly encouraged with the captain acting as leader and system manager. CRM's goal is to eliminate human error accidents wherever possible.

Glass-cockpits and fly-by-wire (and optical fiber) aircrafts are changing the way aircraft are flown. This trend will certainly continue and probably accelerate. New aircraft technologies being studied include the credible such as voice command and control and the incredible such as laser displays on the retina and aircrafts controlled by thought (yes, both of these are real research topics showing impressive results to date). Already, experimental aircraft that are "globally unstable" are being tested. These aircraft are potentially faster, more maneuverable, and will use less fuel than other designs. The trick is that they require constant computer attention to keep them flying—if the computer chokes, the aircraft doesn't glide to the ground. (Fly-by-wire aircrafts have similar weaknesses.)

AQP is a Federal Aviation Administration (FAA) initiative designed to allow U.S. airlines more flexibility in training flight crews. Indeed, training may be accomplished with nearly any set of tools and in nearly any manner that is first approved by the FAA. AQP is expected to shift the bulk of training to less expensive, more innovative simulators.

The Shape of Simulators to Come

Military cutbacks, along with an airline industry slump and such initiatives as AQP encourage the use of less expensive flight training devices. Many of the new devices will be able to compete directly with traditional flight simulators on capabilities, but will be smaller, transportable, and a fraction of the expensive. This trend will lead to decentralized training and "commercially available off-the-shelf" (COTS) flight training devices.

Traditional flight simulators will still be in demand for the new Boeing 777 and Airbus 330 and 340 aircraft. However, some airlines will certainly begin to opt for the new technology now, while others will stay with more traditional, conservative, and better understood flight training methods.

The next ten years will probably see the demise of the traditional flight simulator. Advanced electronic training devices will gradually replace the high-end, while the low-end will be occupied by strictly computer-based training devices. COTS and mix-and-match technologies will offer more training in a more efficient manner at less expense. The future will almost certainly include some sort of fully immersive virtual environment (virtual reality) systems, although the name will likely be something less provocative. The key technologies for the advent of these systems are tactile feedback and real-time, high quality visual displays showing fully interactive three-dimensional worlds of detail.

Who's Gonna Pay?

Military cutbacks in research and development coupled with the airline industry slump are causing funding problems in the short term. However, initiatives such as the AQP will allow small innovative companies to provide inexpensive, high-quality training devices. The training devices are expected to be small and transportable, to support decentralization of training efforts, inexpensive, and widespread enough to become available as COTS training devices.

The military will still require research and development for the next generation of war and defense machines. Funding cuts will ensure that a greater portion of these funds will be borne by the airline industry than in the past. But either way, ultimately the ticket buyer and the taxpayer will pay the price—that is our system.

Concluding Remarks

We have reached the end of this brief journey into the world of flight simulation. Along the way we provided the history of flight and flight simulation. We explored many of the current applications of flight simulation and related technologies. The human operators and their inner workings were discussed with a slant toward how organic sensor systems can be fooled. The current displays used to fool optical, auditory, and haptic biological systems were summarized. And the hazards that poor displays can wreak, such as simulation sickness, were described.

The journey then moved to an engineering-based description of fluid mechanics and aerodynamics—the fundamentals of heavier-than-air flight. We discussed the control surfaces and power plants airplanes use to sustain flight. We walked through some virtual environments, then looked at the latest initiatives being employed to reduce accidents, including CRM and AQP. Finally, we took a look into the future of flight and flight simulation.

You are about to embark on another journey. Through the entrails of a working, albeit somewhat simple (believe it or not!), flight simulator. Flight models and implementation issues will be discussed. Topics from scene and terrain generation to night flying will be covered in detail. This trip is sure to be a treat. This text is wrapped up with appendices; look here for references to delve deeper into the world of flight and flight simulation.

Section V

The Flight Simulator Software

Up to now, you have seen how research in flight simulation has led to the development of many diverse technologies. Funding for some advanced studies in human perception has occurred as a result of simulation projects. Many of the technologies are even useful in fields that seem unrelated to flight simulation. The recent virtual reality craze is as a result of many creative people using flight simulation technology integrated with advanced tactile feedback devices and immersion display systems.

Now it is time for you to see flight simulation technology in a little more detail. How a computer generates the visual scene that you fly through, and how input from a pilot (you) is processed to affect the display that you see is discussed in this part. It is time for you to build your own flight simulator on your PC.

CHAPTER

14

The Concept of a Flight Simulation System

We construct the world according to what is channeled through our senses. Right now I see a not-very-colorful monitor screen, around the monitor I see what appears to be a big room full of fluorescent lights and boring objects, on my rear end I feel a mild pressure from my old chair, every time I p...r...e...s...s...a...k...e...y I feel a reassuring resistance-yielding-resistance that gives me a subconscious okay to press the next key. The only sound is the rustle of the air conditioning and the faint swoosh of the blower on the computer CPU. I'm not aware of any odor, having worked in this room for many years. I would, however, be profoundly perturbed if the room began to sway or lurch in any way. I know I'm not in any kind of traveling vehicle, and I'd never forgive the room for suggesting that (I'd conclude that there was an earthquake, or I was

135

violently ill). The point is that, with appropriate input to my senses, I'd believe just about anything. I might even believe…that I was in an airplane. Which brings us to flight simulators.

The Flight Simulator Environment

What would it take to make a pilot, or a pilot trainee, believe that he or she is flying a plane? Well, first of all, it takes a heavy dose of visuals. Sight is the bully of the senses and generally dictates to the others. (Don't believe it? How long would it take you to flee a theater if you saw the stage burst into flames, whether or not you smelled smoke or heard the crackle of fire?) Vision must be catered to above all, so simulators always sport a sophisticated display screen or screens. The screen shows the runway, lights, markers, other planes, even people and vehicles on the tarmac. They move in real time, without jerks, and in familiar perspective and size as they approach and recede. Everything is in bright, realistic colors. (Since planes have windows of limited size, screens don't have to be colossal monsters to fool the 180-degree human peripheral vision . Helicopters are another story.)

You are strapped into virtually the same seat that is installed in the plane you're training for. The actual, familiar controls will be within arm's reach. We've taken care of sight, so now—let there be sound. A top-notch stereo sound system is a feature of all modern flight simulators. Its function is to produce all those aviation sounds that young kids delight in mimicking—the roar of the engines at takeoff, the scream of the wind, the slap and squeal of the tires on landing. Flight controller conversation is fed to you in the normal way, over headphones.

With our two main senses hoodwinked, what's left? The finishing touches that complete the illusion. Vibration drivers give us the feeling of being in a live environment, humming with energy. Meanwhile, a tiltable platform can serve up realistic portions of roll, pitch, and yaw—to the point of motion sickness. Last but not least, real-time interactions with the controls—programmed into the simulator software—convince us that we are immersed in a virtual world that we have power over. We turn a switch or pull a lever and the "plane" responds instantly, perhaps violently and disastrously. There is a case of soldiers in tank simulators—not so different from aircraft units—who were doing group maneuvers in multiple, linked simulators. They saw their comrades ambushed and under enemy attack. So completely had they come under the spell of the simulators that they unstrapped themselves and poured out onto the laboratory floor to get a better view of the "battlefield." This is simulation at its best.

Creating the Visual Aspects with Computers

It's worth discussing, in a very brief way, how computers can create a virtual world that will support the flight simulator illusions. First, understand that the visuals seen in today's simulators are not movies of real objects. Nor are they panels, such as *The Simpsons*, drawn by human artists. It's all done with polygons. *Polygons*—straight-sided geometrical figures such as triangles and rectangles—are convenient objects for computers to manipulate. Computers are very comfortable with polygons. You can even make curved objects from polygons; for example, you can make a cylinder from a lot of long, skinny polygons. Later, the computer will smooth the rough edges. You also have to deal with color, texture, size, perspective, overlay, light sources, and reflections. Believe it or not, all these things can be expressed mathematically. It isn't always easy, and the results aren't ideal in all cases, but amazing progress has been made—didn't you believe the villain in *Terminator 2*, in all his morphing incarnations?

Technologies for the Flight Simulator Visual System

To understand and develop a visual system that will support the flight simulation illusion, you must understand a basic set of mathematical

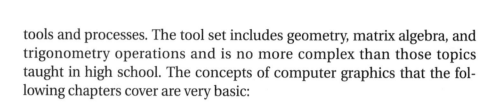

tools and processes. The tool set includes geometry, matrix algebra, and trigonometry operations and is no more complex than those topics taught in high school. The concepts of computer graphics that the following chapters cover are very basic:

- Projection of polygons from a 3-D polygonal world onto a 2-D computer display

- Sorting polygons from farthest to nearest for order of display

- Clipping polygons that fall behind us, and clipping polygons that fall partially or totally off to the sides of the computer display

- Shading and texturing polygons to create a realistic appearance

- Removing hidden polygons that exist on the unseen sides of objects

So let us start our journey into the technical aspects of flight simulation with a conceptual discussion of how all of the technologies work together to produce the effect.

An Overview of a Flight Simulation System

Imagine that you are flying in an airplane. You have a window at the front of the cockpit that allows you to see the world before you. You know that the world outside is made of three-dimensional objects such as trees, mountains, and buildings. However, if you had never been outside to experience these objects up close, the two-dimensional image that you see through the window of your airplane would be all that you would know. Assume your computer screen to be the airplane window.

Imagine that the surfaces of all of those three-dimensional objects in your world are made up of tiny polygonal patches such as triangles and rectangles. That simple building in your view, for instance, could be made of four rectangles for walls, two rectangles for a roof, two triangles to fill in the ends of the roof, and assorted rectangles for windows and doors. The more polygons you use to construct your objects, the more detail your objects will have.

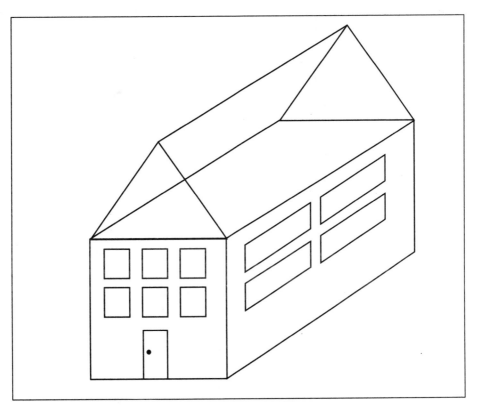

Figure 14.1 *It's a polygonal world—building made of polygons.*

Try to visualize how your complex three-dimensional world might look if it were made only of triangles and rectangles—rather choppy and without any interesting detail. Many simulators pride themselves by coloring, shading, and texturing those polygons. Whether rough or smooth or complex with texture, our objects and their interactions with light can be simulated by mathematical equations.

The Two-Dimensional Cockpit Window

Let us examine where we are. We have a three-dimensional world whose objects are constructed from shaded and possibly textured polygons. We have a computer display that acts like a window into that three-dimensional world. Like the airplane's cockpit window in relation to the real three-dimensional world of real objects, our computer display can assume any position and orientation in relation to our virtual three-dimensional world of polygonal objects. What you see through the cockpit window of your airplane is a projection of the three-dimensional world onto that two-dimensional cockpit window. By performing perspective projection onto the computer display of all of those three-dimensional polygons that make up objects in our virtual flight simulation world, we will see our virtual world through our window.

Imagine next that we can move our window around in three-dimensional space, just like the airplane cockpit window, repositioning it and reorienting it as time goes by. You might now say that we are flying.

In a nutshell, a flight simulator functions like this: you orient and position the viewer (the person sitting in front of the computer display) relative to the screen and relative to the three-dimensional, polygonal-object world. You project all of those polygons from three dimensions into two dimensions with geometric perspective and display them on the computer screen. You may also project any "light points" such as runway lights from the three-dimensional world onto the two-dimensional computer display. The computer takes input from your control devices (keyboard, mouse, joystick, yoke, pedals, wheel, and so on), and the computer reorients and repositions the viewer based on the status of those controls.

Repeating the above process, and given that you have mathematics that accurately model the way the viewer would physically move, bounce, and crash based on input from controls, then you have the beginnings of a flight simulator. Make the display system large enough for a pilot and co-pilot to feel like they are really looking out of a cockpit window, and you are closer to immersion. Add tactile feedback to the controls so that they feel real (for example, in older aircraft with mechanical linkages, you could feel some resistance in the controls when performing dynamic maneuvers), add sound (the change in hum of the engines when banking), and maybe add smell (the greatly undesired fire in the cargo bay), and you have an immersion flight simulator.

Summary

Now, let us look at each part of a flight simulation system in some detail, primarily the mathematics and algorithms for a computer graphics engine. A good graphics engine is the basis for any simulation and virtual reality system. And in most cases, such a graphics engine would be used to generate the images seen on your visual displays in "real time."

Many of the following explanations use our source code as examples to enhance the explanation of concepts. For those needing some support or reference regarding the C programming language, see Appendix D. It covers some of the C language.

CHAPTER

15

The Mathematics of Three-Dimensional Computer Graphics

Given some conceptual understanding of the field of flight simulation, and given a little knowledge of the C programming language (for which there is a tutorial in Appendix D), this chapter begins discussions on computer graphics with a review of the basic tools required. These tools include routines that perform special mathematical functions related to geometry and trigonometry, which are commonly performed through application of matrix algebra.

Most of the functions in this chapter are used to manipulate two- and three-dimensional points and vectors using the basic techniques of linear algebra. Points and vectors are used to describe all of the geometry of the three-dimensional world, including both the positions and orientations of all of the objects in the world, including the viewer position and direction and any available light source positions and directions. The routines described here provide both an efficient and an elegant means of manipulating points and vectors for rotating objects, scaling, translating, viewing, and calculating light intensity.

Three types of routines are found in the mathematics module: numerical, vector, and matrix functions. The *numerical* functions are single-valued functions (except for AlgDefs_POWER) that take as input a single number and compute some function of that number. Functions such as sine and cosine fall into this category. This module also contains the definitions of common mathematical constants such as π and *ln(10)*.

The vector and matrix functions create and manipulate vectors. For these purposes, a *vector* is an ordered collection of numbers (normally 2 or 3) that represent a magnitude of travel and a direction in the 2-D *X-Y* plane or in the 3-D *X-Y-Z* space. Vectors also define directions, such as in what direction a surface is facing (the surface normal points in this direction). This chapter discusses all the standard vector operations such as the vector dot and cross products. Since you often need to transform vectors (such as in rotating an object), several transformation routines are provided. You will see how to transform vectors by multiplication of the vector coordinates by a single three-by-three or four-by-four matrix. One of the most convenient aspects of vector transformations is that each type of three-dimensional transformation can be represented by one four-by-four matrix. These individual matrices may be multiplied together to produce a single transformation matrix that represents all of the desired transformation operations: rotation, scaling, and translation. You will see this concatenation of matrices producing a single matrix which allows you to transform an object by simply multiplying the vertices of the object with the one transformation matrix, instead of inefficiently transforming the vertices with each the rotation, scaling, and translation matrices individually. Transformations such as these allow you to construct complex objects from primitive polygonal objects such as triangles and parallelograms and place them into the virtual flight simulation world.

 N O T E No checking is done between point types and vector types, though both data types are provided. Technically, point types and vector types should be incompatible to enforce type checking between them. A *coordinate free* graphics system (a system that processes vectors, not points or coordinates) prevents nonsense operations such as addition of points, normalizing points, and translating vectors.

Mathematical Constants, Data Types, and Structures

Now take a look at some of the mathematical constants, the data types, and structures and then the functions and macros found in the mathematics modules, and look at some of their uses. This section can be used like a reference guide for three-dimensional computer graphics. Program modules for these functions are listed at the end of this chapter.

Mathematical Constants

These are some of the mathematical constants found in the AlgDefs.H include file, which is included on the disk packaged with this book.

Table 15.1 *Mathematical constants.*

Program constant	Constant
AlgDefs_TWO_PI	2π
AlgDefs_PI	π
AlgDefs_HALF_PI	$\pi / 2$
AlgDefs_QUARTER_PI	$\pi / 4$
AlgDefs_INV_PI	$1 / \pi$

`AlgDefs_TWO_INV_P`	$2 / \pi$
`AlgDefs_INV_SQRT_PI`	$1 / \sqrt{\pi}$
`AlgDefs_TWO_INV_SQRT_PI`	$2 / \sqrt{\pi}$
`AlgDefs_DEG_TO_RAD`	$180 / \pi$
`AlgDefs_RAD_TO_DEG`	$\pi / 180$
`AlgDefs_LN10`	$\ln(10)$
`AlgDefs_INV_LN10`	$1 / \ln(10)$

Precision-Error Constants

A common problem found in digital systems is *precision error*, which can be viewed as the difference between what a number should be, and how it is represented in digital form. For example, rotate a vector a few degrees using your computer to make the calculations and to do the drawing. You first position the vector and give it direction. Rotate the vector by some angle. The vector is now pointing in some other direction. Rotate the vector again by some other angle, and then again. Now rotate the vector back to the original direction. You will probably find that you cannot get the vector precisely back into the original direction. This is a manifestation of *precision error*. Since the computer performs mathematical computations to a certain precision (number of decimal places), rounding or truncating of the true number will occur. By compiling the error (performing many rotations) you find that the vector will not go back to the original direction, that it is slightly off.

To combat precision error problems, give our math some slack...the precision error constant is our answer. If you are trying to see if the value of a number (for example, x) is equal to zero, and you know that precision error is a problem for the types of calculations you are doing, then you might look to see if the number falls between two numbers that are slightly offset from zero. For example:

```
if ((x > 0-AlgDefs_ZERO) && (x < 0+AlgDefs_ZERO))
    pay_taxes;
```

The range from `-AlgDefs_ZERO` to `AlgDefs_ZERO` gives sufficient room (in some cases) for the computer to make the correct decision...instead of

```
if "x is equal to zero"
```

one might say:

```
if "x is more or less equal to zero"
```

These are some of our commonly used precision error constants:

Table 15.2 *Precision error constants.*

Program constant	Constant
AlgDefs_ZERO	1.7e-03
AlgDefs_INFINITY	1.0e+20
AlgDefs_SMALL	1.0e-05
AlgDefs_LARGE	1.0e+05

Mathematical error is introduced based on the available precision to store a number. An example would be how the irrational number PI (π) is represented in a computer. π is irrational, so it does not compute out to any exact number of digits; it goes on infinitely:

$$\pi = 3.14159265358...$$

But since we have limited memory, and very limited patience, we may say that:

$$\pi = 3.14159.$$

This is a finite-sized number. So if we use that number, our calculations will always be a bit off. And if we repeatedly use this number, our calculation will quickly run away from the correct value.

Data Types and Structures

In order to make our job easier and our code easier to understand and maintain, we use many type definitions and structures. The following section explains the usefulness and functionality of each data type.

We will first look at Table 15.3 and the general data types. These are the fundamental types, many of which are found in all C compilers.

Table 15.3 *General data types.*

Data type	Use
AlgDefs_byte	unsigned char
AlgDefs_word	unsigned int
AlgDefs_dword	unsigned long
AlgDefs_char	char
AlgDefs_int	int
AlgDefs_long	long
AlgDefs_float	double (We need the precision.)
AlgDefs_double	double
AlgDefs_boolean	AlgDefs_TRUE or AlgDefs_FALSE
AlgDefs_palette_type	256-color palette

The vector data types found in Table 15.4 are used to create vectors used to define such things as directions and magnitudes of travel and viewing.

Table 15.4 *Vector types.*

Data type	Use
`AlgDefs_vector_2D_int_type`	Describes a 2-D integer vector (x,y).
`AlgDefs_vector_2D_type`	Describes a 2-D vector (x,y).
`AlgDefs_vector_3D_int_type`	Describes a 3-D integer vector (x,y,z).
`AlgDefs_vector_3D_type`	Describes a 3-D vector (x,y,z).
`AlgDefs_vector_4D_int_type`	Describes a 4-D integer vector (x,y,z,w).
`AlgDefs_vector_4D_type`	Describes a 4-D vector (x,y,z,w).

The matrix data types found in Table 15.5 are used to create matrices used for transformations of objects.

Table 15.5 *Matrix types.*

Data type	Use
`AlgDefs_matrix_2x2_type`	Describes a 2 x 2 matrix (mat[2][2]).
`AlgDefs_matrix_3x3_type`	Describes a 3 x 3 matrix (mat[3][3]).
`AlgDefs_matrix_4x4_type`	Describes a 4 x 4 matrix (mat[4][4]).

The point data types in Table 15.6 are used to define such things as screen coordinates and three-dimensional object positions.

Table 15.6 *Point types.*

Data type	Use
AlgDefs_point_2D_int_type	Describes a 2-D integer point (x,y).
AlgDefs_point_2D_type	Describes a 2-D point (x,y).
AlgDefs_point_3D_int_type	Describes a 3-D integer point (x,y,z).
AlgDefs_point_3D_type	Describes a 3-D point (x,y,z).
AlgDefs_point_4D_int_type	Describes a 4-D integer point (x,y,z,w).
AlgDefs_point_4D_type	Describes a 4-D point (x,y,z,w).

The vertex data type in Table 15.7 is used to define the three-dimensional vertex of a polygon in a number of three-dimensional coordinate systems.

Table 15.7 *Vertex types.*

Data type	Use
AlgDefs_vertex_3D_type	Describes a single Cartesian point in *local* coordinates, *world*-transformed coordinates, and *viewer*-transformed coordinates.

The polygon data types found in Table 15.8 are used to define a polygon in various stages of processing—from the raw three-dimensional polygon, all the way to its clipped two-dimensional representation.

Table 15.8 *Polygon types.*

Data type	Use
AlgDefs_horz_line_type	Describes the beginning and ending x coordinates of a single horizontal line (used for polygon filling in the program module AlgPoly.C).
AlgDefs_horz_line_list_type	Describes num_horz_lines horizontal lines, all assumed to be on contiguous scan lines starting at y_start and proceeding downward (used to describe a scan-converted polygon to the low-level hardware-dependent drawing code in the program module AlgScrn.C).
AlgDefs_polygon_3D_bounding_box_type	Describes a bounding box for a three-dimensional polygon (used for calculation of polygon center and for cuboid bounding).
AlgDefs_viewport_clipped_polygon_2D_type	Describes a polygon that has been prepared for viewport display.

`AlgDefs_z_clipped_polygon_3D_type`	Describes a polygon that has been clipped with the front of the view volume in order to remove that part of the polygon which falls behind the viewer.
`AlgDefs_polygon_3D_type`	Describes a polygon
`AlgDefs_polygon_2D_display_list_type`	Describes a list of polygons for display.

The three-dimensional object data type found in Table 15.9 is used to describe an object's position and orientation in the three-dimensional world. It references lists of polygons.

Table 15.9 *3-D object types.*

Data type	Use
`AlgDefs_object_3D_type`	Describes an object in the three-dimensional world.

The three-dimensional world data types found in Table 15.10 are used to define the objects in the world and the viewer.

Table 15.10 *3-D world types.*

Data type	Use
`AlgDefs_world_3D_type`	Describes the three-dimensional world made of objects.
`AlgDefs_viewer_3D_type`	Describes the viewer in the three-dimensional world.

The control data type in Table 15.11 is used to define the control surfaces, and their status variables.

Table 15.11 *Control types.*

Data type	Use
AlgDefs_controls_type	Describes the basic surface and thrust controls of an aircraft for "intuitive" control of the viewer.

Examples of Data Type Use

Now that you have seen the type definitions for our mathematics modules, look at this quick example of their use. Below you will find identity matrices being defined, using the AlgDefs_matrix_3x3_type and AlgDefs_matrix_4x4_type data types.

```
// 3x3 identity matrix
AlgDefs_matrix_3x3_type      AlgMatx_identity_matrix_3x3 =
                             {{  { 1.0, 0.0, 0.0 },
                                 { 0.0, 1.0, 0.0 },
                                 { 0.0, 0.0, 1.0 } }};

// 4x4 identity matrix
AlgDefs_matrix_4x4_type      AlgMatx_identity_matrix_4x4 =
                             {{  { 1.0, 0.0, 0.0, 0.0 },
                                 { 0.0, 1.0, 0.0, 0.0 },
                                 { 0.0, 0.0, 1.0, 0.0 },
                                 { 0.0, 0.0, 0.0, 1.0 } }};
```

Now look at the functions and macros that make up our mathematics library. The next section is followed by a discussion of the theory and the uses of the functions.

Functions and Macros

Basic Mathematics Functions and Macros

The mathematics modules contain some handy numerical conversion functions listed as follows. Note that some of the functions found in AlgDefs.H are not listed, as they are variations of the following functions.

Table 15.12 *Basic mathematics functions and macros.*

Function	Description
AlgDefs_RAD(x)	Converts degrees to radians.
AlgDefs_DEG(x)	Converts radians to degrees.
AlgDefs_COS(x)	cosine (radian argument).
AlgDefs_SIN(x)	sine (radian argument)
AlgDefs_COSD(x)	cosine (degree argument)
AlgDefs_SIND(x)	sine (degree argument)
AlgDefs_ABS(x)	absolute value
AlgDefs_FLOOR(x)	floor
AlgDefs_CEILING(x)	ceiling
AlgDefs_ROUND(x)	round
AlgDefs_TRUNC(x)	truncate fractional part
AlgDefs_FRAC(x)	fractional part
AlgDefs_SQR(x)	number squared
AlgDefs_SQRT(x)	square root
AlgDefs_CUBE(x)	number cubed
AlgDefs_LN(x)	natural logarithm
AlgDefs_LOG(x)	base 10 logarithm
AlgDefs_EXP10(x)	10 raised to power
AlgDefs_POWER(x,y)	float x raised to float y power
AlgDefs_SIGN(x)	-1 if negative 0 if 0 1 if positive

Comparison Functions and Macros

These functions are used for determining which of a set of numbers is the largest or smallest.

Table 15.13 *Comparison functions and macros.*

Function	Description
AlgDefs_MIN(x,y)	Find the minimum of two numbers.
AlgDefs_MIN3(x,y)	Find the minimum of three numbers.
AlgDefs_MIN4(x,y)	Find the minimum of four numbers.
AlgDefs_MAX(x,y)	Find the maximum of two numbers.
AlgDefs_MAX3(x,y)	Find the maximum of three numbers.
AlgDefs_MAX4(x,y)	Find the maximum of four numbers.

Swapping Functions and Macros

These functions are used for swapping numbers (data in structures).

Table 15.14 *Swapping functions and macros.*

Function	Description
AlgDefs_SWAP(x,y,type)	Swaps two numbers (datasets in structures of given type).

Power Functions

These are functions for raising a number to a power.

Table 15.15 *Power functions.*

Function	Description
AlgMath_POWER(x,y)	Raises float base *x* to integer exponent *y*.
AlgMath_INT_POWER(x,y)	Raises integer base *x* to integer exponent *y*.

Pseudo-Random Number Generation Functions

These functions are used for pseudo-random number generation.

Table 15.16 *Pseudo-random number generation functions.*

Function	Description
AlgMath_RANDOM_SEED(x)	Initialize pseudo-random number generator.
AlgMath_RAND(x)	Floating point pseudo-random number.
AlgMath_RAND_INT(x)	Integer pseudo-random number. [0..x–1]

Two-Dimensional Vector Functions and Macros

These are the two-dimensional vector functions. Uppercase letters represent scalar numbers and lowercase letters represent vectors. Values are passed into the functions at the beginning of the argument list and returned at the end of the argume   list.

Table 15.17 *Two-dimensional vector functions and macros.*

Function	Description
AlgVec_2D_MAKE(A,B,v)	Makes a vector **v**=(*A*,*B*).
AlgVec_2D_COMPONENTS(v, A, B)	Returns components of vector **v**.
AlgVec_2D_AVERAGE(a,b,v)	Returns average of vector components.
AlgVec_2D_NEGATE(v)	Returns vector with opposite signed components.
AlgVec_2D_NEGATE2(a,v)	Same as negate, except returns in another vector.

`AlgVec_2D_DOT(a,b)`	Vector dot product.
`AlgVec_2D_LENGTH(v)`	Length of vector.
`AlgVec_2D_NORMALIZE(v)`	Normalizes a vector.
`AlgVec_2D_MINIMUM(a,b,v)`	Returns a vector whose components represent the minimum values of two other vectors' respective components.
`AlgVec_2D_MAXIMUM(a,b,v)`	Returns a vector whose components represent the maximum values of two other vectors' respective components.
`AlgVec_2D_COMPARE(a,b,same)`	Compares the components of two vectors and returns true if all components match in the two.
`AlgVec_2D_COPY(a,b)`	Copy vector **a** to vector **b**.
`AlgVec_2D_ADD(a,b,v)`	Adds two vectors **v=a+b**.
`AlgVec_2D_SUB(a,b,v)`	Subtracts one vector from another **v=a-b**.
`AlgVec_2D_LIN_COMB(A,a,B,b,v)`	Linear combination **v**=A**a**+B**b**.
`AlgVec_2D_SCAL_MULT(A,a,v)`	Scalar multiply a vector **v**=A**a**.
`AlgVec_2D_ADD_SCAL_MULT(A,a,b,v)`	Add scalar multiple to a vector **v**=A**a**+**b**.
`AlgVec_2D_MUL(a,b,v)`	Multiply two vectors **v=ab**.
`AlgVec_2D_DETERMINANT(a,b,t)`	Returns determinant of matrix produced when vector is "cross" multiplied $t=a_x*b_y-a_y*b_x$.
`AlgVec_2D_ZERO(v)`	Zeros a vector.
`AlgVec_2D_PRINT(msg, v)`	Prints a message and a vector.

Three-Dimensional Vector Functions and Macros

These are the three-dimensional vector functions. Uppercase letters represent scalar numbers and lowercase letters represent vectors. Values are passed into the functions at the beginning of the argument list and returned at the end of the argument list.

Table 15.18 *Three-dimensional vector functions and macros.*

Function	Description
AlgVec_3D_MAKE(A,B,C,v)	Makes a vector **v**=(*A,B,C*).
AlgVec_3D_COMPONENTS(v, A, B,C)	Returns components of vector **v**.
AlgVec_3D_AVERAGE(a,b,v)	Returns average of vector components.
AlgVec_3D_NEGATE(v)	Returns vector with opposite signed components.
AlgVec_3D_NEGATE2(a,v)	Same as negate, except returns in another vector.
AlgVec_3D_DOT(a,b)	Vector dot product.
AlgVec_3D_LENGTH(v)	Length of vector.
AlgVec_3D_NORMALIZE(v)	Normalizes a vector.
AlgVec_3D_MINIMUM(a,b,v)	Returns a vector whose components represent the minimum values of two other vectors' respective components.
AlgVec_3D_MAXIMUM(a,b,v)	Returns a vector whose components represent the maximum values of two other vectors' respective components.
AlgVec_3D_COMPARE(a,b,same)	Compares the components of two vectors and returns true if all components match in the two.
AlgVec_3D_COPY(a,b)	Copy vector **a** to vector **b**.

`AlgVec_3D_ADD(a,b,v)`	Adds two vectors **v=a+b**.
`AlgVec_3D_SUB(a,b,v)`	Subtracts one vector from another **v=a-b**.
`AlgVec_3D_LIN_COMB(A,a,B,b,v)`	Linear combination **v**=A**a**+B**b**.
`AlgVec_3D_SCAL_MULT(A,a,v)`	Scalar multiply a vector **v**=A**a**.
`AlgVec_3D_ADD_SCAL_MULT(A,a,b,v)`	Add scalar multiple to a vector **v**=A**a+b**.
`AlgVec_3D_MUL(a,b,v)`	Multiply two vectors **v=ab**.
`AlgVec_3D_CROSS(a,b,t)`	Returns determinant of matrix produced when vector is "cross" multiplied $t = a_x*b_y - a_y*b_x$.
`AlgVec_3D_ZERO(v)`	Zeros a vector.
`AlgVec_3D_PRINT(msg, v)`	Prints a message and a vector.

3 x 3 Matrix Functions for Two-Dimensional Manipulations

These are the three-by-three matrix functions required for the manipulation of two-dimensional vectors. Matrices are represented by **m** and vectors by **v**.

Table 15.19 *3x3 matrix functions for two-dimensional manipulations.*

Function	Description
`AlgMatx_copy_3x3_matrix(m,m1)`	Copy m1 into m.
`AlgMatx_multiply_3x3_matrix(m,m1,m2)`	**m = m1 * m2**
`AlgMatx_zero_3x3_matrix(m)`	Zero the matrix components.
`AlgMatx_identity_3x3_matrix(m)`	**m** = identity matrix.
`AlgMatx_scale_3x3_matrix(v,m)`	Make scale matrix and multiply **m** (**m** = scale * **m**).

```
AlgMatx_rotate_3x3_matrix(theta,m)
```
Make rotate matrix
and multiply **m**
(**m** = rotate * **m**).

```
AlgMatx_translate_3x3_matrix(v,m)
```
Make translate matrix
and multiply **m** (**m** =
translate * **m**).

```
AlgMatx_transform_3x3_matrix(v,m,v1)
```
Transform a vector
v = **v1** * **m**

4 x 4 Matrix Functions for Three-Dimensional Manipulations

These are the four-by-four matrix functions required for the manipulation of three-dimensional vectors. Matrices are represented by **m** and vectors by **v**.

Table 15.20 *4x4 matrix functions for three-dimensional manipulations.*

Function	Description
`AlgMatx_copy_4x4_matrix(m,m1)`	Copy **m1** into **m**.
`AlgMatx_multiply_4x4_matrix(m,m1,m2)`	**m** = **m1** * **m2**.
`AlgMatx_zero_4x4_matrix(m)`	Zero the matrix components.
`AlgMatx_identity_4x4_matrix(m)`	**m** = identity matrix.
`AlgMatx_scale_4x4_matrix(v,m)`	Make scale matrix and multiply **m** (**m** = scale * **m**).
`AlgMatx_rotate_4x4_matrix(v,m)`	Make rotate matrix and multiply **m** (**m** = rotate * **m**).
`AlgMatx_translate_4x4_matrix(v,m)`	Make translate matrix and multiply **m** (**m** = translate * **m**).
`AlgMatx_transform_4x4_matrix(v,m,v1)`	Transform a vector **v** = **v1** * **m**.

All of these routines can be expressed easily in terms of C code, instead of using our routines (that is, $N^*=N$ is the same as $N=\text{Sqr}(N)$). We have provided these routines so that the code will be more readable by people considering conversion of the software to other languages.

How the Functions Work

This section will be of interest to those interested in the theory behind the workings of our 3-D graphics library. The single-valued functions are covered, as well as the affine transformations of three-dimensional objects.

Functions for Conversion between Radians and Degrees

These functions are very useful for manipulating data based on angles. Much of the software described in the book requires these routines for proper calculation of viewing vectors, and for positioning and orienting objects. Most of the time, we need to manipulate angles represented as radians (2π radians = 360 degrees), since the compiler-supplied cosine and sine functions require radian measures. However, we often want to enter and express angles as degrees, since for many of us that is more intuitive. These routines provide for easy conversion between the two angular measures. `AlgDefs_DEG` and `AlgDefs_RAD` are functions used to do just the conversions. The functions make use of the `AlgDefs_DEG_TO_RAD` and `AlgDefs_RAD_TO_DEG` constants. You can see examples of their use in the `AlgDefs_COSD` and `AlgDefs_SIND` functions. Figure 15.1 shows the correspondence of radian measure to degree measure.

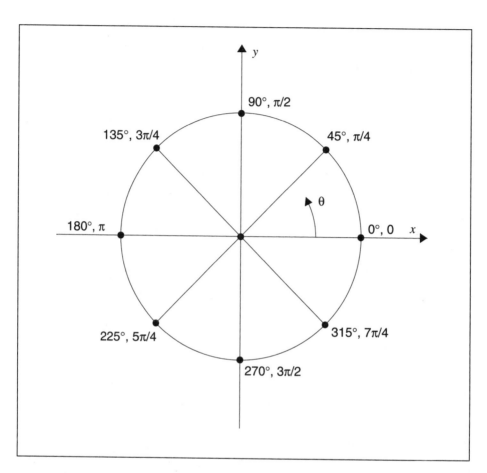

Figure 15.1 *Degrees versus radians.*

The AlgDefs_COSD and AlgDefs_SIND Functions

These functions use the C math library trigonometry functions cos (cosine) and sin (sine), as well as our own degrees-to-radians conversion functions. They perform the same function as the C math library functions, except that they take their argument as an angle expressed in degrees. As you might have guessed from Figure 15.1, these functions walk you around the periphery of a circle as the angle in their argument is increased. Figure 15.2 shows how these functions relate to a circle of radius *r*.

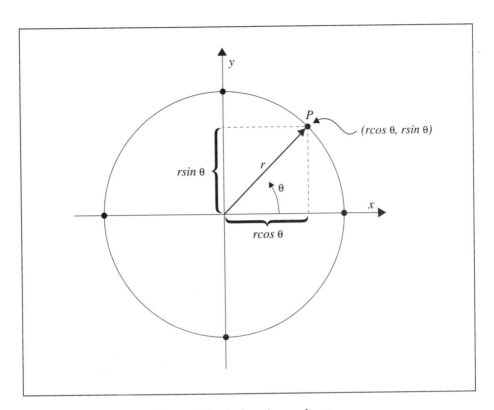

Figure 15.2 *Cosine, sine, and vectors.*

The AlgDefs_POWER and AlgDefs_POWER_INT Functions

These functions have two arguments, a base value and an integer exponent. They return the value of raising the base to the exponent, that is, base^{exponent}. Essentially, base is multiplied by itself an exponent number of times. If the exponent is equal to zero, the function returns a value of 1, since any number raised to the power of zero is 1. Otherwise, the variable power is initialized to 1 and a loop from 1 to the value of the exponent begins. Power is multiplied by base for each iteration of the loop. After the loop has ended, the value in power is returned.

`AlgDefs_POWER_INT` is the same as `AlgDefs_POWER` except that the base is an integer. `AlgDefs_POWER_INT` is a recursive function that raises an integer value to an integer power. *Recursion* implies that a function calls itself. Like the `AlgDefs_POWER` function, if the exponent is equal to zero, the value of one is returned. Otherwise, the exponent is decremented and the function calls itself. Once the exponent is zero through successive calls to itself, the value of 1 is returned to the previous call. One is then multiplied by base and returned to the next previous call and so on until three highest level is reached. The power of the integer is returned.

The AlgDefs_LOG Function

This function finds the base-10 logarithm of a number. Using the C log function, it gets the natural logarithm of the number and then divides this value by the constant Ln10 (the natural logarithm of 10). The floating-point base-10 logarithm is then returned.

The AlgDefs_EXP10 Function

This function finds the value of 10.0 raised to the power of a floating point number. First, the value passed to the function is multiplied by the constant Ln10. Then using the C exp function, we calculate the natural logarithm of the new value. The floating-point result is then returned.

The AlgDefs_SIGN Function

This function is used to find the sign of a number. A value of -1 is returned if the number is less than zero, 0 if the number is equal to zero, and 1 if the number is greater than zero.

The AlgDefs_MIN, AlgDefs_MIN3, AlgDefs_MIN4, AlgDefs_MAX, AlgDefs_MAX3, AlgDefs_MAX4 Functions

These functions determine the minimum value of 2, 3, and 4 numbers, respectively, and the maximum value of 2, 3, and 4 numbers, respectively. The minimum and maximum routines are useful for finding the boundaries of an object (often referred to as the *extent of the object* or the *bounding box* or *cuboid*). By running through the list of points that make up an object (such as vertices of polygon sides of the object) and computing the maximum and minimum points found overall, you can determine the maximum and minimum values for each dimension. For example, a three-dimensional object requires three tests for each vertex of the object. A bounding box can then be defined by two points: the minimum value in each of *X*, *Y*, and *Z* and the maximum value in each of *X*, *Y*, and *Z*. You will see more of this when bounding a polygon to obtain its distance from the viewer (used in polygon sorting for display ordering).

Vector and Matrix Functions

In this section, you will learn about the vector and matrix types used extensively throughout most computer graphics applications. This set of modules allows you to move objects around in space, orient the viewer with the virtual simulation world, prepare projection of polygons onto a two-dimensional display, and perform most standard vector operations.

In order to facilitate this, we have defined several new variable types. The `AlgDefs_vector_3D_type` variable type contains three floating point numbers (x, y, z) representing the components of a three-dimensional vector. In accordance with the normal mathematical notation for vectors, we also refer to the three standard unit vectors (vectors of length 1) **i**, **j**, and **k**. These are simply vectors that point along the positive X, Y, and Z axes. They are defined as:

$i = (1, 0, 0)$

$j = (0, 1, 0)$

$k = (0, 0, 1)$

and may be manipulated as any other vector. Any vector **v** (x, y, z) may be represented as the sum of the vectors **i**, **j**, **k**:

$\mathbf{v} = x\mathbf{i} + y\mathbf{j} + z\mathbf{k}$

This is useful in understanding some of the other vector operations such as rotation and scaling.

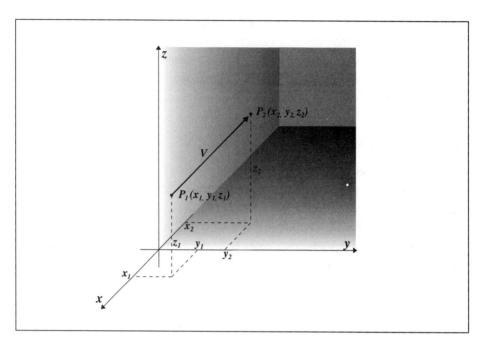

Figure 15.3 *Three-dimensional vectors in the Cartesian coordinate system.*

Examine Figure 15.3. This figure shows a three-dimensional vector that begins at point p_1 and terminates at point p_2. Notice that points p_1 and p_2 are three-dimensional points, having x, y, and z components.

The `AlgDefs_point_3D_type` would be commonly used to express points to distinguish them from vectors.

Finally, the `AlgDefs_matrix_4x4_type` type represents a four-by-four component matrix of floating point values. This data type expresses all of the vector transformation functions as explained later.

The AlgVec_2D_MAKE and AlgVec_3D_MAKE Functions

These functions are used for the actual creation of vectors. The `AlgVec_3D_MAKE` function takes three floating point numbers (A,B,C) and stores them into the `AlgDefs_vector_3D_type` type (**v**) that it creates. The `AlgVec_2D_MAKE` function does the same, except that it stores two into an `AlgDefs_vector_2D_type`. This is a very useful and easy means of working with vectors.

N O T E These macros also work with the `AlgDefs_point_xD_type` types.

The AlgVec_2D_COMPONENTS and AlgVec_3D_COMPONENTS Functions

The `AlgVec_3D_COMPONENTS` function extracts the three values stored in an `AlgDefs_vector_3D_type` (**v**), and places them into three separate variables (*A,B,C*). `AlgVec_2D_COMPONENTS` performs similarly with two components.

N O T E These macros also work with the `AlgDefs_point_xD_type` types.

The AlgVec_2D_AVERAGE and AlgVec_3D_AVERAGE Functions

These functions add two vectors together and then divide each component by 2.

N O T E These macros also work with the `AlgDefs_point_xD_type` types.

The AlgVec_2D_NEGATE and AlgVec_3D_NEGATE Functions

These functions negate the components of a given vector by changing the sign of each component. These functions effectively reverse the direction of a vector, making it point in the opposite direction.

NOTE These macros also work with the `AlgDefs_point_xD_type` types.

The AlgVec_2D_DOT and AlgVec_3D_DOT Functions

These routines compute one of the most useful geometric functions of two vectors, namely, finding their dot product. The dot product of two vectors **A** and **B** is defined as

```
AlgVec_3D_DOT(A,B) = AlgVec_3D_LENGTH(A) *
                     AlgVec_3D_LENGTH(B) * cos(theta)
```

where `AlgVec_3D_LENGTH` computes the magnitude, or length, of the vector and theta is the angle between the two vectors. This is the same as simply multiplying each component of **A** by the corresponding components in **B** and summing all of the products together. The value of the dot product is

$$\mathbf{A}\bullet\mathbf{B} = ab\cos x \qquad\qquad (Equation\ 15.1)$$

`AlgVec_xD_DOT` is the number returned, a and b are the magnitude of vectors **A** and **B**, and x is the angle between the two vectors.

This function has a number of interesting and useful properties :

- If `AlgVec_xD_DOT` = 0, then the vectors are perpendicular to each other.

- If `AlgVec_xD_DOT` = `AlgVec_xD_LENGTH(A)` * `AlgVec_xD_LENGTH(B)`, then the two vectors lie along exactly the same direction.

- If `AlgVec_xD_DOT` = `-AlgVec_xD_LENGTH(A)` * `AlgVec_xD_LENGTH(B)`, then the two vectors point in exactly opposite directions.

Examine Figure 15.4. Here we are taking the dot product of $\mathbf{v}_1$ with $\mathbf{v}_2$. Notice the angle between the two vectors.

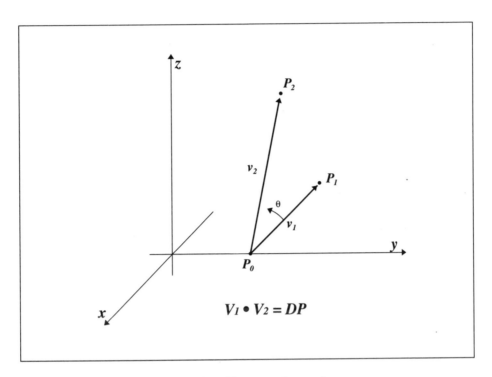

Figure 15.4 *The vector dot product.*

One important use of this function in computer graphics is to determine whether we are facing a particular polygon of an object. If the surface normal of the polygon (the *surface normal* is a vector immediately from the surface in the direction the surface is facing) is dotted with the viewing direction and the resulting number is negative, then we can see the polygon, since the vectors are pointing opposite to each other (the polygon is pointing in our general direction). If the resulting number is positive, then the vectors are pointing in the same general direction and we cannot see the polygon (it is turned away from us).

`AlgVec_2D_DOT` functions similarly to `AlgVec_3D_DOT`, except it pertains to 2-D vectors.

These macros also work with the `AlgDefs_point_xD_type` types.

The AlgVec_2D_LENGTH and AlgVec_3D_LENGTH Functions

These functions find the magnitude or length of a vector. They are basically two-and three-dimensional versions of the Pythagorean theorem. The length is the square root of the sum of the squares of the component values, that is,

$$\text{AlgVec\_2D\_LENGTH}(v) = \sqrt{x^2 + y^2}$$

$$\text{AlgVec\_3D\_LENGTH}(v) = \sqrt{x^2 + y^2 + z^2}$$

This function may also be used to find the distance between two points in three-dimensional space. The vector would contain the differences between each component of the two desired points.

The AlgVec_2D_NORMALIZE and AlgVec_3D_NORMALIZE Functions

A *normalized* vector has the same direction as a given vector, but has unit length or magnitude (length = 1). You can see this in Figure 15.5, where **v2** is the normalization of **v1**, pointing in the same direction, but with length 1. This functionality is needed often, for example, in the computation of the surface normal for a polygon described above. The `AlgVec_3D_CROSS` function computes a vector pointing in the right direction, but the shading model needs a vector of unit length. `AlgVec_3D_NORMALIZE` fills this need by normalizing the vector, thus giving it unit length.

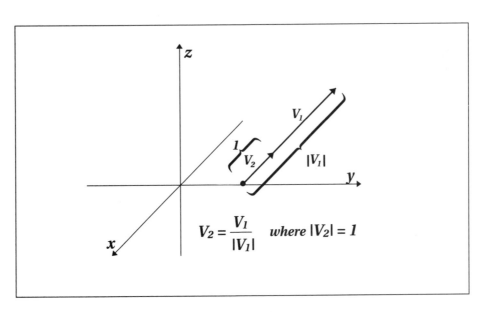

Figure 15.5 *Normalized vector.*

The first thing this routine does is find the length of the vector passed to it. Next it checks to see if the length is zero and, if it is, prints an error message and exits. The reason is that a vector with a length of zero has no direction and therefore cannot be normalized. This is a *degenerate case.* Once you determine that your vector is usable, you find the inverse distance by computing $1.0/\text{length}$. Next we multiply each component in the vector by the inverse distance, giving us our normalized vector.

AlgVec_2D_NORMALIZE functions similarly to AlgVec_3D_NORMALIZE, except that it pertains to 2-D vectors.

 N O T E These macros also work with the AlgDefs_point_xD_type types, even though normalizing a point has no real meaning.

The AlgVec_2D_MINIMUM and AlgVec_3D_MINIMUM Functions

The `AlgVec_3D_MINIMUM` function returns a vector whose components represent the minimum values of two other vectors' respective components. `AlgVec_2D_MINIMUM` functions similarly to `AlgVec_3D_MINIMUM`, except that it pertains to 2-D vectors.

NOTE These macros also work with the `AlgDefs_point_xD_type` types.

The AlgVec_2D_MAXIMUM and AlgVec_3D_MAXIMUM Functions

The `AlgVec_3D_MAXIMUM` function returns a vector whose components represent the maximum values of two other vectors' respective components. `AlgVec_2D_MAXIMUM` functions similarly to `AlgVec_3D_MAXIMUM`, except that it deals with 2-D vectors.

NOTE These macros also work with the `AlgDefs_point_xD_type` types.

The AlgVec_2D_COMPARE and AlgVec_3D_COMPARE Functions

These functions compare one vector with another vector, component by component. A value of `AlgDefs_TRUE` is returned if the respective components match.

NOTE These macros also work with the `AlgDefs_point_xD_type` types.

The AlgVec_2D_COPY and AlgVec_3D_COPY Functions

These functions copy the components of one vector into another vector. The vectors you pass to this function (and several others in this module) perform their operations *in place*, meaning that they modify the vector passed to it. This means that if you need to save your original vector, pass a temporary vector to this function and use the `AlgVec_2D_COPY` or `AlgVec_3D_COPY` functions to store the new values into your destination vector.

 N O T E These macros also work with the `AlgDefs_point_xD_type` types.

The AlgVec_2D_ADD and AlgVec_3D_ADD Functions

The functions `AlgVec_2D_ADD` and `AlgVec_3D_ADD` perform the operations of addition where the vector components are added. Examine Figure 15.6 to see vector addition. Notice here that the beginning of vector $\mathbf{v}_2$ slides up to the end of vector $\mathbf{v}_1$ when added. Note that these macros also work with the `AlgDefs_point_xD_type` types.

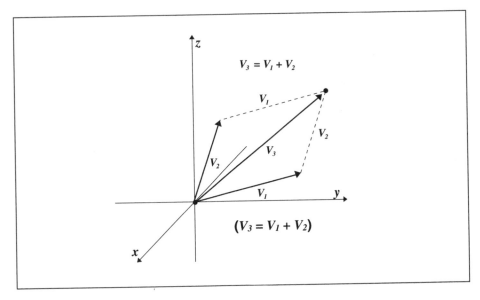

Figure 15.6 *Vector addition.*

The AlgVec_2D_SUB and AlgVec_3D_SUB Functions

The functions `AlgVec_2D_SUB` and `AlgVec_3D_SUB` perform the operations of subtraction where the vector components are subtracted. See Figure 15.7 to visualize vector subtraction. Notice that the subtracted vector $\mathbf{v_3}$ points to $\mathbf{v_2}$, since $\mathbf{v_3} = \mathbf{v_2} - \mathbf{v_1}$.

NOTE These macros also work with the `AlgDefs_point_xD_type` types.

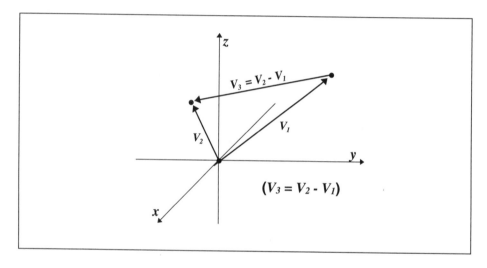

Figure 15.7 *Vector subtraction.*

The AlgVec_2D_LIN_COMB and AlgVec_3D_LIN_COMB Functions

These functions compute linear combinations of two vectors and place the result into a third.

Four variables are passed, two numbers and three vectors (*A*, *B*, **a**, **b** and **v** respectively). The components of **a** are multiplied by *A* and the components of **b** are multiplied by *B*. The results are added and stored into the vector **v**. The operation is

$$\mathbf{v} = A\mathbf{a} + B\mathbf{b}$$

(Equation 15.2)

`AlgVec_3D_ADD` is equivalent to `AlgVec_3D_LIN_COMB(1.0, a, 1.0, b, v)` and `AlgVec_3D_SUB` is equivalent to `AlgVec_3D_LIN_COMB(1.0, a, -1.0, b, v)`.

`AlgVec_2D_LIN_COMB` functions similarly to `AlgVec_3D_LIN_COMB`, except that it pertains to 2-D vectors.

 NOTE These macros also work with the `AlgDefs_point_xD_type` types.

The AlgVec_2D_SCAL_MULT and AlgVec_3D_SCAL_MULT Functions

These functions scale a vector by multiplying each component of the passed vector by a given number and storing the result into a new vector. This operation keeps the vector direction the same, but changes its length. Examine Figure 15.8. It shows that multiplying vector $\mathbf{v}_1$ by **2** yields a vector twice as long.

 NOTE These macros also work with the `AlgDefs_point_xD_type` types.

The AlgVec_2D_ADD_SCAL_MULT and AlgVec_3D_ADD_SCAL_MULT Functions

This is a convenience function, combining several operations into one call. It performs an `AlgVec_3D_ADD` on the input vectors *a* and *b*, followed by an `AlgVec_3D_SCAL_MULT` using the argument *a*. The result is stored in **v**. The operation is

$$\mathbf{v} = A\mathbf{a} + \mathbf{b} \qquad\qquad (Equation\ 15.3)$$

 NOTE These macros also work with the `AlgDefs_point_xD_type` types.

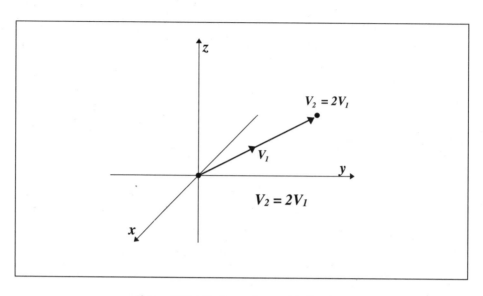

Figure 15.8 *Vector scalar multiplication.*

The AlgVec_2D_MUL and AlgVec_3D_MUL Functions

These functions accept a number and three vectors as input (*A*, **a**, **b** and **v** respectively). The components of vector a are multiplied by the components of vector **b** and the resulting vector is then multiplied by *A*. The results are stored in the vector **v**.

 N O T E These macros also work with the `AlgDefs_point_xD_type` types.

$$\mathbf{v} = A\mathbf{ab}$$ (Equation 15.4)

The AlgVec_2D_DETERMINANT Function

This routine computes the value of the *"determinant"* of a matrix whose elements are the two vectors as rows. (A determinant is a square array of numbers that a value may be associated with according to a rule; matrices are not themselves numbers, they are rectangular arrays

Plate 1. *Virtual building and aircraft. (Source: IVEX Corporation)*

Plate 2. *Runway in the evening. (Source: IVEX Corporation)*

Plate 3. *Behind the scenes of a flight simulator. (Source: IVEX Corporation)*

Plate 4. *Helicopter simulator. (Source: IVEX Corporation)*

Plate 5. *Virtual tank simulation.*

Plate 6. *Inside the virtual cockpit. (Source: IVEX Corporation)*

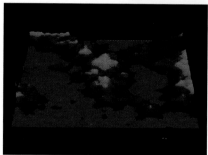

Plates 7–9. *The height field rendered using shaded polygons.*

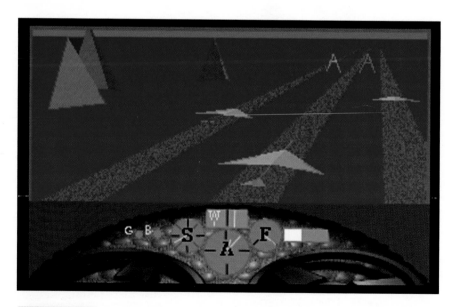

Plate 10. *A scene from the flight simulation program FREEBIRD. Source code and executables for this program are included on the disk accompanying this book.*

of mathematical elements, usually numbers.) The scalar value that is returned is equal to

$$\text{scalar} = (\mathbf{a}_x)(\mathbf{b}_y) - (\mathbf{a}_y)(\mathbf{b}_x)$$
    (Equation 15.5)

NOTE These macros also work with the `AlgDefs_point_xD_type` types.

The AlgVec_3D_CROSS Function

This routine is probably the second most useful tool in computer graphics. It finds the cross product of two vectors. The cross-product generates a third vector that is perpendicular to the plane defined by the first two vectors. The vector cross-product has a length of

$$\mathbf{v} = \mathbf{a} \times \mathbf{b} = AB \sin x$$
    (Equation 15.6)

where **a** and **b** are vectors. *A* and *B* are the magnitudes of the two vectors and *x* is the angle between them. `AlgVec_3D_CROSS` is the resulting vector. The two argument vectors define a plane (if they are not the same vector). `AlgVec_3D_CROSS` is therefore very useful in determining the surface normal for an object polygon.i.polygon;. For example, we can take two of the edges of a polygon as vectors, compute their cross-product, and have a vector representing the direction of the polygon face (surface normal). Subsequently, this surface normal is used in the shading.i.shading; of the facet lying in that plane. The vector cross-product is computed as follows

$$\mathbf{v} = \mathbf{a} \times \mathbf{b} = (\ (\mathbf{a}_y\,\mathbf{b}_z - \mathbf{a}_z\,\mathbf{b}_y),$$
$$(\mathbf{a}_z\,\mathbf{b}_x - \mathbf{a}_x\,\mathbf{b}_z),$$
$$(\mathbf{a}_x\,\mathbf{b}_y - \mathbf{a}_y\,\mathbf{b}_x)\ )$$
    (Equation 15.7)

The directions **i**, **j**, and **k** refer to the x-, y-, and z- axes, respectively. As a simple example, note that **k** is the cross-product of **i** and **j**. The order of the two vectors is important. `AlgVec_3D_CROSS(v2, v1)` is a vector pointing in the exact opposite direction (180 degrees) from `AlgVec_3D_CROSS(v1, v2)`.

Examine Figure 15.9. Notice that vector **v** is the cross-product of $\mathbf{v_1}$ and $\mathbf{v_2}$, and that this vector **v** is perpendicular to the plane defined by vectors $\mathbf{v_1}$ and $\mathbf{v_2}$.

N O T E

These macros also work with the `AlgDefs_point_xD_type` types.

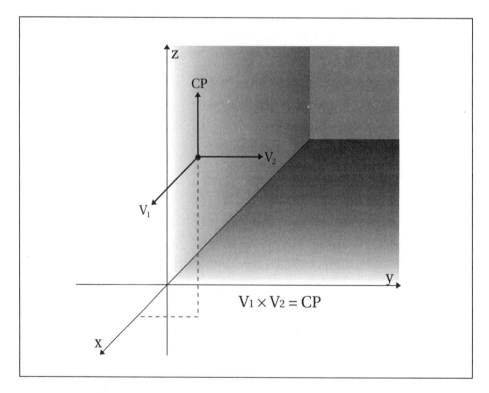

Figure 15.9 *The vector cross product.*

Examine Figure 15.10 for a simple diagram that will always keep the cross product direction straight for you:

$$\hat{i} \times \hat{j} = \hat{k} \qquad \hat{j} \times \hat{k} = \hat{i} \qquad \hat{k} \times \hat{i} = \hat{j}$$

$$\hat{j} \times \hat{i} = -\hat{k} \qquad \hat{k} \times \hat{j} = -\hat{i} \qquad \hat{i} \times \hat{k} = -\hat{j}$$

Figure 15.10 *Directions of cross products based on order of multiplication.*

The AlgVec_2D_ZERO and AlgVec_3D_ZERO Functions

The `AlgVec_2D_ZERO` and `AlgVec_3D_ZERO` functions simply set all components of a vector to zero.

NOTE

These macros also work with the `AlgDefs_point_xD_type` types.

Affine Transformation Routines

This is the heart of all of our geometric manipulations of vectors and points. (*Affine,* literally "by marriage," refers to a functional condition in which *to every finite value of one variable there corresponds a finite value of another variable, and vice versa.*) The affine transformation provides a means for concisely expressing all of the graphics transformations we need to perform on objects, including translation (moving the object in space), scaling (changing the size of the object), and rotation (changing the orientation of the object).

It is natural to wonder why we use a four-by-four matrix when all of our vectors are three-dimensional. The answer is that we wish to

incorporate translation into our single matrix transformation. The first column of the four-by-four matrix (as you will soon see) represents the translation of the vector using standard matrix multiplication:

$$\begin{bmatrix} b0 \\ b1 \\ b2 \\ b3 \end{bmatrix} = \begin{bmatrix} m00 & m01 & m02 & m03 \\ m10 & m11 & m12 & m13 \\ m20 & m21 & m22 & m23 \\ m30 & m31 & m32 & m33 \end{bmatrix} * \begin{bmatrix} a0 \\ a1 \\ a2 \\ a3 \end{bmatrix}$$

(Equation 15.8)

where in most of our use, a0 = 1.0, and (a1,a2,a3) represents our three-dimensional input vector. In addition, m00 = 1.0 and m01 = m02 = m03 = 0.0 for most matrices, so that b0 will also be equal to 1.0 after the transformation.

The routines in this section create matrices for scaling, rotation, and translation. The routines also combine these matrices into a single transformation matrix, and perform various mathematical operations using these matrices. All of the matrix operations use the AlgDefs_matrix_4x4_type type.

Note that there is also a set of 3x3 matrix routines. Those are not described in detail here, as you will not use them for any of the software found with this book. Now let's take a look at the functions and macros.

The AlgMatx_copy_4x4_matrix Function

This function copies a given 4x4 matrix into another 4x4 matrix.

The AlgMatx_multiply_4x4_matrix Function

This function performs the multiplication of two four-by-four floating-point (real-numbered) matrices, effectively combining two separate transformation matrices (transformations) into one. Multiplying x-rotation, y-rotation, z-rotation, scaling, and translation matrices together (concatenating matrices), produces a single *composite transformation matrix* that represents all of our rotations, scalings, and translations in one.

You generate a composite transformation matrix by first setting the matrix equal to the identity matrix (all 1.0 in the diagonal components, 0.0 everywhere else). You then compute each transformation matrix that you need (x-rotation, y-rotation, z-rotation, scaling, and translation) separately. Then you combine these matrices into a composite matrix, using four applications of the `AlgMatx_multiply_4x4_matrix` macro to multiply them all together. The net result is a matrix that represents all of the transformation operations, which you then apply to your vectors (points - vertices) as needed.

WARNING The order of matrix composition is crucial, and that you must keep in mind the task that you are trying to perform. A different ordering of matrix multiplications can produce entirely wrong and unexpected results.

Since each object in a scene may be moved separately, you potentially need different composite matrices for each object in the virtual flight simulation world. These matrices are called *local transformation matrices*. As we will see in our discussions on rendering scenes, all of these matrices are generated using the same basic procedure. It is also common to have a viewer transformation matrix that represents how all objects in the world should be transformed based on the position and orientation of the viewer. This view transformation matrix gets multiplied by the local matrices; then the objects are transformed by this new view-local concatenated matrix for viewing. In a nutshell, the local coordinates for an object (the coordinates that define the shape of an object—independent of the world) get transformed by the local transformation matrix into the virtual world, thus now objects relate to one-another. These objects that exist in the world (*world-coordinates*) get viewed because a viewer transformation matrix transforms the objects based on the position and orientation of the viewer. It is common to multiply the viewer matrix with the local matrices before transforming the vertices of the objects—this sometimes buys performance.

The AlgMatx_zero_4x4_matrix Function

This function zeros out all of the components of a 4x4 given matrix.

The AlgMatx_identity_4x4_matrix Function

This function loads a given matrix with the *identity matrix*. It is called an identity matrix, because it leaves a vector unchanged when applied as a transformation.

The AlgMatx_scale_4x4_matrix Function

This function creates a scaling matrix to scale each component of a vector. The matrix is first set to the identity matrix; then the diagonal elements are set to the three scaling parameters passed to the procedure and a 1.0 in the first position. The origin of a three-dimensional vector will not be changed by this transformation, only the scale of the vector. If all three scale factors are the same, the result will be the same as using AlgVec_3D_SCAL_MULT, leaving the direction unchanged. If they are different, then both the direction and length of the vector may change. The scaling matrix is

$$
\mathbf{s} = \begin{bmatrix} x & 0 & 0 & 0 \\ 0 & y & 0 & 0 \\ 0 & 0 & z & 0 \\ 0 & 0 & 0 & 1 \end{bmatrix}
$$

(Equation 15.9)

The AlgMatx_rotate_4x4_matrix Function

This function creates the matrix to rotate a vector in space about the X, Y, and Z axes. The function first sets the matrix to the identity matrix. Then the cosine and sine of the three angles are placed into certain matrix components, depending on the axis chosen. Note that the rotations about the given axes correspond with roll (Z-axis), pitch (X-axis), and yaw (Y-axis) orientations described later in this book. For an example of vector rotation, see Figure 15.11.

The matrix for rotation about the X-axis is

$$\mathbf{Rx} = \begin{bmatrix} 1 & 0 & 0 & 0 \\ 0 & \cos X & \sin X & 0 \\ 0 & -\sin X & -\cos X & 0 \\ 0 & 0 & 0 & 1 \end{bmatrix}$$

(Equation 15.10)

The matrix for rotation about the Y-axis is

$$\mathbf{Ry} = \begin{bmatrix} \cos Y & 0 & -\sin Y & 0 \\ 0 & 1 & 0 & 0 \\ \sin Y & 0 & \cos Y & 0 \\ 0 & 0 & 0 & 1 \end{bmatrix}$$

(Equation 15.11)

The matrix for rotation about the Z-axis is

$$\mathbf{Rz} = \begin{bmatrix} \cos Z & \sin Z & 0 & 0 \\ -\sin Z & \cos Z & 0 & 0 \\ 0 & 0 & 1 & 0 \\ 0 & 0 & 0 & 1 \end{bmatrix}$$

(Equation 15.12)

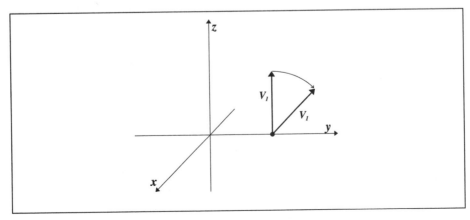

Figure 15.11 *Vector rotation about the y-axis.*

The AlgMatx_translate_4x4_matrix Function

This function creates the linear translation matrix to translate a point (vector) to a new location in space (see Figure 15.12). This matrix starts as the *identity matrix* consisting of a diagonal of ones. Then we set the last components of the first three rows to the negative of the three translation parameters passed to the function. This results in the following matrix

$$\mathbf{T} = \begin{bmatrix} 1 & 0 & 0 & -x \\ 0 & 1 & 0 & -y \\ 0 & 0 & 1 & -z \\ 0 & 0 & 0 & 1 \end{bmatrix}$$

(Equation 15.13)

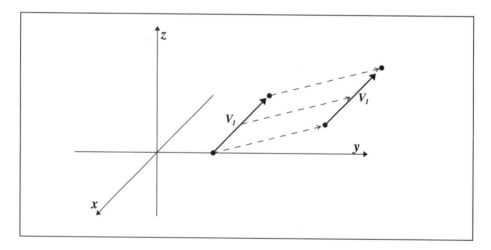

Figure 15.12 *Vector (point) Translation*

 NOTE Technically, only points can be manipulated in this manner, since a vector is always assumed to have reference to the origin—but for this purpose, points and vectors are interchangeable, as we do not fully do checking.

The AlgMatx_transform_4x4_matrix Function

This function performs the multiplication of a three-dimensional vector by a four-by-four matrix. The resulting vector will be the one corresponding to the various transformations represented by the passed matrix.

This function is our fundamental vector transformation function. It multiplies the components of a vector by the components of a 16-component composite `AlgDefs_matrix_4x4_type` matrix using the standard mathematical definition. As stated earlier, this function allows us to transform a vector by rotating, scaling, and translating it in one operation.

Examination of the transform function shows that the fourth component of our vector is assumed to be 1. We do this because we do not need the fourth component (for our work here).

Pseudo-Random Number Generation

These routines create pseudo-random numbers via the power residue sequence approach (explained below) for positive pseudo-random number generation. *Pseudo-random* means that the sequence only appears to be random and can be regenerated exactly by passing the same "seed" value to the routine on initialization. In addition, the sequence is only approximately uniformly distributed in the interval 0.0–1.0.

The pseudo-random number generator starts by initialization with an arbitrary floating-point number, referred to as a *seed value*. New numbers are generated by multiplying a constant (sigma) with the seed value and returning the fractional part, thus guaranteeing that the result is between 0 and 1. Every time the routine is called, a new number in the sequence is generated based on the previous value and, indirectly, on the seed. Therefore, it guarantees that any sequence can always be regenerated, if you know the seed. For instance, if the fractal terrain generation program found in Appendix C using the pseudo-random number generator generates an image that you like, you can regenerate the same image with just the knowledge of the seed value.

The AlgDefs_RANDOM_SEED Function

This function initializes the random number generator with a floating-point number. `old_seed` is set to the passed seed value. `AlgMath_RAN-`

DOM_SEED must be called for usage of both the AlgMath_RAND and AlgMath_RAND_INT functions. Anytime the same value is passed to AlgMath_RANDOM_SEED, the same sequence will be generated by AlgMath_RAND and AlgMath_RAND_INT.

The AlgMath_RAND Function

This function returns a positive floating-point type random number between 0.0 and 1.0. old_rand takes on the fractional part of old_rand times the constant sigma. old_rand is then the returned value. AlgMath_RANDOM_SEED must be called prior to any use of AlgMath_RAND.

The AlgMath_RAND_INT Function

This function returns a positive integer-type pseudo-random number from an AlgDefs_word-type range argument, that is, a value from 0 up to (range-1). We simply get the next value from AlgMath_RAND, which is always in the range 0.0–1.0, multiply this by range, and return AlgDefs_TRUNC of the result.

Software Routines—Vector, Matrix and Type Definition Modules

Examine AlgVec.H, AlgMath.H, AlgMath.C, AlgMatx.H, AlgMatx.C, and AlgDefs.H on the accompanying diskette.

Summary

Now that we have examined some of the basic linear algebra, matrix, and vector geometry for object manipulation and viewing computer graphics, and seen some of the data structures that we will use to define and hold our virtual flight simulation world data, let's get to the nuts and bolts and carry our focus to the polygon primitive as it applies to a graphics system.

Polygon Generation

This chapter discusses the basic issue of generating two-dimensional, color-filled polygons. As described in the previous sections, solid-shaded polygons construct the objects in our virtual three-dimensional worlds for flight simulation. Everything from the mountains and trees to the buildings in a flight simulator are usually constructed from polygons. Polygons can have the size of a screen pixel and thus represent a point, or they can have many vertices and describe some complex 3-D surface. That makes the polygon a very versatile primitive tool.

The Polygon

Simply stated, a *polygon* is a shape formed from straight lines placed end to end, where the end of the last line touches the beginning of the next line. Drawing just these lines on your computer display would constitute a wire-frame version of whatever object you are displaying, using polygons. For these purposes we fill in polygons to make solid objects. A *color-filled polygon* has all of the pixels colored that are inside the closed loop of lines that make up the polygon.

Polygons come in three classes—*convex, nonconvex,* and *complex.* See Figure 16.1 for illustration.

Convex Polygon

Non-Convex Polygon

Complex Polygon

Figure 16.1 *Convex, nonconvex, and complex polygons.*

Polygon Definitions

Convex polygons are the type of polygon that our flight simulator's polygon-rendering module can handle. A convex polygon for these purposes is one for which any line horizontally drawn through the polygon will cross the left edge only once and the right edge only once (excluding any horizontal or zero-length edges of the polygon). Simply stated, neither the left edge nor the right edge of a convex polygon will ever reverse direction from up to down, or down to up. The left and right edges cannot cross each other (though they may touch). This makes for a polygon that can be color-filled quickly and easily.

Nonconvex polygons can have edges that go in any direction, as long as those edges never cross. This makes the color-filling process slower and more complicated, but it is still manageable.

Complex polygons have no limit as to where the edges can go. Since edges can overlap in a complex polygon, it becomes interesting to figure out which interior parts of the polygon to color-fill.

We use convex polygons because we need performance. The computation cost of nonconvex polygons and especially complex polygons is so high that we could not make a renderer with a suitable screen update-rate with them. All objects can be constructed from convex polygons; therefore, this is no real limitation.

Color Filling the Convex Polygon

The fundamental principle of filling a polygon on a *raster display* (a computer monitor or TV display in which the whole image is created by a series of horizontal shaded lines) is the decomposition of a polygon into an array of horizontal lines. We must draw a horizontal line representing a horizontal slice of the polygon for each raster display scan line (horizontal row of pixels) within the polygon. We will call this process *rasterization of the polygon.* To rasterize convex polygons you start at the top of the polygon and follow down the left and right edges—one scan line (vertical pixel) at a time, filling in the area between the two edges on each scan line as you go, until you reach the bottom of the polygon. Note that this approach is valid only for convex polygons.

Therefore, scan-converting polygons is a bed of roses, right? Wrong! There are a couple of thorns in the rose patch that make this conceptually simple process a rather difficult one to implement.

Problems in Converting Polygons

The first problem is the limited efficiency of polygon rasterization. See Figure 16.2. It is hard to develop efficient code that simultaneously follows two edges from the top of the polygon down and fills in the pixels between them. A simple solution is to decouple the computation of the horizontal lines (the scan conversion of the polygon into a horizontal line list) from the actual drawing of those horizontal lines. This separates what should be device-independent routines such as the horizontal line list computations from the device-dependent horizontal line display.

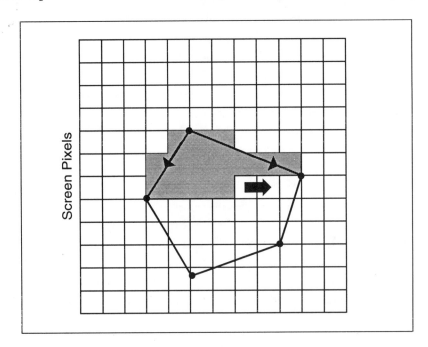

Figure 16.2 *Filling a polygon.*

The second difficulty exists because we want our polygons to fit close together. See Figure 16.3. Our objects are created from clusters of adjacent polygons. If we use some standard line-drawing routine to compute the polygon edges, we will get points that fall outside the polygon. This occurs because a line is a one-dimensional creature, and we merely approximate the actual line with our computer display by coloring pixels nearest to the actual line on either side of it.

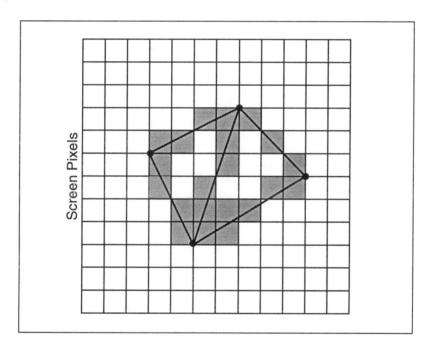

Figure 16.3 *Adjacent polygons on a raster display.*

Well, you might see where we are headed; the key word is "adjacent." We need adjacent polygons, and if we are placing points that fall on either side of the actual line, when we place a second polygon adjacent to an already-drawn one, the second will overwrite the first, possibly making an unacceptable image.

> **N O T E** Standard line drawing routines in place of our advanced routines can be useful when polygons do not overlap, especially when they do not overlap and you want to add borders (different colored edges) to your polygons.

As you might guess, this discussion leads to an algorithm for adjacent polygon drawing.

Drawing Adjacent Polygons

For starters, any *edge-following* or *tracing* algorithm that defines what the edges of the polygon are, must select only pixels (small colored picture elements that make up the image on your screen) that are inside the polygon—pixels cannot lie on either side of the line that defines the polygon edge. This equates to shifting a standard line drawing routine to the left or to the right by one-half pixel, always toward the interior of the polygon.

That leaves us with two cases, pixels that are exactly on the boundary and pixels that lie on *vertices*. See Figure 16.4. For those two cases, we draw these pixels only once. To do that, we stipulate that pixels located exactly on non-horizontal edges are drawn only if the interior of the polygon is to the right. That means that left edges are drawn and right edges are not. Pixels that are located exactly on horizontal edges are drawn only if the interior of the polygon is below them. That means that horizontal top edges are drawn and horizontal bottom edges are not. A vertex is drawn only if all lines ending at that vertex meet the other two conditions; therefore, no right or bottom edges end at that vertex. See Figure 16.5.

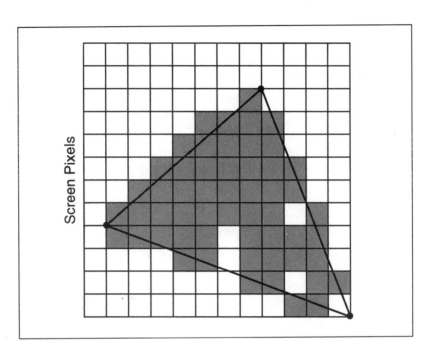

Figure 16.4 *Interior pixels must be below and to the right of edges for them to be drawn.*

All polygon edges, excluding flat tops and bottoms, will be considered edges. The left edge is the line that starts from the top of the polygon and tends to the left. The right edge is the line that starts from the top of the polygon and tends to the right.

Following these rules guarantees that a pixel of the first polygon will not be overwritten by a pixel of the adjacent second polygon. So we now have an algorithm that we can implement.

The Polygon-Filling Routine

The function `AlgPoly_draw_convex_polygon_to_screen_buffer` is our polygon-filling routine. It expects a list of vertices that describes a convex polygon. The last vertex is assumed to be the first vertex. The function creates the horizontal line list described above and passes it to the device-dependent `AlgScrn_draw_horz_line_list_to_screen_buffer` for drawing into a screen buffer.

`AlgPoly_draw_convex_polygon_to_screen_buffer` starts by finding the top and the bottom of the given polygon. It then figures from the top point the ends of the top edge.

If the two ends are at different locations, the top is flat. It the top is flat, it will be easy to find the starting vertices and directions through the vertex list for the left and right edges. Also, the top scan line of the polygon should be drawn without the rightmost pixel colored. This is because only the rightmost pixel of a horizontal edge that makes up the top scan line can be part of a right edge.

If the two ends are at the same location, the top is not flat, it is pointed, and the top scan line is not drawn. It is part of the right edge by our rules. When the top is not flat, it is difficult to determine in which direction through the vertex list the left and right edges go, as both edges start at the same (top) vertex. To resolve this problem, we compare the slopes of the two edges. See Figure 16.5 for a comparison of flat and non-flat tops.

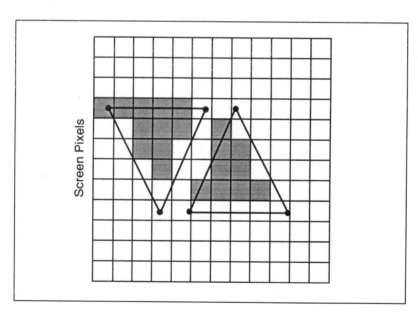

Figure 16.5 *Comparison of flat and non-flat polygon tops.*

Now that we know where the left edge starts in the vertex list, we can perform our scan conversion of the left edge of the polygon from top to bottom, producing the starting x positions for our horizontal line list. Note that the nearest x coordinate on or to the right (interior of the polygon) is chosen. This avoids drawing a vertex twice and also avoids drawing the bottom scan line. Note that the first scan line of our polygon is not drawn if the top is not flat.

Now that we have a list of scan-converted left points for our horizontal lines, we must produce the corresponding list of right points. This is very similar to computation of the left list, except that every edge in the right edge is moved one pixel to the left before scan conversion. This gives us the nearest point to the left of the edge, but not on the edge.

Software Routine For Generating 2-D Polygons

Examine `AlgPoly.H`, `AlgPoly.C`, `AlgScrn.H`, and `AlgScrn.C` on the accompanying diskette.

Summary

We now know how a polygon is generated by a computer, and how they are useful for the construction of three-dimensional objects. So, now let's take a look at cleaning up the jagged edges of our polygons, through *anti-aliasing*.

Polygon Anti-Aliasing

This chapter discusses problems with aliasing and discusses possible solutions through various anti-aliasing techniques.

Issues of Image Quality and Spatial Aliasing

Aliasing is defined in engineering as the appearance of spurious, low-frequency signals resulting from insufficient sampling of a high-frequency signal. The high-frequency signal then masquerades (or aliases) as a low-frequency signal in the sampled data. The most common form (though by no means the only one) in computer graphics is the "jaggies" or "stair-step" edges of raster scanned polygons and lines. Anti-aliasing techniques, the processes of removing aliases, comes to our rescue.

The bane of computer graphics is the many and sundry aliasing problems. The problem results from the fact that the screen represents a finite sampling, the pixels, of an infinitely high, *spatial frequency signal,* an edge or a texture pattern. When we create the scan-converted polygons described above, we are *sampling*. It is easy to see how, in the absence of any other techniques, simply color-filling a polygon frequently misses edges by a fractional amount. This becomes most apparent in any kind of motion such as a flight simulation, in which the aliasing problems become very distracting along object edges. The problem is also evident when texture patterns are used. As the objects move into the distance, the pattern is sampled less and less frequently, resulting in sampling errors.

Some of the more common graphics *aliasing artifacts* (jaggies and stair steps) are shown in images where a bright line is drawn on a computer display against a dark background. The "jaggies" are everywhere. Other common images that show off aliasing artifacts are the checker pattern to the horizon and the *zone plate* (repeating waterdrop-like pattern) to the horizon.

Let us explore the problem of aliasing further and see how various anti-aliasing techniques can help minimize the artifacts.

Anti-Aliasing

As mentioned in the previous section, aliasing problems result when a high-frequency signal is sampled at too low a *sampling rate*. Imagine that you have a sine wave, you can take samples at different points of the sine wave and approximate it. The number of samples you take per unit time is the sampling rate. See Figure 17.1. With a regular sampling pattern, these high-frequency signals appear as low-frequency, or *beat* frequency signals. One of the worst case tests of any anti-aliasing schemes is the *checkerboard texture* (alternating black and white) projected on a flat plane. As the pattern goes off into the horizon, the frequency of the checkerboard gets higher and higher (black and white squares appear closer together) due to the perspective. Eventually, the spacing is smaller than adjacent screen pixels, and this causes aliasing problems. The regular sampling scheme creates new patterns in the image that look almost unrelated to the checkerboard spacing. The human eye is very sensitive to such sampling artifacts and we generally find such images objection-able. Figure 17.2 shows an example of an image with aliasing and the anti-aliasing of that image.

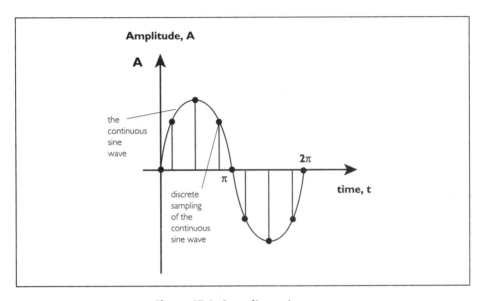

Amplitude, A

A

the continuous sine wave

discrete sampling of the continuous sine wave

π

2π

time, t

Figure 17.1 *Sampling a sine wave.*

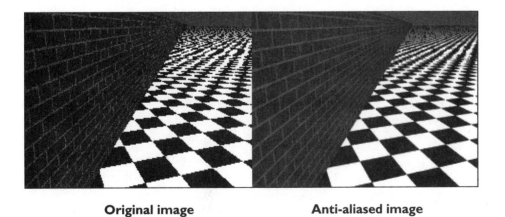

Original image   **Anti-aliased image**

Figure 17.2 *Anti-aliasing of an Image*

Given that some sort of *adaptive supersampling* (extra samples taken where needed) must be used to combat the aliasing artifacts, the trick now is to apply the supersampling selectively only on pixels that intersect object edges or pixels in areas of high contrast, such as in a spotlight or a textured area, thus the term *adaptive*. If half of the final image is covered by the background or by a large smooth object, and supersampling is applied everywhere, then half of the computing time has been wasted on regions that did not need it.

For the most part, adjacent screen pixels will intersect the same polygons of objects just at slightly different positions. Also, only the areas of high contrast exhibit noticeable aliasing problems. Therefore, let's concentrate on these areas, and not on large areas of smooth changes or on the background. The job then is to detect the edges and/or high-contrast transitions as in the checkerboard pattern. This leads us to *adaptive anti-aliasing*. The renderer decides how to smear, and thus fix the image (locally average colors) by comparing colors of adjacent pixels to see if they are within some user-defined threshold value (or alternatively, that they both intersect the background).

Now that you know what aliasing is and you have been introduced very briefly to a method for performing anti-aliasing, look at the problem of aliasing when you move or the objects in your simulation world are moving.

Motion Anti-Aliasing

Moving the viewer, and moving objects within a world, introduce yet another potential problem into our imagery, namely that of *temporal* aliasing. Just as *spatial aliasing* (aliasing, like jaggies and stair steps caused primarily by the way a polygon is spatially sampled) causes problems in the quality of imagery, temporal aliasing can produce equivalent problems in a scene in motion.

Wagon Wheels and Temporal Aliasing

Too much aliasing can destroy the *suspension of disbelief* effect (effect created when the simulator participant actually believes that the simulation is real) that a simulator should provide. The basic situation is the same as in rendering the scene; we are sampling the motion at discrete points in time and at a finite rate. If the motion is too rapid, it will be sampled incorrectly and odd artifacts result. The classic case of this is watching the wagon wheel spokes in old cowboy movies. Movies record a scene at 24 frames per second (fps). Each frame is chopped, giving an equivalent 48-fps display. When the wheels turn rapidly, the camera undersamples the rotation and may give false appearances, such as the wheels seeming to rotate backward. The same effect can occur with any type of motion where changes occur more rapidly than the frame rate can effectively sample.

Motion Blur

The wagon wheel motion problem can be solved partially by the temporal equivalent of anti-aliasing. The technique is also commonly referred to as *motion blur*. A motion-blurred wagon wheel will have spokes that run together rather than being individually identifiable. As happens so often in technology, you have gained one thing but lost another—you have traded off the aliasing artifacts for lower resolution in time. You can no longer discern quite as fine and rapid a motion as you can in the non-motion-blurred case. However, it usually does not matter, since you can't trust the non-anti-aliased image anyway (you have seen these movies where a wagon wheel seems to turn in the opposite direction that you would expect—the carriage moves forward—but the wheel seems to turn backwards).

Textures and Aliasing

Anti-aliasing is important when using *texture mapping*. Texture mapping is where you use an image or mathematical equation to shade a particular polygon (like a polygon that is used for a picture of the Mona Lisa on the wall.) The problem gets worse in a scene with motion. The reason, of course, is that now the actual texture map— *pixel intersections*—varies slightly from image to image in the motion. Any aliasing problems will be compounded and appear as the "crawlies" or random dot motion in the texture. Motion blur is an effective method for reducing the crawlies.

Progressive Refinement

And a final note on the efficiency of anti-aliasing the motion-filled simulations such as flight. A technique called *progressive refinement* says that you can hold off on anti-aliasing the image until the motion stops. This way, you can use all of those compute cycles to work with motion and image update rates, and worry about the "jaggies" and "crawlies" only later when the image on the computer display is static (the viewer is not moving, or the objects in the scene are still). The edge of larger surfaces (such as mountains) should always be anti-aliased to some degree, as large "jaggies" will probably break the suspension of disbelief.

Summary

So far, we have seen how polygons are generated, and how anti-aliasing can enhance image quality. We will now take a look at how our three-dimensional polygons are projected into two dimensions.

CHAPTER

18

Polygon Projection

You may remember that you need to get polygons from the virtual three-dimensional and mathematically defined world onto the very real two-dimensional computer display. Remember that the computer display acts like a window into the virtual flight simulation world for us, much as the airplane cockpit acts as a window into the real world for the pilot. We see a likeness of the world through the window.

You may also recall that you perform many projections of polygons from the three-dimensional polygonal world onto the two-dimensional screen, using geometry and trigonometry. All of the objects in the world are transformed relative to the viewer, so that the objects that you should see are projected onto the screen in their correct relations.

This chapter describes the mathematics required to perform *perspective projection* (projection that will generate images where objects appear larger when they are closer). *Perspective projection* is required,

203

since you want to see your virtual flight simulation world in your display system, just as we would see the real world though a window.

Perspective Projection

For perspective projection, assume that the computer display is to be parallel to the xy plane, and that our viewer is looking along the z axis (surface normal-vector pointing straight from surface) of the view plane. To form a projection, you extend perspective lines from each vertex of the polygon until they intersect the plane of the computer display. See Figure 18.1 for an example of perspective projection. The point of intersection with the computer display is called the *projection of the vertex*. If you project the three-dimensional polygon world coordinate points in the order in which they were defined in the database, you get a two-dimensional representation of the polygon (again, as it would be seen through a window). This representation is passed to a solid polygon generation routine (the polygon filling routine described in Chapter 17) for display.

In the case of perspective projection, the z coordinate is very important. The z coordinate gives us a way to "taper" the scene based on increasing distance from the viewer to the horizon. In perspective projection, the farther away an object is from the viewer, the smaller that object appears. This size change of an object based on the object's distance from the viewer is a very important depth cue. When many objects are in a scene, the relative sizes of similar objects help the brain sort the objects according to distance. You need this cue, since you have just a single image for both eyes. Without stereo vision for depth cues, you have to have perspective and correct apparent sizing of objects to make sense of the world. (Look at a mural from ancient Rome—before perspective was discovered—and see how hard it is to tell if the dog is in front of the table or behind the table).

In perspective projection, the lines of projection are not parallel lines. They converge at a single point called the *center of projection* (*COP*), known to artists as the *vanishing point*. The intersection of all of these lines from the COP. with the plane of the screen determines the projected image. The lines of projection from the object's vertices to the center of projection correspond to the paths of light rays coming from the object to the viewer's eye. Once again, see Figure 18.1 for an illustration of perspective projection.

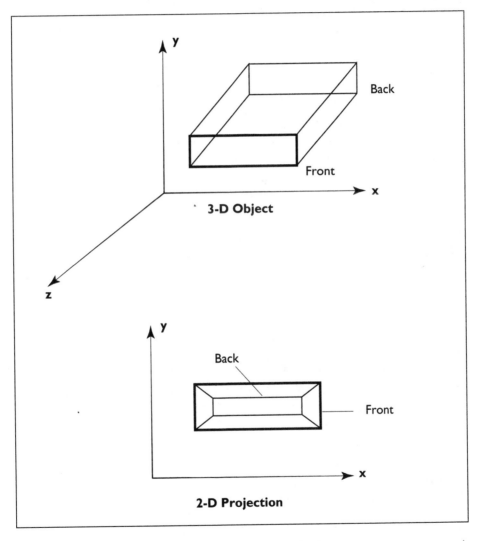

Figure 18.1 *Perspective projection.*

Remember when, as a kid, you were on a trip with your parents and you were looking out the car windows at layers of trees and mountains, listening to your father speak in colorful metaphors about missing an exit and that he really knew where he was going on that shortcut. Well, you may remember that the mountains usually moved by more slowly than the trees, and the lines in the road and the telephone poles flew past you. Well, this is an example of perspective. Objects that are nearby appear larger and move quickly by you, while objects that are at a a distance move more slowly and appear smaller. As you would expect, we need to create mathematical functions that simulate these effects, and perspective projection gives us that capability.

The way perspective projection works, at least for our simple flight simulation renderer, is that we perform the projections of the object's polygon vertices. If the z coordinate of the object vertex is small, meaning that the object vertex is nearby, we scale up the xy position of projection. If the z coordinate is large, meaning that the object vertex is far away, we scale down the xy position of projection. To do this, we divide the x and y components of our coordinate by the z coordinate, and scale these new x and y values (our projected values) by a number that represents the distance to the perspective plane. The larger this value, the larger the objects appear, as the plane is closer to those objects. Finally, we offset these perspective projected coordinates so that they are in the center of the screen.

Software Routines for Projecting 3-D Polygons into 2-D

Examine AlgProj.H and AlgProj.C on the accompanying diskette.

Summary

So, now we know how to get our three dimensional polygons into two dimensions. What remains is how to prepare our polygons for display. This will involve clipping polygons behind us, and off to the sides, and that is the topic of the next chapter.

19

Polygon Clipping

Previous chapters discussed ideas about how polygons that comprise objects are projected, and how those projected polygons are scan-converted for display on a rasterized computer screen. The techniques to generate images in simulation are similar for both personal computer displays and many large projection systems. For the projection of objects, one condition of interest occurs when sitting within a group of objects. As you sit reading this book, you probably do not see the lamp located behind you, or the pillow you're leaning against (you probably do see your cat—they squat on top of what you are trying to read).

If you think about a virtual representation of this world (your living room), and of what the mathematics for perspective projection does when virtual objects lie behind us, you see that the equations basically create a display of mirrored and tangled objects. You obviously should not see the objects that lie behind you, in any form.

The projection technique described in Chapter 18 is fine for looking at objects in the distance in front of you, but for any virtual reality or flight simulation system where interaction is usually necessary, you

207

need access of movement throughout the complete virtual world, whether it is visible to a given observer or just potentially visible.

There are solutions to this problem, and the solution that we will use is called *polygon clipping.* Polygon clipping removes parts of polygons or whole polygons that fall behind the viewer or partially off to the sides of the computer display. Clipping, when used in conjunction with perspective projection, gets us one step closer to creating an interactive graphical display system in which the viewer can move freely throughout the virtual flight simulation world. See Figure 19.1 for an example of line clipping for screen display.

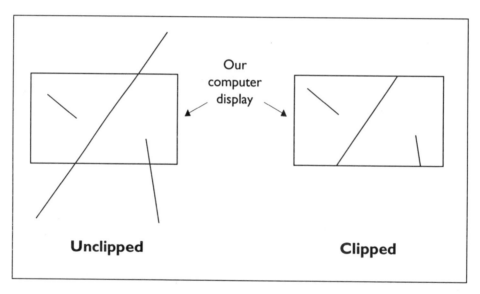

Figure 19.1 *The 2-D clipping of some lines.*

In the *clipping algorithm* (that you will soon learn how to write), it is necessary to determine how a line is positioned relative to some clipping boundary. In Figure 19.1, the rectangle representing the computer display is the *clipping boundary,* and you need to display any lines or parts of lines that fall within this boundary. In a clipping system, you examine each line scheduled for display to determine whether it lies completely inside or outside the boundary, or crosses the boundary. If the line is inside, it is displayed. If it is outside, it is trivially clipped — suppressed—and nothing is drawn. If it crosses over the boundary, the point of intersection of the line and boundary must be determined and the portion of the line that lies within the boundary drawn.

The next extension of this concept is to our primitive object, the polygon. Since a polygon is nothing more than a collection of lines called *edges*, we can apply the algorithm multiple times to clip each edge of the polygon with some boundary. That boundary can be a plane that exists in a three-dimensional world, or it can be a collection of bounding lines that form another polygon. In the preceding example, the edges of the computer display form a rectangle (four-sided polygon). We clip the polygon against each of these screen edges individually. See Figure 19.2. This is the *Sutherland-Hodgman* polygon clipping algorithm applied to clipping a polygon to a screen rectangle. We will use this algorithm for *z*-clipping (clipping polygons partially or totally behind the viewer) of the polygon.

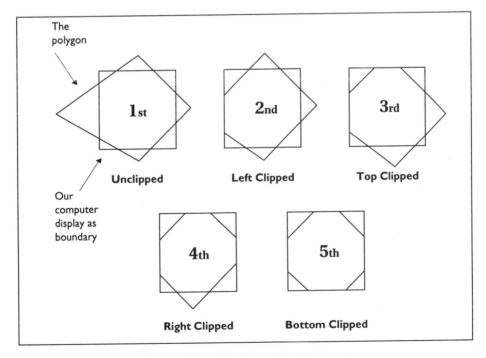

Figure 19.2 *Clipping against the screen.*

Our simulation system requires two types of clipping routines so that we can fly through and around the objects in our virtual flight simulation world. The first form of clipping is one that clips the polygons in the z dimension (the z dimension represents distance from the viewer along the direction in which the viewer is looking). This is called z-clipping and will effectively remove all of those polygons or parts of polygons that fall behind the viewer (or in this case, the pilot). This clipping must be performed before perspective projection, to have any useful effect. The second form of clipping occurs after projection, and it is clipping of the polygons that did not make it fully into the viewable screen area.

We will now look at the two types of clipping used in our graphics system in more detail. The *Sutherland-Hodgman* method of polygon clipping is used for clipping polygons in the z dimension before projection. Then a technique called the *Liang-Barsky* polygon clipping method will be used for the display clipping of those already z-clipped and projected polygons.

Z-Clipping Polygons using the Sutherland-Hodgman Method

So far, you have learned about clipping two-dimensional lines and polygons with a two-dimensional boundary. It is now time to think in three dimensions, where it is not a two-dimensional rectangle that bounds our polygons, but some three-dimensional volume. We call this volume a *view volume*, a *clipping volume*, or a *view frustum*. A view volume is shaped like a box. See Figure 19.3. According to when and how you are clipping, its shape can be that of a rectangular prism (like a cube or cuboid) or some frustum-shaped volume (a frustum is the base of a truncated solid whose sides converge to a point). Polygons within the view volume are displayed, while those outside it are not. Polygons that cross the boundary of the view volume are cut. Only that portion of the polygon that falls within the view volume is displayed.

Every edge of a polygon must be tested with each side of the view volume individually (i.e., we determine what polygon edges cross the view volume boundaries, and how edges that do not cross the boundaries are orientated with the boundaries (on what side)). This is analogous to testing all of the edges of a two-dimensional polygon with each screen edge, where all edges of the polygon are tested with the left side of the screen, then all edges are tested with the top of the screen, then all edges are tested with the right, and then with the bottom of the screen.

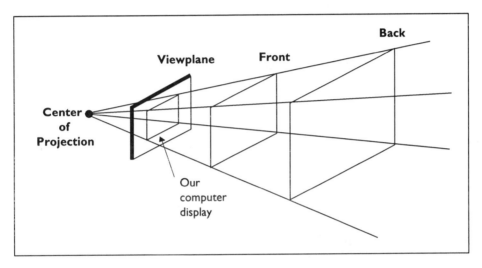

Figure 19.3 *The perspective view volume.*

For our flight simulation program, we will use only the front of the view volume (closest plane making the viewing frustum). We clip our polygon with this single front plane. We do this to remove or clip the polygons that are part of objects that fall behind us. Once again, we do this before projection of the polygon.

We do not use a back-to-the-view volume and clip against it (that is a clipping of objects greater than a certain distance from the viewer). We determined that since the virtual flight simulation worlds are simple, this additional clipping would decrease the program performance. If the virtual world were more complex, such clipping could be used to remove objects that are so far ahead of the viewer that no details could be seen. Therefore such an object should be reduced in detail or removed anyway.

For *z*-clipping a polygon, each edge of the polygon is tested with the front clipping plane portion of a view volume. A view volume is never actually defined, only the AlgPClip_Z_CLIPPING_PLANE value found in the code listing AlgPClip.H which defines the *z*-clipping plane. This value is positive (instead of zero) to guarantee proper calculation of clips. This routine returns a polygon that has been *z*-clipped and is ready for perspective projection.

Note that we did not z-clip against the whole volume (just the front plane) because we will use a clipping routine that is best suited for screen clipping after we have done the projection of the polygons into two dimensions.

Notice that polygons that have been clipped into non-existence set the trivial reject flag to AlgDefs_TRUE. This keys in the calling routine that it should not add this given polygon to the list of polygons for display, as the polygon is out of sight.

Screen-Clipping Using the Liang-Barsky Method

Though multiple applications of the Sutherland-Hodgman method yield nicely screen-clipped polygons (applied to polygons in three dimensions or applied to projected polygons in two dimensions), we will use a two-dimensional polygon-clipping method called the *Liang-Barsky* method. We choose the Liang-Barsky method because it lets us quickly clip two-dimensional polygons with rectangles. We also use this method to show that there are other ways to look at the polygon clipping problem. The performance of the Liang-Barsky method is comparable to (and only slightly better than) the Sutherland-Hodgman method for purposes of screen clipping our polygons.

To understand this algorithm, it is best to start with a pseudocode representation. The following listing shows the Liang-Barsky polygon clipping algorithm in pseudo-code. See *Computer Graphics, Practice and Principles* by Foley, van Dam, Feiner, and Hughes for a detailed description of this algorithm.

```
for (each edge of the polygon)
  {
      determine the direction of the given edge

use this direction to determine which bounding lines for the clip
region the containing line hits first

      find the t-values for the exit points

      if (t_exit_point2 > 0)
          find t-value for second entry point

      if (t_entry_point2 > t_exit_point1)
      {
          no visible segment
          if (0 < t_exit_point1 <= 1)
              output_vertex(turning vertex)
      }
      else
      {
          if ((0 <  t_exit_point1) and
                (1 >= t_entry_point2))
          {
              there is some visible part
              if (0 <= t_entry_point2)
output_vertex(appropriate side intersection)
              else
                  output_vertex(starting vertex)

              if (1 >= t_exit_point1)
                  output_vertex(appropriate side intersection)
              else
                      output_vertex(ending vertex)
          }
```

```
        }

    if (0 < t_exit_point2 <= 1)
            output_vertex(appropriate corner)
  }
```

To follow this algorithm, we must think of a polygon edge in its *parametric form*. This means that we assign the starting vertex for the edge 0.0 and the ending vertex for the edge 1.0. Values between 0.0 and 1.0, called *t-values*, carry us a distance along the edge from the starting vertex. This can be represented in parametric equation form as

$$P(t) = (1 - t)P_0 + tP_1$$

To be precise, we use values $0.0 < t <= 1.0$ to represent points on the edge, omitting the starting point. As with the polygon filling routine discussed earlier, this guarantees that each vertex of the polygon is contained in exactly one of the two edges that meet there.

We start our discussion with diagonal polygon edges. Such edges must cross each of the lines that determine the boundary of the screen window. If we divide the viewing plane into nine regions, where the center region is the screen, you can see that every diagonal line passes from one corner region to the opposite corner region. Each window thus divides the plane into two half-planes. We refer to the region containing the screen the inside half-plane. The regions in Figure 19.4 are labeled by the number of inside half-planes they lie in. The screen is the only one lying in four. Regions at the corners lie in two and are called *corner regions*. Regions directly above, below, to the left, and to the right of the screen region lie in three and are called *edge regions*.

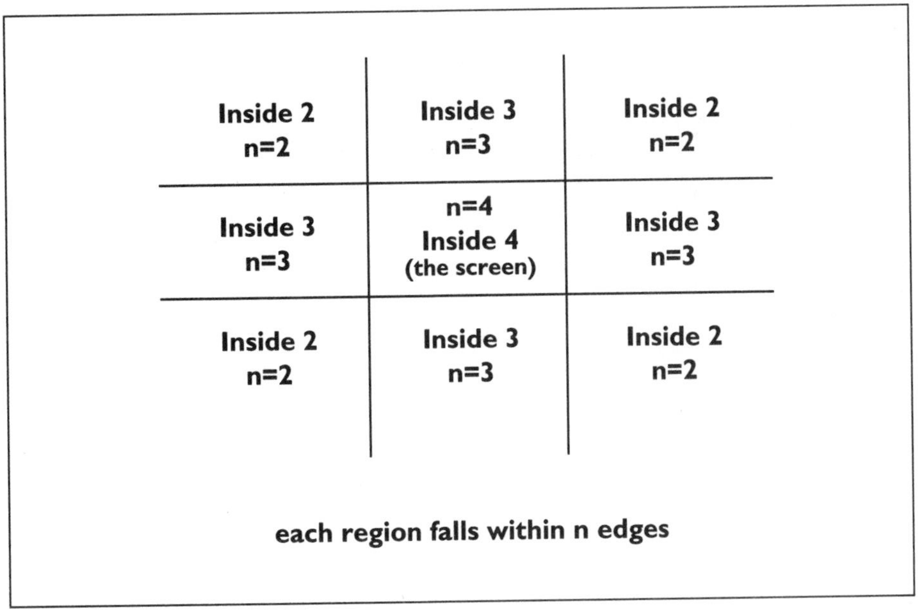

Inside 2 n=2	Inside 3 n=3	Inside 2 n=2
Inside 3 n=3	n=4 Inside 4 (the screen)	Inside 3 n=3
Inside 2 n=2	Inside 3 n=3	Inside 2 n=2

each region falls within n edges

Figure 19.4 *The 9 regions for the Liang-Barsky method.*

If some part of the edge lies in the screen, that part must be part of the output polygon. The vertices that this edge contributes to the output polygon can be either the ends of the edge (if the edge lies totally inside the screen), or the intersections of the edge with the window edges (if the edge lies totally outside the screen), or there may be one vertex inside the screen and one outside the screen.

Given that both endpoints of an edge lie outside the screen, the next edge may intersect the screen on its journey back into the screen. See Figure 19.5.

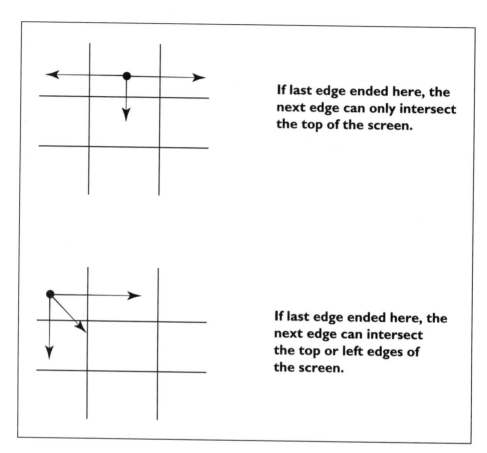

If last edge ended here, the next edge can only intersect the top of the screen.

If last edge ended here, the next edge can intersect the top or left edges of the screen.

Figure 19.5 *Totally outside edges.*

If the next edge intersects the screen, the place where it intersects is determined by its starting point. An edge starting in the upper-edge region can begin its intersection with the screen only by hitting the top edge of the screen, whereas an edge starting in the upper-left corner region can begin its intersection with the screen along either the top boundary or the left boundary.

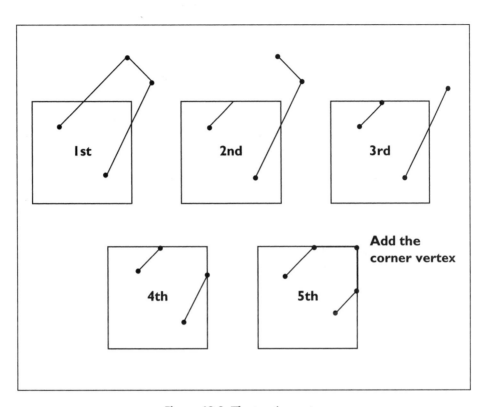

Figure 19.6 *The turning vertex.*

Imagine that the last edge to intersect the screen generated a vertex at the top of the screen. And the next edge to intersect the screen will do so on the right edge of the screen. The output polygon will then have to contain the upper-right corner of the screen. This means that we must add a vertex for the upper-right corner of the screen. Since we are processing the polygon edge by edge, we must add this corner vertex now (called a turning vertex by the conceptualizers), in anticipation of the next intersection with the screen (see Figure 19.6). If the next edge intersects the top edge of the screen, this additional vertex will be redundant, but we can remove it later.

N O T E   Our polygon filling routine will not crash if two vertices in a polygon are the same. The reason for adding the vertex is that any intersection point added by the next edge must be able to be reached from the last vertex that we output.

As with our Sutherland-Hodgman implementation, polygons that have been clipped into non-existence will set the `trivial_reject` flag to `AlgDefts_TRUE`. This alerts the calling routine that it should not proceed in adding this given polygon to the list of polygons for display, as the polygon is out of view. More on this issue of trivially rejecting polygons later.

Software Routines for Clipping Polygons

Examine `AlgPClip.H` and `AlgPClip.C` on the accompanying diskette.

Summary

To date we have seen how polygons are clipped in the z-axis to remove those polygons in part or in whole behind the viewer (pilot). We have seen how polygons are then projected into two dimensions and clipped for screen display, and how polygons are actually drawn to the display device. In the following chapter, we will take a look at the one last display issue—the removal of those polygons that fall on the far sides and backs of objects. With this step, we will have all of the parts required for a generic three-dimensional polygon visualization system.

20

Polygon Removal for Hidden Surfaces

The virtual worlds for flight simulation systems commonly contain many objects that are not aeronautical. Simulators may have buildings, control towers, trees, mountains, runways, those darned tax collectors, cars and trucks, other aircraft and seacraft, and many other three-dimensional structures.

The field of realistic three-dimensional computer graphics requires three-dimensional models that completely define the surfaces and internal structures of objects. A virtual control tower would need to have polygons defining all outside surfaces of the building, as well as any inside floors, rooms, and elevators of the building. You need this structural detail for virtual reality and simulation systems, because you might want to move through or around any part of the building.

You must find ways to remove those polygons that are parts of interesting objects, but at a given moment are out of the viewer's sight (like the back-sides of walls). The polygons that we must remove are determined by the position and orientation of the viewer, as well as by the positions and orientations of the objects in the scene. Note that objects may also be moving within the world, for example, fuel trucks and luggage carts scurrying about the plane before takeoff.

There are many solutions to the hidden-surface problem. None of them are without drawback or limitation. This chapter discusses many approaches, but only one simple, incomplete, and efficient approach will be implemented. The discussion starts with the backface removal algorithm

The Backface Removal Algorithm

Since hidden-surface tests are generally expensive, it is important to reduce the number of polygons that must undergo such tests. One method for quickly reducing the number of polygons for single convex objects is to detect the direction that each polygon is facing, relative to the direction that the viewer is facing.

Polygon faces that point away from the viewer are considered *backfaces*. These faces cannot be visible, as the other, closer half of the object blocks the view. This does not solve the hidden-surface problem, since part of the object may block polygons that are facing us and on the object itself(such as objects with set back or indented surfaces). But this simple test can usually remove about half of the polygons from the scene at one time.

To follow the algorithm, we must think of a polygon as having two sides. One side is hidden (invisible) from our point of view, the other is visible. We can define which side is which for our polygon by ordering the vertices in a counterclockwise fashion for the visible side. Looking at the polygon from the invisible side, the vertices will appear clockwise; see Figure 20.1.

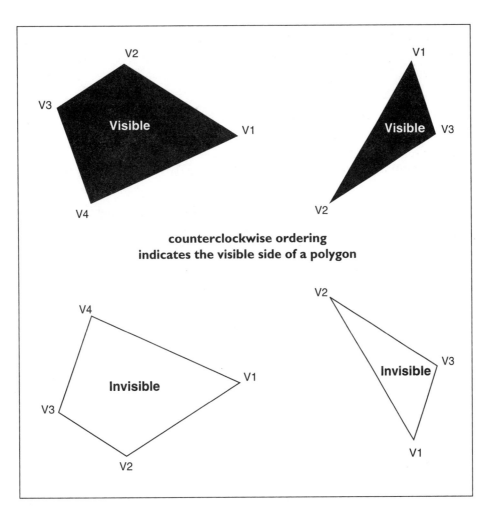

Figure 20.1 *Ordering of vertices for visible side of polygon.*

Some simple mathematics help determine the direction in which the polygon is facing. We will use the *vector cross* product as defined in the mathematics, Chapter 16. The vector cross-product of two three-dimensional vectors gives a third three-dimensional vector that is perpendicular ("normal") to the plane formed by the first two vectors. The formulas for the three-dimensional cross-product of vectors in our right-handed coordinate system are:

$$v = v1 \times v2$$

$$v_x = (v1_y)(v2_z) - (v1_z)(v2_y)$$

$$v_y = (v1_z)(v2_x) - (v1_x)(v2_z)$$

$$v_z = (v1_x)(v2_y) - (v1_y)(v2_x)$$

Given that two sides of a polygon describe two vectors in the plane of that polygon face, the cross-product of those two vectors gives us a normal to that face of the polygon.

Now that there is a surface normal to the polygon, we just need to know if the polygon is facing towards or away from us. To do that, we need to know if the two sides represented by the two vectors form a *convex* (obtuse) or *concave* (acute) angle.

If the polygon has two adjacent sides that meet at a convex angle (> 180°, meaning that moving one edge to the next turned us slightly to the left, if we follow the vertices in a counterclockwise fashion) at the vertex, the vector cross-product yields a vector pointing out of the viewable side of the polygon. This the *surface normal* of the polygon.

Simply stated, this means that the surface normal for a visible polygon should point toward us, and the surface normal for an invisible polygon must point away from us. This invisible polygon should be removed from the polygon display list to save needless computations later, greatly improving performance.

To determine whether the surface normal vector points toward the viewer, examine its z component. If this z component is negative, the polygon faces the viewer and is not a backface. If this z coordinate is positive, the polygon faces away from the viewer, this polygon is a backface, and should not be added to the polygon display list.

You might remember from the section on dot products of vectors in Chapter 16 how useful the dot product is for determining whether two vectors point in the same direction. The formula for computing the dot product is as follows:

$$dot\_product = v1 \cdot v2$$

$$dot\_product = (v1_x)(v2_x) + (v1_y)(v2_y) + (v1_z)(v2_z)$$

For the backface check using the dot product, one vector is the normal to the polygon and the other (the view vector) acts as the direction of increasing depth. You can determine this direction by including another vertex of the polygon because the polygon was locally and view transformed (transformed for placement into the world, and then transformed for viewing), before entering the test routine.

Now you have seen a quick and dirty method for removing some of those backface polygons from a virtual flight simulation world. This method is implemented in our software, and it will work well for single convex objects. You may find the algorithm inadequate for virtual worlds with many objects and objects with concave surfaces.

Now you can examine some other methods for properly displaying polygonal simulator virtual worlds.

The Painter's Algorithm

This algorithm given by Newell (1972) is named for the way oil painters create their works of art. An artist begins an oil painting by painting the background of an image. The artist then paints the objects farthest from the viewer on top of the background. Then the painter adds objects that are closer, painting over parts of the far objects and the background. Fortunately for us, a *frame buffer* (a memory buffer that stores the generated image for immediate or later display) can be used in the same way, with usually efficient results for simple scenes. We have implemented this algorithm in our software.

When we project a polygon into the frame buffer for subsequent display on the computer screen, we might overwrite pixels in that buffer colored with an earlier projected polygon. If you sort the polygons from farthest to nearest before you project them and write them into the frame buffer, you create your scene correctly with hidden surfaces removed (overwritten).

 NOTE There are some drawbacks to this technique. Polygons that cut through other polygons (intersecting polygons) will not be displayed properly. The polygon chosen for later display overwrites the first polygon, producing an incorrect image. You must find a way to break up polygons into non-intersecting polygons and then sort them for display.

Position Comparison Tests for Polygons and The Binary Space Partitioning Algorithm

Fuchs (1980) suggests that in order to break up polygons into non-intersecting ones, a series of simple geometric tests can be performed. We have several tests at our disposal for determining the relative positions of two polygons. Not all of these tests can be used with all hidden-surface algorithms, and some of the tests are not rigorous and conclusive. The goal is to use simple tests for as many cases as possible and use the more involved costly tests only when necessary.

A commonly used technique is called the *boxing test*. It is also known as the *cuboid test* and the *minimax test*. This test is useful when we need to know only the orderings of polygons that overlap and not necessarily the orderings of all of the polygons. This test shows quickly if two polygons do not overlap.

You start the test by placing tight boxes around each polygon so that each box totally encloses its own polygon. See Figure 20.2. Each bounding box is defined by two points: the maximum and minimum points. You obtain the minimum point by looking through the vertices of the polygon and finding the minimum x and y values. You obtain the maximum point by looking through the vertices of the polygon and finding the maximum x and y values.

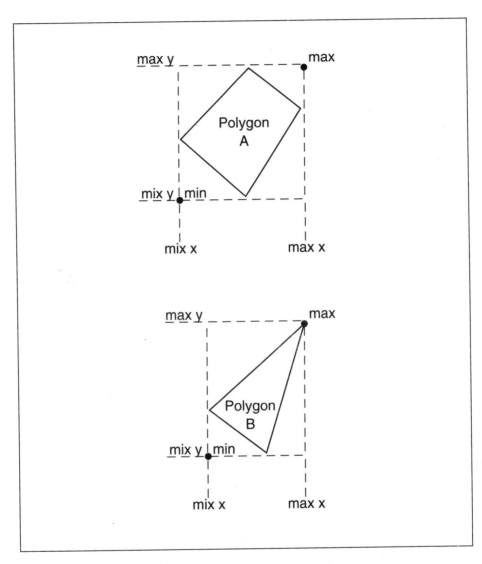

Figure 20.2 *Making boxes for the boxing test.*

If the two boxes obtained for the two polygons do not overlap, then there is no chance that the two polygons overlap. If the boxes do overlap, then the polygons may or may not overlap and we need to do more testing. See Figure 20.3.

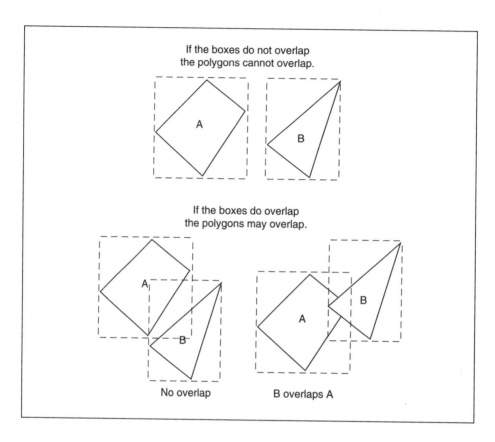

If the boxes do not overlap
the polygons cannot overlap.

A   B

If the boxes do overlap
the polygons may overlap.

A   B

A   B

No overlap   B overlaps A

Figure 20.3 *Box overlapping.*

A boxing test applied to the z coordinates of two polygons often indicates the relative ordering of two polygons that do overlap in x and y. If the smallest z coordinate for polygon A is greater than the largest z coordinate for polygon B, you can assume that polygon A is in front of polygon B. See Figure 20.4.

Another very useful test is one that tells you if all of the vertices of one polygon (A) lie on the same side of the plane containing another polygon (B). See Figure 20.5. If the vertices of polygon A lie on the same side of polygon B as the viewer, then this polygon A is closer and in front of polygon B. If the vertices of polygon A lie on the other side of the viewer, then polygon B lies in front of polygon A.

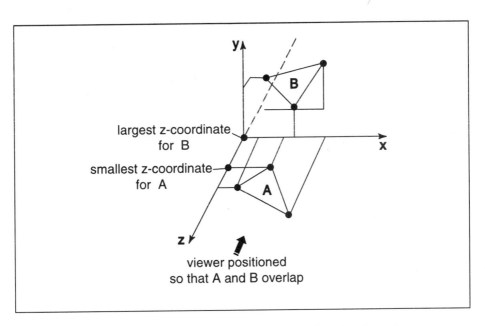

Figure 20.4 *Boxing test applied to z-coordinates of overlapping polygons.*

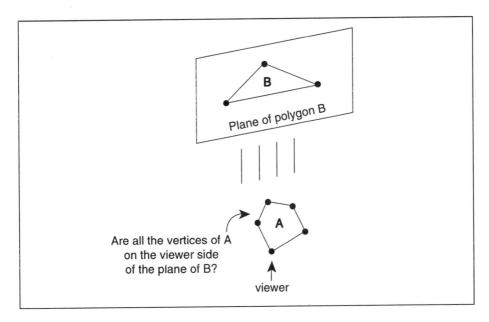

Figure 20.5 *Test to see if a polygon lies entirely on the side of another polygon.*

But what if the plane of polygon B also intersects polygon A? You can try comparing the vertices of polygon B with the plane of polygon A and make similar deductions as above.

If this test also fails, then we may cut the polygons into pieces so that the preceding tests succeed.

For a quick look at how we test to see if a vertex of one polygon lies on a given side of the plane of another polygon, look at the following equation:

plane equation $= MAx + NAy + OAz + P$

This is the equation of a plane, and M, N, O, and P are coefficients of that plane. The coefficients can be derived from any three points (vertices) of the polygon (B) whose plane will be used to test the other polygon's (A) vertex. Given that polygon (B) has the vertices B1, B2, and B3 such that

$B_1 = (Bx_1, By_1, Bz_1)$

$B_2 = (Bx_2, By_2, Bz_2)$

$B_3 = (Bx_3, By_3, Bz_3)$

we can compute the coefficients of the plane as

$M = By_1 (Bz_2 - Bz_3) + By_2 (Bz_3 - Bz_1) + By_3 (Bz_1 - Bz_2)$

$N = Bz_1 (Bx_2 - Bx_3) + Bz_2 (Bx_3 - Bx_1) + Bz_3 (Bx_1 - Bx_2)$

$O = Bx_1 (By_2 - By_3) + Bx_2 (By_3 - By_1) + Bx_3 (By_1 - By_2)$

$P = - Bx_1 (By_2 Bz_3 - By_3 Bz_2)$

$\quad - Bx_2 (By_3 Bz_1 - By_1 Bz_3)$

$\quad - Bx_3 (By_1 Bz_2 - By_2 Bz_1)$

We have the coefficients of plane equation, so now it is time to test our vertex of polygon A. Given that this vertex of polygon A is A=(Ax, Ay, Az), we substitute Ax, Ay, and Az into our plane equation with our newly found coefficient values. If the plane equation equals zero, the vertex of

(A) lies in the plane of (B). If the equation is less than zero, then the vertex of (A) lies on the counterclockwise vertex ordered side of (B). (Remember the visibility test in Figure 20.1.) If the equation is greater than zero, then the vertex of (A) lies on the clockwise vertex-ordered side of (B). Testing all of the points (vertices) of (A) will tell you on what side polygon (A) lies relative to polygon (B).

Sorting Polygons for Painter's Display

Now that we have a set of tools to perform basic positional tests, let's look at the ideal way to sort our polygons for Painter's display. The basic idea of *binary space* partitioning (successively breaking a space into smaller and smaller spaces, with each space having an eighth the volume of before) is to sort the polygons for display from farthest to nearest just as in the Painter's algorithm. Here we use the position comparison test mentioned in the previous section that compares the vertices of one polygon with the plane of another polygon. We extend this test so that if the plane intersects the polygon, we will divide the polygon along the plane. Using this test, we can pick one polygon and compare all of the other polygons to it. From the comparisons, we get two groups, the polygons that are in front and those that are behind. For each of these two new groups, we can again select two polygons and use them to partition the groups, respectively. You repeat this process until all polygons are sorted. The result of this quick-sort (if you will) is a *binary tree*, with each node representing a polygon. See Figure 20.6. One branch contains all of the polygons that lie in front of the plane of this polygon; the other branch contains polygons that lie behind the plane of this polygon. An *in-order traversal* of the tree gives farthest-to-nearest order of the polygons for display (the sort yielded an ordered tree, so by taking polygons from the deepest tree-branch and moving across all that level, on up to the top and then handling the other branch will yield the proper display order). See Figure 20.7.

See Steven Harrington's most excellent computer graphics text, *Computer Graphics, A Programming Approach* for an implementation of this algorithm.

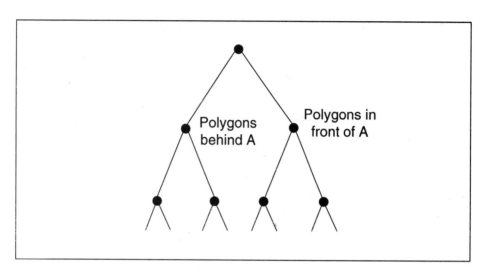

Figure 20.6 *Binary tree.*

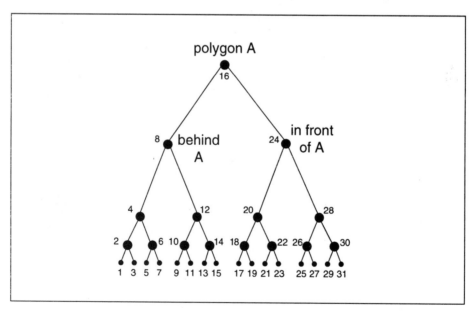

Figure 20.7 *In-order traversal of the binary tree.*

The Z Buffer Algorithm

For our final method, contrived by Catmull (1974), let's look at an approach ideal for hardware systems. If you use a frame buffer to compose images before they are copied to the computer screen, you can look at the hidden-surface problem like this: you want to arrange the frame buffer so that the color displayed for any given pixel of the buffer is the color of the surface that is closest to the viewer from that point. To create this, you must compare all of the pixels projected onto that given pixel and sort for the closest one. This is called a *geometric sort* and is essential to most hidden-surface removal algorithms.

A *Z buffer* is a large frame buffer (array) with a z coordinate entry and color entry for every pixel on your screen. Each z coordinate is set for a very large number representing the background distance, and each color is set to the background color. As the algorithm transforms and projects the polygon for viewing, it makes pixel-by-pixel comparisons 230 of the polygon's preprojected z coordinate with the z coordinate sitting in the Z buffer. Note that comparisons are made only for those pixels (elements of the buffer) that the projected polygon could affect. If the polygon's z coordinate is smaller than the one in the Z buffer, the color of the polygon is copied into the Z buffer, and the z coordinate in the Z buffer is updated with the polygon's preprojected z coordinate. If the polygon's z coordinate is larger than the one in the Z buffer, the Z buffer is not updated, as the polygon is not the closest one for that point in the image.

This technique is expensive in memory requirements and processing time. It is, however, a simple method that lends itself to hardware implementation. It is a very good solution to the hidden-surface problem.

Software Routines for Removing Hidden Polygons

Examine `AlgPClip.H` and `AlgPClip.C` on the accompanying diskette.

Summary

We now have all but one of the basics under the belt for the creation of our flight simulation visual system—the one being shading—which is the topic of the next chapter.

Shading, Texturing and Special Effects

As mentioned in Chapter 14, "Concept of a Flight Simulation System", it is very important for any flight simulation or virtual reality system to have a graphics engine that can generate images that have a certain degree of realism. Perspective projection is a must for creating depth, but that is not always enough. Without images that effectively fool the sense of vision into thinking that they are real, immersion is not truly possible. The techniques of shading and texturing will help us in our quest for photorealism.

Shading Models

Shading models (mathematic models of how light interacts with objects and how these objects reflect light into our eyes) are commonly based on simplified physical models of the real world—simplified because complete physical models cannot be computed in a finite (reasonable) amount of time. Additionally, lighting models have generally been "fudged" to create the desired visual effects. However, even with assumptions and approximations, most models produce quite acceptable results. Our model is no different. All of the color terms described in Table 21.1 are additive; that is, we compute each one individually and sum the terms to produce the net color. Furthermore, we take advantage of the fact that light energy obeys the superposition law. That is, we may compute the effects for each light in the scene individually and add the results together.

Now, let's look at some terminology and definitions. An *incident ray of light* is a light ray that hits an object. This ray is represented mathematically as a three-dimensional vector. The *surface normal*, N, is a vector that is normal to the surface of the object at the point of intersection of the incident ray with the object. The vectors for *reflected rays R* and the rays to the *light sources L_n* are generated using the basic laws of *optical reflection* (the angle of incident light on an object is equal to the angle of reflected light from the object). Here are some of the shading model mathematical constants and variables.

Table 21.1 *Mathematical constants and variables.*

Ka	Ambient Coefficient
Kd	Diffuse Coefficient
Kh	Specular Highlight
Ns	Specular Exponent
Ks	Specular Coefficient
Kt	Transmitted Coefficient
N	Surface Normal at Intersection Point
V	Vector of Incident Ray

R	Vector for Reflected Ray
E	Vector from the Eyepoint to the Intersection Point
L_n	Vector toward nth Light Source
H_n	Reflected L_n Vector. This is the direction light reflects directly off the surface.
I	Total Illumination (the final color)

We mentioned that our process is additive. To get the total illumination value, I, we sum together the components:

$$I = ambient + diffuse + specular + transmitted + specular\ highlights$$

In the following discussions, we work only with a single light source, computing I_n. The I_n are then summed over all light sources to produce the total illumination I.

Background Ambient Illumination (Ka)

We begin with the simplest lighting component, the background or *ambient* lighting. Ambient light comes from all around the environment, points in all directions, and is thus uniformly distributed throughout the virtual world. We treat this as the light intensity assigned to rays that do not intersect any of the objects or lights in the scene. A daylight scene will have a much brighter ambient component than a nighttime one. An object may have an ambient lighting component as well. This is used to model self-luminous objects such as street lamps, fireflies, plutonium or radium on a good day, and so on.

Diffuse Illumination (Kd)

The *diffuse color* of an object is essentially the color of the object under white light. A green ball is green because it reflects the green component of light on the surface and absorbs the others. If you shine a light on a green ball, the light is not reflected as a mirror would reflect—just in one direction—but is reflected in all directions. The part of the surface facing the light receives the most intensity per unit area, while the parts facing away receive no light at all (for example, an opaque object such as our green ball). Therefore, we see the areas facing the light source (surface normal pointing in the direction of the light source) as the brightest, independent of our viewing direction. This is because a diffuse surface is assumed to scatter light equally in all directions. See Figure 21.1. Because of this viewer direction independence, the *diffuse intensity* is a function of the angle between the surface normal and the light direction, or, equivalently, a function of the dot product of the two:

$$Kd = -N \cdot L_n$$

The *Lambertian diffuse reflectance model* (which models the diffuse reflection of light, named after the physicist Johann Lambert) tells us that the light intensity is directly proportional to this dot product, see Figure 21.1. If the diffuse value is less than or equal to 0, it is treated as 0. These correspond to the portions of the surface facing away from the light and are thus automatically shadowed from the light source. In the absence of shadows and texture, we can simply multiply the *intrinsic diffuse color* of the object (a vector that is a triplet of red-green-blue, that represents what color the object really is) by the *diffuse value* (perhaps from the light source color) to get the net *diffuse intensity* (what color the object appears to be in our scene based on lighting colors) at this point. But wait—what if we shine a red light on a blue ball? We must take the diffuse color vector and multiply each component (red, green, and blue) by the corresponding light color components. A red light would typically have color (1, 0, 0). Note that the diffuse color would be 0 if the ball were purely blue or green (a most nonphysical situation).

Our model includes a factor for reducing the light intensity as a function of distance from the intersection of the light ray with the object. Physically, light intensity of a point source falls off as *one-over-the-square* of the distance. However, because of the approximations that we have made about the diffuse and ambient light in the environment, we get a better-looking result using one-over-distance intensity scaling. This kind of intensity scaling works for light sources such as light bulbs, but is not needed for daylight scenes. The sun intensity does not change appreciably over the distances of your average scene (unless you are viewing a cosmic virtual scene from virtual outer space).

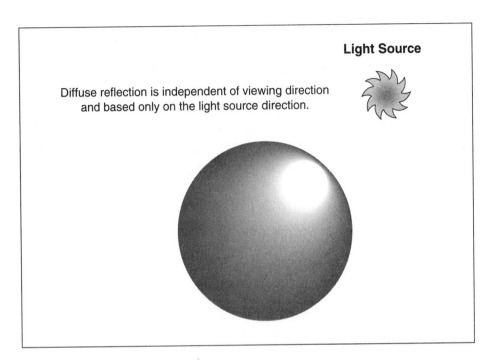

Light Source

Diffuse reflection is independent of viewing direction and based only on the light source direction.

Figure 21.1 *Diffuse reflection.*

Specular Illumination (Kh)

Many surfaces have mirror-like qualities. Think of a car in the sun. Metal and plastic surfaces at least partially reflect the light source directly as "hot spots." This is referred to as a *specular effect (speculum* was the Latin word for mirror). An image of the light source itself is reflected off the surface. For this reflected light to reach our eye, we must be positioned such that the light source reflects in the direction of our eye. The angle between the eyepoint vector and the surface normal must be close to the angle between the light vector and surface normal. Unless the surface is a perfect mirror, the light will always be slightly diffused, forming a reflective spot on the surface known as the *specular highlight*. This spot will be the color of the light source because it is, after all, a distorted reflection of the light source. See Figure 21.2.

The vector H_n is the direction in which the light would be reflected if the surface were a perfect mirror. As with the *diffuse intensity*, the perceived intensity is a function of the angle between the vector H_n and the eyepoint vector E. Unlike the diffuse component case, we must face the proper direction to perceive the spot. Note that if you are viewing a shiny flat surface, the image of a light source reflected on the surface moves as you do. The model used in virtually every rendering program is the *Phong* model. The standard equation for computing the specular highlight is

$$Kh = (-Hn \cdot E)^{Ns}$$

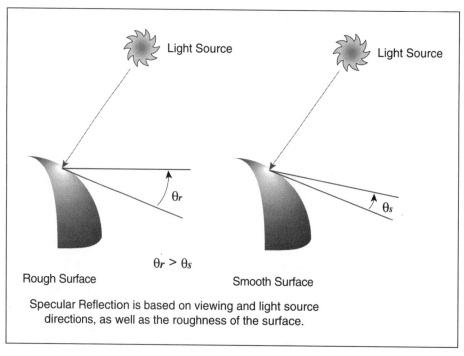

Specular Reflection is based on viewing and light source directions, as well as the roughness of the surface.

Figure 21.2 *Specular reflection.*

By introducing the exponent Ns we can control the apparent spot size. The larger Ns is, the tighter the spot size. This is not a particularly physical model, but rather one that we can easily control to produce the desired result, namely specular highlights that look as they do in the real world. The computation of diffuse and specular highlights is performed for each light source. As we are talking about light sources, we need to discuss shadows.

Shadows

Shadows are another important cue to the brain, to fool the brain into thinking that a virtual world is real. Many flight simulation systems do not compute shadows because they are usually expensive and do not add much to the flight simulator virtual environment. There are many methods for computing shadows in computer graphics, but like the hidden-surface problems, the techniques are usually involved.

One polygon graphics technique is to treat parts of the polygon being rendered as if they were your eye, and "render" the parts of the polygon looking from the polygon to the light source. This shows just how to shadow your polygon, and perhaps the environment around your polygon. Another technique that yields much more accurate results is called *ray casting* and is commonly found in *ray-traced* computer graphics. See the book "Photorealism and Ray Tracing in C" by Christopher D. Watkins and Stephen B. Coy fir more information. Shadows are evaluated by casting rays from a ray intersection point toward each of the light sources. If the ray intersects any opaque objects in between, the light is not visible and thus does not contribute to that lighting computation. If the ray intersects a transparent object, then the light intensity is reduced by the transmissivity of the intervening object. If the ray reaches the light (or equivalently, goes out of the scene), then the light is visible and its full intensity is used, remembering to scale for *distance falloff* (how light decays in intensity with distance). Point light sources require only a single shadow ray to be cast from the intersection point. Finite-extent light sources, such as spherical light sources, require multiple shadow rays to be cast in order to approximate the effect of the finite size. This can yield *soft shadows* (penumbras). The ratio of shadow rays that hit the light to the total number of rays determines how far the point is in the shadow. In either case, the shadowing coefficient is used to scale the light intensity used in the calculations. Both the diffuse and specular components will be scaled down in proportion to the shadow coefficient.

The net mathematical effect of shadowing is that we generate an intensity scaling factor which is either 0 (light is blocked), 1 (light is totally unblocked), or between 0 and 1 (intersection point is in shadow penumbra, that is, you can partially see the light). The color is then scaled by the shadow coefficient and added to the ambient lighting terms to produce the total light contribution due to the surface alone. We still, however, must consider the light coming from other surfaces by examining the reflected and refracted rays of light.

Reflection (Ks) and Refraction (Kt)

The coefficients Ks and Kt determine how much of the light is actually reflected and transmitted (refracted), respectively. If Ks is 0, then the surface is diffuse and there are no specularly reflected rays. Similarly, if Kt is 0, the surface is completely opaque. The reflected ray color is then weighted by Ks and the refracted ray is weighted by Kt. All contributions are then summed over all light sources and this total color, I, is returned as the color of the ray.

Ks and Kt are rgb (red, green and blue component) vectors, since we may want to weight the color components differently. This allows the simulation of colored glass in which certain colors are transmitted and others reflected. For instance, blue glass might have Kt of (.1,.1,.7). You might be interested in how the reflection and refraction of light is modeled mathematically. Modeling reflection at a specular surface is simple: The angle at which a light ray is reflected from an object is equal to the angle at which the ray was originally incident on the object. See Figure 21.3.

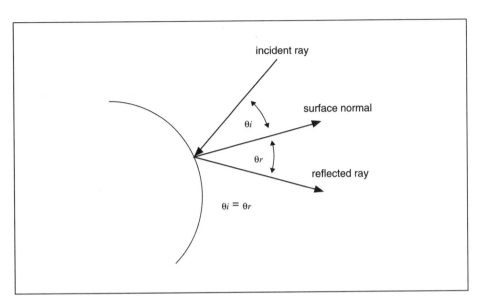

Figure 21.3 *Reflection of light rays.*

An equation that models this reflection in vector form is:

$$reflected\_ray\_direction = incident\_ray\_direction + 2 * \\ (incident\_ray\_direction \bullet \\ surface\_normal) * surface\_normal$$

This equation states that the reflected ray direction is equal to the incident ray direction, plus two times the dot product of the incident ray direction with the surface normal, times the surface normal vector. Both reflected ray direction and incident ray direction are three-dimensional vectors (for our purposes). Modeling the transmission and refraction of light rays into materials such as glass and water is slightly more complex. You might remember Snell's law from elementary school physics. It relates the angle of an incident light ray to the angle of a transmitted (refracted) light ray. See Figure 21.4.

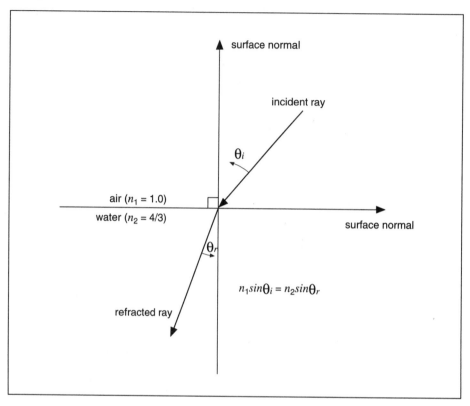

Figure 21.4 *Refraction/transmission of light rays.*

Snell's law models the bending of light when light leaves the material in which it is traveling for another material. (For example, a ray of light travels through the air, and then intersects a bowl of water. The ray direction bends toward the surface normal when it enters the water because light travels more slowly in water). The equation that models this phenomenon is

index_of_refraction_for_incident_ray_material*sin (incident_ray_angle) =

index_of_refraction_for_refracted_ray_material*sin(refracted_ray_angle)

The index_of_refraction constants are based on the material characteristics. These values are computed as

$$index\_of\_refraction = \frac{speed\_of\_light\_in\_a\_vacuum}{speed\_of\_light\_in\_the\_given\_material}$$

The index of refraction for air is very close to that of a vacuum. It varies greatly for glass and water. The following table shows some indices of refraction for common materials in yellow (600 nm) light.

Table 21.2 *Indices of refraction.*

GAS	
Air	1.0003
Carbon Dioxide	1.0005
LIQUID	
Ethyl Alcohol	1.36
Water	1.33
SOLID	
Diamond	2.42
Glass	1.48 – 1.89

Texture Mapping and Textures

The concept of *texture mapping*, the mapping of an image onto another surface, is simple. To render a point on the surface of an object, you determine the color for that point is determined by transforming the three-dimensional intersection point to a two-dimensional point in the texture map image. The color of the texture map at that point is input to the shading model to determine the color of the surface at the intersection point. Using this technique, you can render relatively simple geometric models with a great amount of apparent complexity. While texture mapping is a very powerful technique, it does have its limitations. The most obvious problem is the mapping a two-dimensional image onto a three-dimensional object without distorting the texture mapped image excessively. Flat surfaces are no problem, but surfaces with complex shapes can be difficult to map. Even for a relatively simple surface, such as a sphere, the texture map must be distorted to get it to fit onto the three-dimensional surface. On spheres this results in the compression of the texture at the poles.

Peachey (1985) and Perlin (1985) simultaneously developed the idea of *solid texturing* to solve this problem. The underlying principle of solid texturing is to create a three-dimensional texture map from which the textured object appears to be carved. This texture map may either be defined explicitly as a three-dimensional array of values, consuming huge amounts of memory, or can be defined by a procedural function. The procedural function takes an (x,y,z) point and returns the surface characteristics at that point. See Figure 21.5. Perlin introduced the *noise function* (a function that has almost fractal qualities in that it is random, with interpolation that gives it uniformity) to generate many of his procedural textures. To this day, the images he produced for his SIGGRAPH paper (Perlin 1985) are considered some of the best in computer graphics.

Another useful texturing technique is known as *bump mapping*. In bump mapping, the surface normal is perturbed to provide the surface with a bumpy or wavy appearance. The idea was championed by the guru of computer graphics, Jim Blinn. He was studying the problem of modeling wrinkled surfaces. On a finely wrinkled surface, such as an orange, our perception of the wrinkles is not because we cannot see the folds themselves, but because of how the light bounces off the surface folds. The surface normal is highly variable, even though the surface itself is relatively smooth. Thus, he reasoned that you did not have to model the folds but instead could simply vary the surface normal vector in a random fashion across the surface. When this normal is used by the lighting calculations, the variations will cause the surface to appear rough and uneven, when in fact it is still perfectly smooth. Bump mapping is extremely useful for creating rough or wavy surfaces for virtual reality and flight simulation systems.

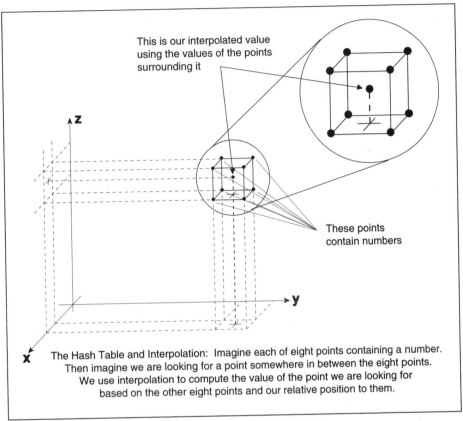

This is our interpolated value using the values of the points surrounding it

These points contain numbers

The Hash Table and Interpolation: Imagine each of eight points containing a number. Then imagine we are looking for a point somewhere in between the eight points. We use interpolation to compute the value of the point we are looking for based on the other eight points and our relative position to them.

Figure 21.5 *The Perlin noise function lattice.*

The first, and still most popular, type of texture mapping is the mapping of an image onto a surface. The solid texturing and bump mapping approaches are used for the *nonplanar primitives* (primitives other than polygons—like spheres). The basic operation is to convert the three-dimensional intersection point into an index for the texture map. Since the two-dimensional value will normally be floating point, we will alter adjacent pixel values in the texture map to get the texture value to use at the intersection point. By default, this texture value is used as the diffuse color at this point. However, you can also use it modulate any of the other attributes, most notably the transparency Kt.

Noise

The noise function provides repeatable seemingly random numbers under rotation and translation, and they have a narrow limit in frequency. This constancy is required to allow textured models to be moved in space while keeping their surface texture constant. For example, as a chair with a wood texture is moved, its grain pattern should not shift and change as a result of the movement. The narrow frequency band requirement is beneficial because given a noise curve of a known frequency it is fairly easy to create a curve of any desired frequency characteristics by scaling and summing the simpler curve. A narrow frequency range means that, as the fairy tale goes, the function doesn't vary too much and doesn't vary too little but changes just the right amount over space. The noise function is also a continuous function over space.

Totally New Waves

In addition to using *stochastic noise* (random noise) to perturb textures, *sine waves* can give many pleasing effects. These functions act like *compression waves*, alternately pushing and pulling the point passed to the texture function along a line from the point of intersection to the source of the wave. Waves should be defined by a source, wavelength, amplitude, phase, and damping factor. The *source* specifies the point from which the wave emanates, and the *wavelength* defines the distance between wave peaks. The *amplitude* determines how far the point is pushed by the wave. The *phase* is a number that determines the situation of the wave at the source point (whether the wave is up, down, 0, or somewhere in between). The *damping factor* determines the falloff with distance that the wave's amplitude experiences. You should be able to affect a surface by more than one wave source. The offsets generated by the waves are summed to produce the total offset for the intersection point. Waves seem to have limited use in generating interesting solid textures; they are used primarily in procedural bump mapping, described next.

Bump Mapping

The noise and wave functions used by the procedural solid texturing may also be used to provide procedural bump mapping. The results from the functions are used to perturb the surface normal, *N*, based on the point of intersection. This perturbed normal is then used in the shading calculations. Since the surface's brightness, highlights, reflection, and refraction are all dependent on the surface normal, a small change is all that's needed to make a large difference in the resulting image.

 NOTE The cost of evaluating the wave function at each intersection point is fairly high, especially if there is more than one set of waves to evaluate.

Atmospheric Effects

You can enhance the realism of outdoor environments in flight simulators by adding atmospheric effects such as fog and haze. In the real world, fog and haze are evident by scattered light over a distance, due to minute particles of matter in the atmosphere. Exponential decay is the simplest model of such scattering. It assumes a uniform scattering medium. The object color is blended with a background haze color using the equation:

alpha = exp(- distance / haze_distance)

*color = alpha * object_color + (1-alpha) * haze_color*

where *haze_distance* is the visibility distance, *distance* is length of the vector *E*, and *haze_color* is normally the background color. As objects get farther away, they slowly merge into the haze. You can achieve a fog effect can be achieved by evaluating alpha as a function of the intersection point position as well as the distance. For example, you can produce a layered fog effect by setting alpha = 1.0 if the point is above the top of the fog layer. Otherwise, evaluating the foregoing equation when the point in question drops below the fog height.

Software for Shading and Texturing

Examine `AlgShade.H`, `AlgShade.C`, `AlgTex.H`, and `AlgTex.C` on the accompanying diskette.

Summary

Many of the techniques discussed in this section are a bit too computationally expensive for us to work with on our IBM PCs. Our implementation of interactive shading is nonexistent, and our implementations of procedural texturing that we do have take liberties with proper projection. We resort to techniques for transparency such as drawing every other pixel of a polygon (thus you see what was behind this "transparent" polygon). In any case, we hope that you have a better idea about how shading and texturing work and how they can be important to virtual reality graphics systems. For an excellent dissertation of image warping and projection techniques for texturing, see *Digital Image Warping* by George Wolberg. For those interested in the implementation of some of the above shading algorithms, look for the excellent book *Photorealism and Ray Tracing in C* (M&T Books) by Christopher D. Watkins and Stephen B. Coy.

CHAPTER

22

Database Structure

This chapter is a discussion of databases for three-dimensional computer graphics and simulation systems. The basic layout for the flight simulation graphics system and database hierarchy are discussed here. See *Virtual Reality ExCursions* and *Photorealism and Ray Tracing in C* for more information on general graphics database formats.

World Order

In most things, humans desire order, usually hierarchical order (hopefully not one new world order). The area of computer graphics is no different. To make it easy for someone to use your graphics engine, you must organize it in such a fashion that they have easy access to sections of the database at different levels. One transformation may affect only one object in the world (like a spinning propeller), while another may

249

affect all of the objects in the world (like the change in direction of the aircraft). Never force the user to deal with the details of the database. The user should be able to choose whether to meddle with a particular part of the database.

You can look at a flight simulation virtual-world database as if it were constructed of children's building blocks. Some sets of blocks may be built up into runways and control towers, while others may be built up into aircraft. One can make copies of the runways and aircraft and place these copies anywhere in the world. This is called the *instancing* of an object. Instancing is a kind of mathematical cookie cutter, using math to copy and reposition and reorient objects.

You should now see that your virtual flight simulation *world* is made of such building blocks called *objects*. You should also know that those objects must be made of something too, just as most life on Earth is made of carbon, hydrogen, oxygen and nitrogen. And yes, the objects are made of something, and for our purposes they are made from the infinitesimally thin planar building blocks called *polygons* (we use triangles and quadrilaterals for our polygons). Based on how you put your polygons together, you can build almost any object. Much like positioning and orienting objects in your world to create it, you position and orient individual polygons to create your object. Picture a soccer ball and the 32-sided mesh of five- and six-sided patches (polygons) that make up its surface. Thirty-two flat polygons approximate the near-spherical soccer ball, and polygons will approximate our virtual world.

Polygons are defined by two- or three-dimensional coordinates called *vertices*. A vertex is a point where two edges of a polygon meet. If the polygon has three edges (a triangle), it will have three vertices. If the polygon has four edges (a square, a rectangle, a parallelogram, or a quadrilateral), it will have four vertices. When a polygon exists on the display screen, it is more than likely represented by two-dimensional vertices. When the polygon is used to define part of a surface of one of the three-dimensional objects in the virtual flight simulation world, it is represented in the database by three-dimensional vertices.

To summarize things so far, *worlds* have *objects* in them that are constructed from *polygons* that are defined by *vertices*. One more time:

our virtual

  world contains

    objects that are constructed from

      polygons that are defined by

        vertices.

Until this point, we have blithely assumed that the creation and definition of a three-dimensional world or environment was a piece of cake. It is as if the world environment specification was the easy part and polygon rendering of the world was the hard part. In fact, the opposite is very much true. The rendering proceeds with only your input as to where to look and an occasional interaction that you might have with an object (hopefully not a mountain). Initially positioning objects, setting surface characteristics, and especially building complex models requires extensive use of your mathematical and artistic skills, and most importantly your time.

Choosing a good database structure is essential for maintaining and manipulating world databases. You receive several benefits by approaching your database efforts in a hierarchical fashion, and it is interesting to note that they are similar to the benefits provided through following classic structured programming techniques. These benefits can be summarized as follows:

Reuse	Objects can be used repeatedly within the same world or across several worlds such as the runway object or the airplane object.
Flexibility	Since each instance of an object is a separate entity within the world, each can be independently scaled, rotated, translated, textured, and so on.

Locality and Extensibility

What if, after all your laborious 3-D modeling work to build your databases, it turns out that the aircraft manufacturer has made a major revision to a wing? The new wing has a different tip construction. After gathering new measurement data, you alter the wing object database to reflect the design changes. All your future models will be correct, and since all the past models used instances of the wing object (that exists in the model once) rather than hard-coded descriptions of the wing (which would exist in the model many times), all of your aircraft renderings and visualizations will be correct the next time they are visualized. In this way you have taken advantage of the localized nature of the data describing the wing and its tip.

Now consider that the manufacturer offers a special wing-tip light cover as an option. You couldn't change the standard wing model, since a given aircraft might not have the wing-tip light cover. You could, however, make a different model based on the standard wing that includes the wing-tip light cover. Or better yet, you could simply model the wing-tip light cover as its own object, then create a higher-level object that contains the standard wing object and the light cover object. In either case, you have extended the applicability of your wing model.

Efficiency

Once you model an object you can spend time more effectively on creating new objects, and on the process of integrating objects into new simulation worlds.

There are further benefits of the hierarchical approach when you want to interact with a given object. For example, if you decide to fly virtual aircraft using an aircraft object, you'll need to rotate the prop to provide the illusion of motion. This is a simple matter when the prop is a separate object, but would be very difficult if the description of the prop were integrated with the rest of the aircraft model.

A Flight Simulation Modeler

So far, we have talked a lot about databases and hierarchy. Now let's take a quick look at what makes up a basic flight-simulation virtual-reality world modeler and visualizer.

Materials Factory	All objects are made of something. This module defines what the materials are and their physical properties (for example, intrinsic color, surface texture, deformability, reflectivity—how the control tower appears).
Laws of Nature Maker	It seems that a world has objects and has universal rules for object-object interactions and object-world environment interactions. This module helps define those rules. That is, does an aircraft bounce when it hits a runway or crash...and if it bounces, how does it bounce?
Object Builder	This is a tool for creating object descriptions and databases. It uses paradigms for object construction/description, including the polygon/vertex list (the paradigm used in our flight simulation software). Here we may also define object mechanics.

World Builder	This is a tool for defining the extent and contents of the virtual flight simulation world. It allows you to place objects within the world and establish "initial conditions," since you expect that objects will be manipulated in time. This includes an interactive rate viewer, since manipulation of objects within the world occur at real time rates.
Stimulus/Response Linker	This tool links a certain stimulus from the environment to a particular action based on object mechanics previously defined.
Involver/ Simulator	This is the interactive rate viewer (that is, the simulator).

Freebird's Database Hierarchy: Primitives, Objects, and Worlds

First of all, let us introduce you to Freebird. Freebird has the basic functionality of a flight simulation system, without all of the bells and whistles to confuse you about its functionality.

Now that we have to this point extolled the virtues of hierarchical database construction, let's look at how this approach is supported within Freebird. Freebird supports a database hierarchy consisting of primitives, objects, and worlds.

Once again, the primitive of our choice is the polygon; we use it to construct our objects. Examine the following sample .FS (flight simulator) scene file:

```
alg_object
{
    name            landing_strips
```

```
surface          outside
collision        permeable
translate        0.0      1.0      0.0
rotate           0.0      0.0      0.0
scale            150.0    150.0    1.0
motion
{
      status           static
      translate        0.0      0.0      0.0
      rotate           0.0      0.0      0.0
      scale            0.0      0.0      0.0
}
vertex_list
{
      num_vertices     12
      vertex -120.0    0.0      1000000.0
      vertex -120.0    0.0      -2000.0
      vertex  -80.0    0.0      -2000.0
      vertex  -80.0    0.0      1000000.0
      vertex  -20.0    0.0      1000000.0
      vertex  -20.0    0.0      -2000.0
      vertex   20.0    0.0      -2000.0
      vertex   20.0    0.0      1000000.0
      vertex   80.0    0.0      1000000.0
      vertex   80.0    0.0      -2000.0
      vertex  120.0    0.0      -2000.0
      vertex  120.0    0.0      1000000.0
}
polygon_list
{
```

```
num_polygons    3
polygon
{
        RUNWAY
        num_vertices    4
        vertex_index    0
        vertex_index    1
        vertex_index    2
        vertex_index    3
        color           gray
        intensity       15
        texture         grit_map
}
polygon
{
        RUNWAY
        num_vertices    4
        vertex_index    4
        vertex_index    5
        vertex_index    6
        vertex_index    7
        color           gray
        intensity       15
        texture         grit_map
}
polygon
{
        RUNWAY
        num_vertices    4
        vertex_index    8
```

```
            vertex_index      9
            vertex_index      10
            vertex_index      11
            color             gray
            intensity         15
            texture           grit_map

        }

      }

    }
```

What you see is a landing-strip-object built from polygons. Examination of the `alg_object` object definition shows that it contains a polygon list. The polygons that make up this list are in turn built from the vertices found in the vertex list at the beginning of the `alg_object` object definition. The numbers inside a polygon structure called `vertex_index` are the actual references into the vertex list. For our first polygon:

```
    num_vertices      4
    vertex_index      0
    vertex_index      1
    vertex_index      2
    vertex_index      3
```

This tells us that the particular polygon that is constructing part of the object is a quadrilateral (it has four vertices), and that those vertices are:

```
    vertex  -120.0    0.0    1000000.0
    vertex  -120.0    0.0     -2000.0
    vertex   -80.0    0.0     -2000.0
    vertex   -80.0    0.0    1000000.0
```

These vertices are vertex 0, 1, 2 and 3 from the `vertex_list`. Notice how with one list of vertices, we can define all of the polygons. This is because some of those polygons share vertices (that is, they share the same three-dimensional coordinate, thus they share the same vertex). Also notice how color and texture information is stored for each polygon within the list, and how the object that is built from the polygons can be manipulated (scaled, rotated, translated) as a single entity, through manipulation of the scale, translate, and rotate vectors/parameters.

To reiterate, you should see that the world defined by the .FS file is constructed from objects. The objects in the world are constructed from polygons. In turn those polygons are defined by three-dimensional vertices.

Lastly we will take a look at the actual structures found in the `AlgDefs.H` file. These are the annotated structures for the object, the polygon, and the vertex types. The hierarchy can be seen from these structures, in that variables from one structure are the type of another.

We begin with the world:

```
// describes the three-dimensional world made of objects
typedef struct
{
    AlgDefs_word              num_objects;
    AlgDefs_object_3D_type    *object;
}
AlgDefs_world_3D_type;
```

Notice that the world is made of objects. An object structure is as follows:

```
// describes an object in the three-dimensional world
// made from polygons
typedef struct
{
```

```
    AlgDefs_vector_3D_type              scale;
    AlgDefs_vector_3D_type              rotate;
    // origin in world coordinates
    AlgDefs_vector_3D_type              translate;
    AlgDefs_word                        num_polygons;
    AlgDefs_polygon_3D_type             *polygon;
}
AlgDefs_object_3D_type;
```

The objects, as we have said so many times, are made from polygons. Note that each object has its own local scale, rotate and translate vectors for *local transformation* (positioning and orientation into the world).

```
// describes a polygon constructed from vertices
typedef struct
{
    AlgDefs_byte           color;
    AlgDefs_word           texture;
    AlgDefs_word           num_vertices;
    AlgDefs_vertex_3D_type **vertex;
}
AlgDefs_polygon_3D_type;
```

And the polygons, once again, are made from vertices. Note that our structure for a vertex actually stores three coordinate representations of the vertex. The first is the local coordinate of the vertex, which is the vertex of the polygon/object in the actual model of the object. The second is the world coordinate of the vertex, which is the vertex after it has been transformed for placement into the virtual world. And the third is the viewer coordinate of the vertex after the transformation of the world coordinate by the viewing transformation, so that we "see" it properly.

```
// describes a single Cartesian 3-D vertex (point) in
//      local coordinates, world coordinates and viewer
//      transformed world coordinates
typedef struct
{
   AlgDefs_point_3D_type     local;  // local coordinate
   AlgDefs_point_3D_type     world;  // world coordinate
   AlgDefs_point_3D_type     viewer; // viewer transformed world
                                     //         coordinate
}
AlgDefs_vertex_3D_type;


// describes a 3-D point
typedef struct
{
   AlgDefs_float   x;     // x coordinate
   AlgDefs_float   y;     // y coordinate
   AlgDefs_float   z;     // z coordinate
}
AlgDefs_point_3D_type;
```

Software Routines for Database Structure

Examine AlgFSPrs.H, AlgPrs.C, AlgFS.H, AlgFS.C, and AlgDefs.H on the accompanying diskette.

Summary

By now you are probably tired of hearing about worlds made of objects, objects made of polygons, and polygons defined by vertices, so let's focus our attention on how one controls a flight simulator,

The Controls and the Flight Model

Modeling and simulating reality are some of the more practical and common uses of the computer for scientists and engineers. Computer simulation of physical laws allows manufacturers and developers to predict how their products and inventions will function out in the real world; this is for aircraft and children's toys alike. Events as complex as space missions can be launched and safely completed in the computer laboratory with no risk to human life (beyond a little eye strain and an occasional reaction to caffeine, or maybe not enough caffeine as the case may be). Many of the video games that you see are also based on basic computer simulations.

Any simulation system must allow the user to interact with the virtual simulation world in a very real way. Controls or input devices are necessary for any interaction to take place. These controls can be basic, like the keyboard, the mouse, or the joystick, or they can be more complex like the six degrees of freedom spaceball, or a yoke-and-pedals for a flight simulator. Data gloves, human eye position sensors, voice and gesture recognition, and many other advanced controls are also available, some of which are being employed in our space-age aircraft.

Interactions with the virtual flight simulation world can be simple. Changing the throttle position and yoke position changes the speed and direction with which we move through our virtual environment. This is a basic operation of a flight simulator. Interaction could be a little more advanced by blocking the user's motion or simulating a crash, if the user flies into a wall or mountain. This is referred to as *viewer-object collision detection*—if our craft were to shoot a missile at another craft in a warfare simulator, and if it were to hit the other craft, that would be an example of *object-object collision detection*. Perhaps the interaction is as complex as a real flight simulation, where the way the user sets the controls at a given instant affects the feel and response of the same controls in the future.

These interactions must be modeled mathematically. *Kinematics* and *dynamics* are fields of study that allow us to do just that. The results of evaluating the kinematic or dynamical mathematical expressions may affect the view, the positions of objects, or how the controls feel. We call this *simulation*. If you think of a simulation as complex as flight simulation, you will see that the positions and orientations of the controls (such as the yoke) feed numerical information to mathematical expressions. The mathematically processed information is used by the graphics processors to show you how your control decisions affect the positioning and orientation of your aircraft. If your aircraft is experiencing a strong virtual crosswind, then the mathematical expressions tell the controls (the yoke) to be a bit more physically resistive to movement in certain directions. This tactile/haptic feedback (called *force feedback*) is essential for realistic simulation.

The mathematics of simulation are usually complex in practice but based on many simple fundamental physical principles. An aircraft in flight is affected by gravity, crosswinds, air-pressure changes, drag, lift, its thrust, ram velocity, and many other physical phenomena. An aircraft in landing mode experiences frictional forces from surfaces that it contacts. In all cases, an aircraft is ruled by its own physical characteristics (such as mass and surface) that define how it reacts to force. We generally find that we must take liberties with the physics if we want great performance in simulating real-world events; that is, we must make approximations. When you simulate for appearance and not accuracy, you can make even more approximations. It is all based on what you are trying to learn from or accomplish with the simulation.

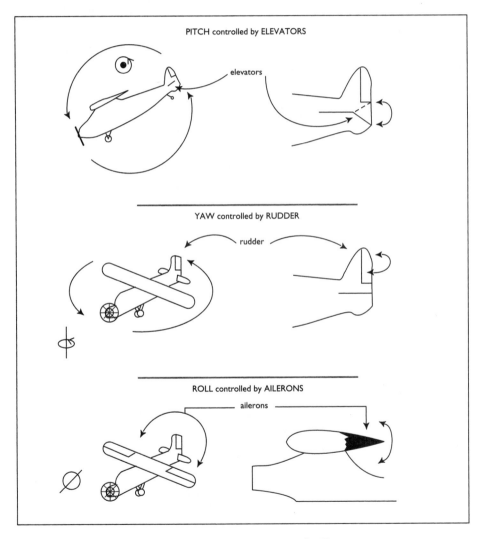

Figure 23.1 *Pitch, yaw, and roll.*

The Software and How it Works

The flight simulation software accompanying this book allows full control over viewer pitch, yaw and roll. This means that the viewer can effectively fly in any direction within the virtual flight simulation world. (See Figure 23.1 for an understanding of pitch, yaw, and roll.) These are aeronautical terms, referring to the control surfaces of an aircraft. For our purposes the elevator controls aircraft pitch (the nod of your head up and down), the rudder controls aircraft yaw (your head turning left and right), and the ailerons control aircraft roll (like the familiar "barrel roll"—you look out the end of the barrel, or your head is tilted side to side). These are our possible rotational movements as defined by our control surfaces.

Translational movement is controlled by the *throttle*. The throttle determines the thrust that the aircraft can impart. The viewer moves in the direction defined by the control surfaces at some rate defined by thrust, and the viewer can change direction by simply changing the positions of the ailerons, rudder, and elevator to eventually point him in the desired direction of travel.

If you have used the software, you may have noticed that the longer you hold down a key for a given motion (translations or rotations), the more of that movement you will get, up to a maximum limiting value. When you release the key for the given movement, the movement slowly decreases and comes to a rest. The routines found in `AlgCtrl.C` govern these control reactions. Basically, by holding down a given key, you increase the amount of change for some movement. The longer you hold down the control (key), the more times the control has contributed to some variable that represents the change in movement. When releasing the control, you no longer contribute to this variable. You might think that the movement would continue forever. Well, that would be true, except that we add a dampening factor for each control that will always try to bring that movement-change variable back to zero, stopping any rotational movement after a bit of time. One interesting effect is created by using the roll control keys to "rock" the view from side to side. This motion may remind you of looking off the end of a boat.

How We Visualize

Up to now, we have talked about rotations and translations for the viewer, but we have neglected how the program actually performs these functions. Examine the listing in the following program listings section referred to as "transform objects from local and world coordinates to view coordinates." This section of code comes from the `Alg3DEng.C` module, and it creates a master transformation matrix by which all polygon vertices will be multiplied in order to transform them for proper viewing. This master transformation matrix is composed from the multiplication of two matrices, the viewer transformation matrix and the object's local transformation matrix.

In the creation of the viewer transformation matrix we first initialize our viewer transformation matrix to the identity matrix (the top-left to bottom-right diagonal's elements are set to 1, all others reset to 0). Then we create a viewer translation matrix and multiply it by our existing viewer transformation matrix. This in effect will be used to reposition all objects in the virtual world relative to the viewer. Then a viewer rotation matrix is created and multiplied by the existing viewer transformation matrix in order to rotate our previously shifted (translated) objects around the viewer, so that we see a proper view. Note that both the translation and rotation vectors are negated for proper view.

Now that we have the viewer transformation matrix part of the master transformation matrix under control (that is, the viewer transformation matrix that is to be applied to all of the objects in the virtual flight simulation world), it is time to perform local transformations on individual objects, based on how each of those objects is positioned, oriented, and scaled in the virtual flight simulation world. So, for each object, we create a local transformation matrix by first setting the local transformation matrix to the identity matrix. We then simply create scaling, rotation, and translation matrices for the objects and multiply these matrices together to form the local transformation matrix.

We now have both the viewer and local object transformation matrices; so to create our master transformation matrix, we simply multiply the two together.

NOTE Remember always that when multiplying matrices, the order of multiplication is significant as the operations are not commutative (ask your neighbor for the lawnmower *before* you insult his wife, not the other way around).

To finish the transformation routine, we multiply all of the vertices in the virtual flight simulation world with our master transformation matrix. This multiplication yields vertices for objects that are properly placed for projection from the three-dimensional virtual world to your very real two-dimensional computer display.

After using the software, you will find that performance can be increased slightly (according to the model) by taking advantage of the world vertex found in the `AlgDefs_vertex_3D_type` structure. If you comment out the `#define total_transformation_matrix_approach`, you will make the software use the world vertex. With this commented out, you transform vertices from local to world in the conditional statement where the local transformation matrix is built. You then effectively remove the multiply of this local transformation matrix with the viewer transformation matrix, and then transform all vertices from world to viewer. The routine exists the way that it does to show that you can further transform points by multiplying (concatenating) matrices, and to allow you to choose the type of calculation for given types of 3-D world models.

As we mentioned, mathematics is used to simulate physical events. We will now take a brief look at what some of those mathematical expressions might look like for damped motion.

How Our Controls Work

As we have mentioned at the beginning of this section, our control surfaces have been damped. They function like a sliding particle under gravity being damped by friction. The viewer releases the key that he was pressing to cause a roll rotation with the ailerons, and the roll slowly decreases to no roll. For the algorithm from `AlgCtrl.C` following, you can imagine that the aileron positions are moving back to their zero positions; thus they have no effect. You can use a similar idea to simulate frictional surfaces cheaply. A quick look at the algorithm shows that damping of the control position toward its initial inactive state (position of control = 0) will always happen. Additions are made to the control position only if the key is being held down. These additions should be greater than any damping values; thus the control position (and in turn the roll rate) increases. The algorithms for control of the rudder and of the elevator are similar to the control of the aileron.

```
// control roll with ailerons

if (*aileron_position < -ALG_ZERO)
    *aileron_position += *aileron_dampening;
else
    if (*aileron_position > ALG_ZERO)
        *aileron_position -= *aileron_dampening;

if ((*aileron_left_down) &&
    (*aileron_position < *max_aileron_position))
{
    *aileron_position += *delta_aileron_position;
    *aileron_left_down = ALG_FALSE;
}
else
{
    if ((*aileron_right_down) &&
        (*aileron_position > -*max_aileron_position))
    {
        *aileron_position -= *delta_aileron_position;
            *aileron_right_down = ALG_FALSE;
    }
}
```

To summarize, your direction of travel will be the direction in which you, the viewer, have momentum at that moment. Use the *throttle* to increase or decrease the *rate* of travel. The *ailerons* control the *roll*. The *elevators* control the *pitch*, and the *rudder* controls the *yaw*. In a real aircraft, pedals control the rudder, a forward-and-back motion of the stick controls the elevators, and a left-to-right motion of the stick controls the ailerons. Figure 23.2 shows a summary of keyboard commands:

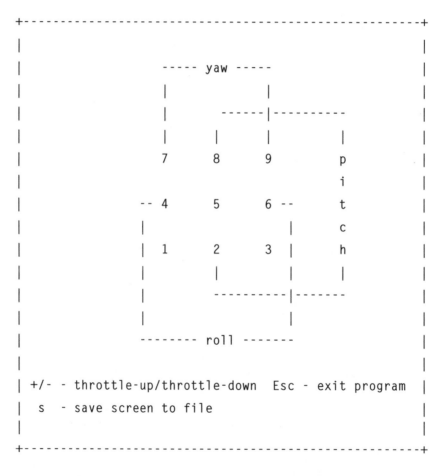

```
+-------------------------------------------------------------+
|                                                             |
|                                                             |
|                 ----- yaw -----                             |
|                    |           |                            |
|                    |    ------|----------                   |
|                    |    |     |        |                    |
|               7    8    9              p                    |
|                                        i                    |
|            -- 4    5    6 --           t                    |
|               |            |           c                    |
|               | 1    2    3 |          h                    |
|               |    |     |   |         |                    |
|               |    ----------|-------                       |
|               |              |                              |
|           -------- roll -------                             |
|                                                             |
| +/- - throttle-up/throttle-down   Esc - exit program        |
|  s  - save screen to file                                   |
|                                                             |
+-------------------------------------------------------------+
```

Figure 23.2 *Keyboard commands for roll, pitch, and yaw.*

The controls mentioned above respond to your key presses based on a set of parameters fixed in the .FS file. The following listing is a section of a file showing these parameters. This section shows how the positions, limits on positions, and dampening of certain controls are set to create the feel of the controls (that is, how the screen responds to your control input).

```
alg_controls
{
        max_aileron_position        18.0
        delta_aileron_position       1.0
        aileron_dampening            0.2
        max_elevator_position       18.0
        delta_elevator_position      1.0
        elevator_dampening           0.2
        max_rudder_position          9.0
        delta_rudder_position        0.8
        rudder_dampening             0.2
        max_throttle_position      250.0
        delta_throttle_position     10.0
        throttle_dampening           1.5
}
```

These values are stored in the `AlgDefs_controls_type` structure that is located in `AlgDefs.H`. It is as follows:

```
// describes the basic surface and thrust controls of an
// aircraft for "intuitive" control of the viewer
typedef struct
{
        AlgDefs_boolean             aileron_left_down;
        AlgDefs_boolean             aileron_right_down;
```

```
        AlgDefs_float           aileron_position;
        AlgDefs_float           max_aileron_position;
        AlgDefs_float           delta_aileron_position;
        AlgDefs_float           aileron_dampening;

        AlgDefs_boolean         elevator_up;
        AlgDefs_boolean         elevator_down;

        AlgDefs_float           elevator_position;
        AlgDefs_float           max_elevator_position;
        AlgDefs_float           delta_elevator_position;
        AlgDefs_float           elevator_dampening;

        AlgDefs_boolean         rudder_left;
        AlgDefs_boolean         rudder_right;

        AlgDefs_float           rudder_position;
        AlgDefs_float           max_rudder_position;
        AlgDefs_float           delta_rudder_position;
        AlgDefs_float           rudder_dampening;

        AlgDefs_boolean         throttle_inc;
        AlgDefs_boolean         throttle_dec;

        AlgDefs_float           throttle_position;
        AlgDefs_float           max_throttle_position;
        AlgDefs_float           delta_throttle_position;
        AlgDefs_float           throttle_dampening;
    }
AlgDefs_controls_type;
```

How Our Very Simple Flight Model Works

In an actual commercial flight simulator, the flight model is rather complex, and incorporates many micro and macro effects. The actual contours of the wings and fuselage, the effects of gear being up or down, and all of the basic physical laws such as gravity, drag, and lift are considered. The set of controls available in a commercial flight simulator extends beyond the simple set that we have. Given that we have the basic set of controls for the ailerons, for the rudder, and for the elevator, and given a throttle with which we can apply thrust, let's examine our simple flight model.

To understand our flight model, we must take a look at the fundamentals of flight. There are four forces that act on an airplane in flight at any given time. These forces work in different directions. Two of these four forces (lift and thrust) keep the plane in the air, thus they tend to act in a forward or upward direction; the other two (drag and gravity) tend to pull the airplane back to Earth, thus they tend to work in a backward, or downward direction. It is how you balance these forces that determines how you land (nose first, or smoothly), bank, loop or just simply fly. See Figure 23.2 below.

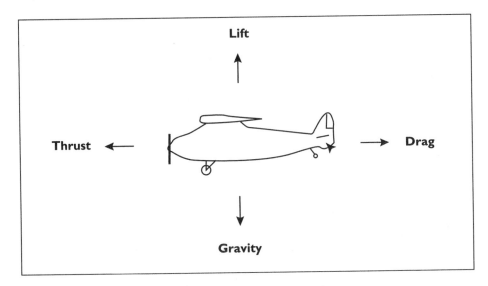

Figure 23.2 *Thrust, drag, lift, and gravity.*

Lift and Thrust in Flight

Lift is the force that acts upwardly on the aircraft. In order to produce lift, one needs thrust. As described in detail in Section III, *The Fundamentals of Flight,* you learned that all propulsion systems impart momentum to the oncoming air (for air-bound vehicles). The way this is accomplished defines the primary differences between propulsion systems. Typical aircraft propulsion systems include propellers, jet turbines, and rocket engines. All of these systems employ *Newton's third law* to provide thrust; that is, every action (force) produces an equal and opposite reaction (force). A force generated to change the momentum of the air produces an equal and opposite force, thrust, which propels the aircraft forward. There are two basic methods by which momentum is imparted (that is, thrust is created), the first is *reaction mass* (thrown particles), and the second is the more useful *pressure differentials* (differing pressure across a boundary).

The thrust generated through reaction mass can be seen as simply the recoil of a gun when it is fired. Note that in this case you are massive, and the bullet is rather small, hence you do not move as fast or as far as the bullet, yet you do feel a recoil. Another example is rocket engines that use propellants such as oxygen to provide reaction mass. When liquefied oxygen is quickly expanded through heating, and the molecules (atoms) of the expanding oxygen are directed through a nozzle at the back of a rocket engine, these atoms provide reaction mass, like many bullets being fired constantly.

Thrust generated through pressure differentials is more commonly found in our standard aircraft. The spinning blade of the propeller (prop) of a plane is shaped so that air will move at different speeds on different sides of the blades. The pressure will be greater on the plane side of the blade than in front of the blade; this acts to "push" the plane along in the direction of lower pressure (you might also say that the plane is being "pulled" along to equilibrium). Therefore, our pressure differential is producing thrust.

You might remember from high-school or college physics—*the Bernoulli principle.* It is the explanation for the above propeller being pushed through the air, dragging the plane behind it. If the pressure is made higher on the underside of a wing than the lower side, the wing will tend to rise. In a real aircraft, the shape of the wing actually creates a low pressure volume above the wing, thus the air pressure below the wing is greater. The faster the wing travels, the greater the pressure differential across the wing, and the greater the lift. When lift overcomes gravity, we are flying...but as we accelerate, drag becomes the negatively directed force that slows us.

Drag in Flight

Drag stems from *ramming*, where air that does not move easily over the wing *collides* with the wing and with the craft, and from vortices that form off the back of the wing (kind of like air-pressure "molasses"). The angle of attack, which is the angle of an aircraft wing with respect to the angle of the oncoming air flow, provides a way to control the lift and balance the drag. So by now, you see how intimately tied thrust, lift and drag are.

Software Routines for Controls and Flight Model

Examine `AlgCtrl.H`, `AlgCtrl.C`, `AlgKbd.H`, `AlgColl.C`, `Alg3DEng.H`, and `Alg3DEng.C` on the accompanying diskette.

Summary

Given our very simple explanation of how an airplane flies, our flight model incorporates constantly acting forces such as gravity, lift, thrust, and drag. Even wind gusts may be incorporated, as will be angle-of-attack effects such as stall.

Now that we have most of the basics, let's take a look at our control panel and gauges, and dive into the very interesting topic of light points.

Light Points and a Brief Overview of the Console and Gauges, and Special Effects

There is one last set of topics to discuss before bringing it all together to build a simulator from the building blocks discussed in the past few chapters. The issue of light points for runway lights, the simulator console and set of gauges, and special atmospheric effects must be discussed.

Light Points

Commercial flight simulators commonly have *light points*. Light points are generated by the renderer and an represent runway landing lamps. Great care must be taken in producing these light points in simulation, since simulator pilots sometimes use them to gauge their landing in fog, darkness, or inclement weather. This is much like in the real world, where a pilot uses the runway landing lamps. Someone examining a simulator to see if it meets certain requirements will certainly look at the light points. He may look to see if a certain number of light points are visible for certain weather conditions. If he expects to see five light points in fog, he had better see five light points. According to how light points and many other issues are handled, recognition as a Phase I, II, III, or IV simulator will be given.

In our system, light points have fixed intensity values. We may even make them vary in intensity with distance—the idea of *atmospheric attenuation* (decrease in intensity with distance). Light points in our system are treated as a primitive, much like a polygon, where they are sorted for display with the polygons (you should not see a runway light point that lies behind a building, out of view). Light points are computationally inexpensive additions to our simulator that can add quite a bit to the simulator's overall appearance. If we are flying at night, we will see the light points as runway lamps. But why not also use these luminous points for the lamps on other aircraft, stars, planets, UFOs that are made by Georgia Tech students—created to bother the people that really believe in UFOs, streetlights, trucks, cars, buildings, and even distant cities? You will be amazed at how a simple light point can add so much to a scene.

As mentioned, light points are a new primitive for us, so let's look at their structure. Since light points are commonly found in strands, it makes sense to create linear sets of light points. Examine Figure 24.1 for a strand of light points.

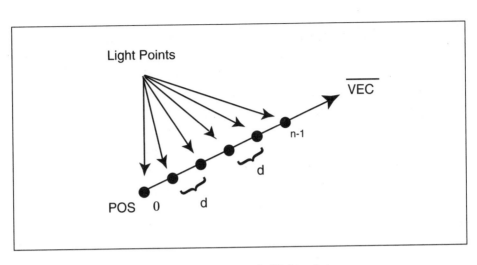

Figure 24.1 *A strand of light points.*

There is a three-dimensional position **pos** that defines where the first light point will appear. There is **vec** which defines in what direction we will find the light points. The distance **d** defines the spacing of the light points, and **n** is the number of light points in the given strand. Following is our basic structure for a strand of light points:

```
typedef struct
{
        // number of light points in strand (n)
        AlgDefs_word          num_points;
        // distance between light points in strand (d)
        AlgDefs_float         distance;
        // the strand base position (pos)
        AlgDefs_point_3D_type   position;
        // the vector direction for light point placement (vec)
        AlgDefs_vector_3D_type  direction;
}
AlgDefs_light_point_strand;
```

As mentioned earlier, individual light points within a strand are treated in many cases like polygons, in that they get sorted with the polygons, and clipped if they are out of sight (that is, behind the viewer, off the side of the screen, behind a polygon, and so on). Light points are treated as polygon vertices in that they are transformed and projected similarly. To begin the process, we initialize our light point strands from information in the .FS file. When we view-transform our polygon vertices, we also view-transform our light points. Creation of the polygon display list incorporates the light points, so as to remove light points that are behind the viewer. When we depth-sort our polygon list, we sort the light points as well from furthest to nearest, to guarantee that light points that we should not see are hidden. Next, the clipping routines do not need to perform z-clipping because that was done when we generated the polygon/light-point display list. Projection of the light points from three dimensions into the two-dimensional screen buffer is performed along with projection of the polygons, so that our Painter's algorithm approach to image generation functions properly.

With some understanding of light points (given by this rather short dissertation), we will move along to how the gauges and console/cockpit image works.

Gauges, Indicators and the Console

No flight simulator would be complete without some gauges and a cockpit window. As you may have noticed, our simulator has a cockpit console that is loaded over part of our simulation screen, along with some basic gauges. This cockpit image originates as a .PCX file (`cockpit.pcx`).

A typical simulator will have many of the following indicators and gauges (and probably many more):

- an artificial horizon
- a compass

- a throttle level indicator

- a brake indicator

- an ignition indicator

- a landing-gear down indicator

- an air speed gauge

- an altimeter

- a fuel gauge

We have many of these gauges in our simulator, which creates a simulated 3-D view of the virtual flight simulation world into a two-dimensional screen buffer. The gauge positions and indicator levels are continuously updated and drawn onto the simulated view in the buffer. A memory copy from a buffer holding the cockpit image composites it with the simulator view buffer, and displays it to the actual screen.

Atmospheric Effects

Manufacturers of commercial flight simulators usually go to a lot of trouble to simulate atmospheric effects. Glare, fog, smog, smoke, haze, and heavy rain are some of their favorites. A nice gradient sky with clouds, and a convincing horizon line is always nice. On our PCs, we can simulate some of these effects by manipulating the palette (a topic for another text). See the discussion in the chapter on shading.

Sound Effects

Another important issue is sound effects. The rumble of the engines when banking and the sputtering sound heard when about to stall are certainly important feedback to any pilot. Such feedback lets him know how to react with the pedals and stick to either prevent or get out of a nasty situation. Incorporating sounds into simulation equipment is mandatory, and in many cases the sound systems create stereo sound images. In some cases, sound equipment is used to vibrate the motion platform, to create just the right rumbling feel.

Surroundings: Ideas for Objects for your Simulator World

Typical objects for flight simulation programs are bushes, trees, clouds, houses, aircraft hangars, storage bays, rivers, runways, control towers, mountains, lakes, office buildings, skyscrapers, bridges, industrial complexes, intersections, cloverleafs, other aircraft, seacraft, cars, and trucks.

Software Routines for Light Points and Gauges

Examine `Alg3DEng.H`, `Alg3DEng.C`, `AlgPClip.H`, and `AlgPClip.C` on the accompanying diskette.

Summary

We have journeyed far, from polygons to light points...now it is time to build and fly our simulator.

25

The Flight Simulation Software

This chapter discusses the overall workings of the flight simulation program, as well as how to compose 3-D virtual flight simulation worlds for it.

Freebird the Flight Simulator

Well, it is now time to bring together all that you have learned so far and apply it to the development of a flight simulation system called *Freebird*. Since you are probably familiar with most of the basic concepts by now, this chapter discusses the functionality of the flight simulator using a

281

diagram showing the simulator's general conceptual flow. Tied to the functional diagram are simple helpful explanations.

Conceptual Program Flow for the Flight Simulator

Begin Program

Following is a conceptual program flow for Freebird. It discusses all initialization procedures, as well as those routines found in the main loop.

- *Initialization of the control system*—all simulator control surfaces (ailerons, rudder, elevator, and throttle) are set to their initial zero positions. Status variables for control surfaces are set initially to false (status variables indicate whether a surface's contribution to the viewer motion is increasing for this program loop).

- *Load the virtual flight simulator world into memory*—loads the three-dimensional virtual flight simulation world model and allocates memory for it and the polygon/light-point display list.

 Initially for our three-dimensional models, the positive *z* axis comes out of the screen, the positive *y* axis points to the bottom of the screen, and the positive *x* axis points to the left of the screen. Also note that polygons must have counterclockwise vertex ordering for the visible face, as the backface calculation uses these vertices to determine the surface normal; thus ordering is important.

- *Initialization of the keyboard*—creates the keyboard as the input device for the controls. Replaces keyboard interrupt.

- *Initialization of light points*—creates the light points from information loaded from the .FS file.

- *Initialization of the screen frame buffer*—allocates memory for the temporary screen frame buffer. The image is composed here in the memory buffer and subsequently copied to the graphics display.

- *Load the cockpit image*—loads the cockpit.pcx file that will act as a screen overlay.

- *Initialization of the graphics display*—initialize 320 x 200 8-bit color graphics mode.

- *Simulate flight by looping until an escape keypress*—**the main loop.**

The Main Loop

- *Get any input from the keyboard and set the status variables*—based on keystrokes, we set the appropriate control surface status variables to true.

- *Process status variables to determine positions for controls*—based on which control surface status variables were set to true, compute the new positions for the given control surfaces.

- *Compute viewing parameters from interpreted controls*—based on the positions of controls, modify the three-dimensional viewing parameters in order to move and reorient the viewer.

- *Transform vertices for our objects and light points*—transform objects and light points from local coordinates, then into world coordinates, and then into viewer coordinates based on viewing parameters.

- *Test for collision of the viewer with our objects*—determine whether we (heaven forbid() hit an object like a building or a mountain.

- *Create the polygon/light-point display list*—create a list of polygons and light points for display into the screen frame buffer. Remove all polygons and light points that fall totally behind the viewer (they are totally behind the z-clipping plane), and remove all polygons that are backfaces (you should not see these, as they are the other sides of objects). The polygon-viewer and light-point-viewer distances are computed here for depth sorting later.

■ *Perform depth sort on the polygon/light-point display list*—the depth sort is performed on the polygon/light-point display list to guarantee that the farthest polygons and light-points are drawn first and the nearest are drawn last. This is the *Painter's display algorithm.*

■ *Initialization of the screen frame buffer to the background (sky) color*—simply clear the viewport in our temporary screen frame buffer to the sky color. We will build our virtual image on top of it (using the Painter's algorithm again).

■ *Z-clip, project, viewport-clip, (shade) and draw polygons and light points in the polygon/light-point display list to the screen frame buffer*—z-clip the polygon or light-point with the z half-plane (the front of the "view volume"), then if the polygon or light-point is not totally z-clipped, project it. Then viewport-clip the polygon or light point, and if some of a polygon still exists, draw it into the screen frame buffer. These polygons are flat shaded and can be textured. Light-point intensities were defined in the .FS file.

■ *Draw the cockpit to the screen frame buffer*—draw the cockpit.pcx image to the bottom of the screen frame buffer.

■ *Copy the screen frame buffer to the graphics display*—copy the screen frame buffer into the graphics display for viewing.

After the Main Loop

■ *Exit the graphics display*—exit graphics for text mode.

■ *Delete the screen frame buffer*—free memory for the screen frame buffer.

- *Delete the keyboard*—return to using original keyboard interrupt.

- *Delete the simulation world three-dimensional model from memory*—free memory for the three-dimensional virtual flight simulation world model and polygon/light-point display list.

- *Display the text exit/copyright message*—display copyright notice and exit.

Freebird: the Flight Simulator

Freebird is the polygonal world flight simulation program containing all the executables and all source code. Freebird is the basis for any virtual reality graphics engine or flight simulation system.

Using Freebird: The Controls

Using Freebird is easy, there are a number of template *.FS* files that contain three-dimensional worlds to work with and modify. Two of these files are Flight.FS and Night.FS.

At the DOS prompt, type this to visualize the flight.FS virtual flight simulation world.

Freebird flight

With a skillful hand, a few little gray cells, and some patience, you can use the keyboard controls to interact with the virtual world. Your direction of travel is the one in which you, the viewer, have momentum at that moment. Use the *throttle* to increase (+ key) or to decrease (– key) your *rate* of travel. The *ailerons* (left and right arrows on keypad) control your *roll*, the *elevator* (up and down arrows on keypad) control your *pitch* (up-down motion), and the *rudder* (**Home** and **Pg Up** keys) control your *yaw* (left-to-right motion). Remember that in a real aircraft, pedals control the rudder, a forward and back motion of the stick would control

the elevators, and a left-to-right motion of the stick would control the
ailerons. Figure 25.1 shows a summary of commands:

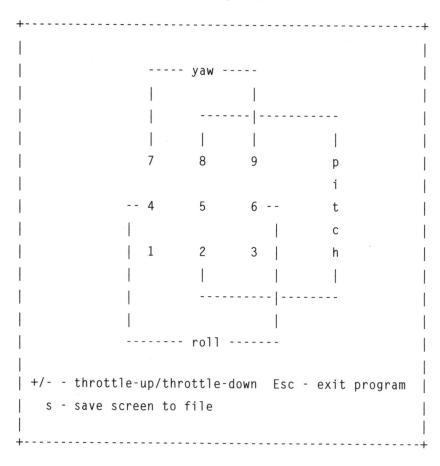

Figure 25.1 *Yaw, pitch, and roll.*

The controls mentioned above respond to your key presses based on a
set of parameters fixed in the .FS file. A section of a .FS file showing these
parameters follows. This section shows how the positions, limits on
positions and dampening of certain controls are set to create the feel of
the controls (that is, how the screen responds to your control input).

```
alg_controls
{
max_aileron_position       18.0
delta_aileron_position      1.0
aileron_dampening           0.2
max_elevator_position      18.0
delta_elevator_position     1.0
elevator_dampening          0.2
max_rudder_position         9.0
delta_rudder_position       0.8
rudder_dampening            0.2
max_throttle_position     250.0
delta_throttle_position    10.0
throttle_dampening          1.5
}
```

 N O T E You must make sure that there are no extra characters on any of the lines, and that there are no extra blank lines inside of the `alg_controls` structure.

The Viewer

The following listing shows a section from the `flight.FS` file, defining the initial position and orientation (viewing direction) of the viewer.

```
alg_viewer
{
  translate  0.0  500.0  14000.0
  rotate    0.0  0.0    0.0
  perspective_plane_distance  350.0
}
```

 You must make sure that there are no extra characters on any of the lines, and that there are no extra blank lines inside of the `alg_viewer` structure.

The World

The following listing is a section from the `flight.FS` file, defining the virtual flight simulation world sky color and intensity, and the maximum number of objects that can be found in the virtual simulation world. This statement must come before any object definitions in a .FS file.

```
alg_world
{
    background_color        cyan
    background_intensity    23
    num_objects             18
}
```

 You must make sure that there are no extra characters on any of the lines, and that there are no extra blank lines inside of the `alg_world` structure.

Viewer-Object Collisions

The `flight.FS` virtual flight simulation world model is set up to allow you to fly through the virtual world and interact (collide) with some of its objects. Some objects are *permeable*, thus they allow you to fly in and out of them, even if they are solid. Other objects (such as the cars) are *pushable* and *rotatable*; thus if you hit them, they will fly off into space, assuming your traveling direction before the collision, and also assuming any rotation (such as roll) that you, the viewer (aircraft) had before collision. Some objects are only *pushable* and can only be moved, while others are just *rotatable* and can just be rotated based on the viewer rotation. Other objects (such as mountains and control towers) are *solid*, and cannot be moved; you the viewer will bounce off of or crash into these objects, if you hit them.

A skillful hand on the controls can have objects flying off into all directions with any rotations that you can imagine. For example, you can sweep down and hit the car, while you are in a roll and a slight yaw rotation, and watch it fly—note that this should only be tried in virtual simulation environments, in the real world, hitting cars at high rates of speed with an airplane in a swerve can ruin your whole day!

A brief list of collision types is as follows:

- solid
- pushable
- rotatable
- pushable_and_rotatable
- permeable

Object Orientations

Objects can assume any position, orientation and scaling in a virtual simulation world. These parameters have components in all three dimensions. This is the format of the world position, orientation and scaling parameters for an object:

```
translate    x    y    z
rotate       x    y    z
scale        x    y    z
```

Object Motions

As described earlier, objects can be in motion. Motions have components in all three dimensions and they can take the form of changing position (translation), orientation (rotation) and scale. An object can be either **static** or **active**. Note that a collision may override the motion status (*static* or *active*) parameter for an object, if that object is *pushable*, *rotatable*, or both. the following listing shows the format of the motion parameters for an object.

```
motion
{
    static or active
    translate     x     y     z
    rotate        x     y     z
    scale         x     y     z
}
```

Object Surfaces

You may remember from earlier discussions on polygons that a polygon is only visible from one side; this aids in polygon backface removal for increased performance. Our vertex ordering scheme for polygons states that counter-clockwise ordering of vertices gives the visible side (think of making a right-handed x-axis cross y-axis to yield the z-axis motion). Some objects (such as mountains that are far away, are *solid* and thus cannot be penetrated) are likely to be represented by an *outside* surface only. Other objects may be *permeable*, thus we need to have two polygons produced, one for the inside and one for the outside, since we could be on either side of the polygon, thus we have *inside_and_outside* surfaces. An *inside* surface is just an *outside* surface with the vertices in clockwise order. Following is a list of the surface types:

- inside and outside
- inside
- outside

Object Colors

Each polygon that makes up any object in the scene can have its own color. There are seven colors from which to choose. Each color can have 36 intensity levels, from black to color saturated. See the following list. Note that each polygon must have an intensity value associated with its color, and that polygons that are inside and outside surfaces must have colors and intensities defined for both the inside and outside polygon (as a polygon that is an *inside_and_outside* surface is actually two separate polygons facing in opposite directions—as defined by the vertex ordering scheme mentioned earlier). Here is the list of colors:

- blue
- green
- cyan
- red
- magenta
- yellow
- gray

Object Textures

No simulation world would be acceptable without a little texturing to help fool the sense of vision. The following is a list of polygon texture types. The *flat* shading provides the basic polygon solid color fill. The four transparent textures, `transparent_hatch`, `transparent_diagonal_stripe`, `transparent_vertical_stripe`, `transparent_horizontal_stripe`, help us to see through polygons by drawing only certain pixels of those polygons into the screen buffer. Since we are using the Painter's algorithm for display, polygons that were drawn before the transparent polygon will be partially covered with the sparse pixels of our transparent polygon. We therefore see both polygons. The *checkerboard* texture is a computed texture, producing a checkerboard pattern on an object.

The *map* textures create fast, complex surface textures. Because these textures are pre-computed into memory arrays, you have no control from the .FS file of their color (the color and intensity input is thrown away—perhaps a future modification will be some palette manipulation to allow control). The `checkerboard_map` texture produces a black-and-white checkerboard pattern. The `grit_map` texture produces a gray grit/sand (runway) texture. The `marble_map` and `wood_map` textures use the Perlin noise function to create black-and-white marble and light brown wood textures, respectively. The `waves_map` texture produces a wicked wavy blue texture. A list of the textures is as follows:

- flat
- transparent_hatch
- transparent_diagonal_stripe
- transparent_vertical_stripe
- transparent_horizontal_stripe
- checkerboard
- checkerboard_map
- grit_map
- marble_map
- wood_map
- waves_map

Some Object Definitions

Now that you know a little about how objects work in a .FS file, take take a quick look at the actual format for an object in a .FS file. Notice that the ground (the first example object) that runs out to the horizon line of the world is nothing more than a very large square polygon. Also notice that the minimum height of flight is 5 (as hard-coded in AlgCtrl.C). All objects below this point (such as the ground and runways) can be permeable, as they are never reached by the viewer. A runway object from one of the .FS files is as follows:

```
alg_object
{
    name            runway
    surface         outside
    collision       permeable
    translate       0.0       1.0       0.0
    rotate          0.0       0.0       0.0
    scale           150.0     150.0     1.0
    motion
    {
        status          static
        translate       0.0       0.0       0.0
        rotate          0.0       0.0       0.0
        scale           0.0       0.0       0.0
    }
    vertex_list
    {
        num_vertices    4
        vertex -120.0   0.0       1000000.0
        vertex -120.0   0.0       -2000.0
        vertex  -80.0   0.0       -2000.0
        vertex  -80.0   0.0       1000000.0
    }
    polygon_list
```

```
        {
                num_polygons      1
                polygon
                {
                        RUNWAY
                        num_vertices    4
                        vertex_index    0
                        vertex_index    1
                        vertex_index    2
                        vertex_index    3
                        color           gray
                        intensity       15
                        texture         grit_map
                }
        }
}
```

NOTE You must make sure that there are no extra characters on any of the lines, and that there are no extra blank lines inside of the `alg_object` structure.

Programs Files And Directories

Installing from the 720K 3.5-inch floppy disk creates the following directory structure. You should work the compiler from the C:\FSBOOK\SOURCE\BIN directory. The project files call on program modules found in the C:\FSBOOK\SOURCE\LIB directory. Copy compiled programs into the C:\FSBOOK\SOURCE directory and run them from there since that is where the .BGI file is kept.

C:\FSBOOK\SOURCE\LIB

Alg3D.C Alg3D.H	PC (certainly not politically correct) general 3-D graphics routines
Alg3DEng.C Alg3DEng.H	creation of polygon display list
AlgCal.C AlgCal.H	Gregorian/Julian calendar routines
AlgColl.C AlgColl.H	viewer-object collision detection
AlgCtrl.C AlgCtrl.H	interpreting keyboard input for control surfaces (and crash)
AlgDefs.H	miscellaneous definitions and types
AlgError.C AlgError.H	Alg-module error handling
AlgFS.C AlgFS.H	.FS file creation routines
AlgFSPrs.C AlgFSPrs.H	parse the .FS file and create world
AlgGraph.C AlgGraph.H	PC (certainly not politically correct) 2-D graphics routines
AlgHids.C AlgHids.H	hidden-surface and sorting algorithms
AlgKbd.C AlgKbd.H	keyboard input routines

`AlgMath.C` `AlgMath.H`	mathematics functions
`AlgMatx.C` `AlgMatx.H`	matrix macro functions
`AlgMem.C` `AlgMem.H`	memory allocation/deallocation/reallocation
`AlgMotn.C` `AlgMotn.H`	object motion
`AlgMouse.C` `AlgMouse.H`	mouse input
`AlgPClip.C` `AlgPClip.H`	Sutherland-Hodgman and Liang-Barsky polygon clipping algorithms
`AlgPCX.C` `AlgPCX.H`	load .PCX image file into buffer (cockpit overlay)
`AlgPoly.C` `AlgPoly.H`	convex polygon drawing routines
`AlgProj.C` `AlgProj.H`	3-D to 2-D projection
`AlgScrn.C` `AlgScrn.H`	screen-buffer and screen routines
`AlgShade.C` `AlgShade.H`	shading algorithms
`AlgTex.C` `AlgTex.H`	procedural and procedural map textures
`AlgVec.H`	vector macro functions

C:\FSBOOK\SOURCE\BIN

```
FREEBIRD.C          flight simulation program
FREEBIRD.DSK
FREEBIRD.PRJ

DOY_JD.C            Gregorian Date to Julian Day converter
DOY_JD.DSK
DOY_JD.PRJ

DOY_MJD.C           Gregorian Date to Modified Julian Day converter
DOY_MJD.DSK
DOY_MJD.PRJ

JD_DOY.C            Julian Day to Gregorian Date converter
JD_DOY.DSK
JD_DOY.PRJ

MJD_DOY.C           Modified Julian Day to Gregorian Date converter
MJD_DOY.DSK
MJD_DOY.PRJ

PARTSYS.C           particle system simulator
PARTSYS.DSK
PARTSYS.PRJ

PI.C                computer
PI.DSK
PI.PRJ

PRIMES.C            prime number computer
PRIMES.DSK
PRIMES.PRJ

SPARKGAP.C          fractal sparkgap
SPARKGAP.DSK
SPARKGAP.PRJ
```

```
TERRAIN.C      fractal terrain generator
TERRAIN.DSK
TERRAIN.PRJ
```

C:\FSBOOK\SOURCE

`SVGA256.BGI`	Borland graphics driver by Jordan Hargrave

`FREEBIRD.EXE`
`FLIGHT.FS`
`NIGHT.FS`
`COCKPIT.PCX`
`*.FS`
	flight simulation program with .FS world models

`DOY_JD.EXE`	Gregorian Date to Julian Day converter
`DOY_MJD.EXE`	Gregorian Date to Modified Julian Day converter
`JD_DOY.EXE`	Julian Day to Gregorian Date converter
`MJD_DOY.EXE`	Modified Julian Day to Gregorian Date converter
`PARTSYS.EXE`	particle system simulator
`PI.EXE`	computer
`PRIMES.EXE`	prime number computer
`SPARKGAP.EXE`	fractal sparkgap
`TERRAIN.EXE`	fractal terrain generator

Software Routines for the Flight Simulator

Examine `Alg3DEng.H`, `Alg3DEng.C`, `AlgMotn.H`, `AlgMotn.C`, `AlgFSPrs.H`, `AlgFSPrs.C`, `AlgColl.H`, and `AlgColl.C` on the accompanying diskette.

Summary

Well, there you have it—your own PC flight simulator. You may have noticed other interesting programs in the listings as well; these are explained in Appendix B. Let's now move on to look at the opossible future of flight simulation visual systems.

26

Flying Forward

So here you are, the last chapter of the book. You have learned about such topics as how flight simulation came into being and how it has evolved. You gained some understanding as to how aircraft stay in the air through simple and sophisticated propulsion systems and aerodynamic structures. You studied a bit about human perception, and its importance to flight simulation. As we have discussed where flight simulation is headed in a more commercial/industrial and financial sense, it is time for us to take a look at where it all might be headed from a purely image generation point-of-view.

Other Rendering Methodologies

Our primary goal in the production of computer-generated imagery is to create images that can pass for photographs of real or imagined objects. Many techniques are used to render three-dimensional scenes, each

301

with its own set of good and bad points. Computer graphics has expanded in many directions with great numbers of people researching various techniques for improving image quality, fidelity with the real world, and visualization of complex data sets. Many problems, such as realistic human animation, have yet to be solved. Certainly many of the problems with real-time image generation exist even today, as they have always.

Realistic models require a sophistication and complexity that bring many high-powered computing systems to a screeching halt. High polygon counts and complex textures for detail and complex mathematical models for accurately simulating physical effects such as the environment and object-object interactions make flight and vehicle simulation impossible on many generic computing systems. Silicon Graphics has the right approach with their high-speed graphics engine—the Reality Engine—with its environment texture mapping (mapping a bitmap image of the environment to the surface of an object) and general texture mapping capabilities.

This section describes two other rendering technologies that get us closer to photorealism: ray tracing and radiosity. But, as mentioned before, each has its good points and its bad points. It is likely, though, that neither of these methods will ever be used for flight simulation, unless each screen pixel has its own dedicated processor for computation of that piece of the image.

Ray Tracing

Ray tracing is an excellent technique for rendering worlds that contain specularly reflective (shiny) objects. The ray tracing technique offers an approach that can truly simulate how a camera (or human eye) might see a scene. The concept is actually quite straightforward: namely, you simulate how light interacts with objects by tracing light rays through a scene to see what objects they interact with. This approach models how light interacts physically with objects. Since we are concerned only with the light rays that eventually reach our eye (or pass through the computer screen), we follow the light rays in reverse. Rays are followed from the eye, through the "screen," and out into the scene. The rays are traced as they are reflected, refracted, diffracted, absorbed, and focused following the basic laws of optics.

The Ray Tracing Algorithm

The ray tracing algorithm is quite simple. The screen is defined as an array of pixels, set up in a viewing geometry (that is, the viewer's eye is placed a distance in front of the screen as though he is looking at the screen center, and objects exist behind the screen). For each screen pixel, we generate an initial ray starting at the eyepoint, passing through the screen, and out into some environment that is already defined. The environment consists of three-dimensional objects, lights, and background models. The ray tracing algorithm then proceeds as follows:

- Find the nearest object that the ray intersects (if any) and determines the point of intersection of the ray with the object.

- Calculate the ambient color of the object surface at the point of intersection based on the object's characteristics and the light sources.

- Cast "shadow" rays from the point of intersection to each light source in the scene. These generate the diffuse and specular lighting of the surface. The shadow rays also determine whether the point of intersection is shadowed from a light source by another obstructing object, either wholly or partially.

- If the object surface is reflective, compute a new ray starting at the intersection point and pointing in the "reflected" direction. Find the effective color of this ray by recursively calling the same procedure.

- If the object surface is transparent, compute a new transmitted ray, again starting from the intersection point. Find the color of this ray and adds it to the color of the other rays.

- Add the object color to the color of the reflected and transmitted rays, and then returns this as the color of the pixel.

This procedure has several interesting properties:

- It is inherently recursive, which makes C and other such languages ideally suited. Each time a ray is cast, we simply call the procedure again with the new ray.

- It is based on a model of light interacting with objects. We can accurately model how light is reflected and refracted through the scene in ways that more traditional methods simply cannot handle.

- It is very amenable to parallel processing (having multiple CPUs work on different parts of a picture). Each pixel can be processed independently of the other pixels in the scene—as mentioned above, this might be the only way that ray tracing is used for flight simulation.

Using Ray Tracing for Testing

While ray tracing satisfies our main goal of producing high-quality imagery, it also provides another important tool in computer graphics. Namely, it gives us a method for testing our understanding of how light interacts with an environment. Many researchers have adapted their physical models of the interaction of light with matter to ray tracing programs to see if they produce images that look like the real thing. If so, then we have greatly increased our confidence that our theoretical model of the world and light is an accurate description of the processes that are taking place. This is especially true in modeling very complex phenomena such as waves, clouds, and terrain. Thus, the tools given by ray tracing allow you to produce high-quality imagery and to test complex models of light. In the approval of flight simulation systems, how real things look is very important to achieving a certain level of approval. The way that light-points (that make up our runway lights, lights on other craft, and more) are presented influences greatly the approval rating given to a simulator. See Appendix C for more details.

Interactive-Rate Ray Tracing for Flight Simulation?

Ray tracing algorithms have never really been used in any type of real-time visualization system because today the computer horsepower simply isn't available to perform the sorting operations (building the hierarchical tree and determining the nearest object for each ray) quickly enough. The standard projective rendering programs (such as the software with this book) have the advantage that they need only sort the object lists, from farthest to nearest, one time per frame. If you use only one level of recursion, then a ray tracer could do the same thing, but then you lose the improved image quality and realism of ray tracing (reflections, refractions, certain object surface characteristics, and so on). One of the real hopes for ever achieving this goal is in parallel computing. Remember that in a parallel processing system each pixel might be processed independently, and thus the image calculation can be spread across several processors that have access to the same scene description. As the cost of these types of machines decreases, we can expect to see more people attempting to run ray tracing in near real time. It should be noted, however, that we can always saturate any ray tracing computation by increasing the recursion level, computing depth-of-field effects, and adding more complicated shadow and lighting computations.

Radiosity

The entire subject of the physical modeling of the interaction of light and surfaces within a scene is called *radiosity*. Radiosity is an excellent technique for rendering worlds that contain many diffusely reflecting objects like interior walls and ceilings. This type of modeling tries to create a complete physical model of how light reflects throughout a scene. It is based on the theory of radiative heat transfer between surfaces. An object surface receives light not only from the light sources and specularly reflective objects, but also from the diffuse illumination of surfaces.

Imagine an interior wall. A radiosity model would actually compute the entire diffuse light contribution from the entire wall reflecting onto the surface of some object. Compare this with modeling a mirrored surface. With a mirror, we looked only for specular reflections and needed to cast only a single ray. With a radiosity solution, we must integrate the contributions from all of the diffuse surfaces within a scene. Additionally, a radiosity approach makes no particular assumption about the ambient and diffuse lighting of a scene. All of the light contributions are computed as integrated contributions rather than single-point evaluations. This applies to specular as well as diffuse components. Recall that in ray tracing the specular contribution came from the light sources only. A full radiosity solution also includes specular effects of diffuse surfaces. For even a simple scene, such as a typical office, these are very extensive computations. These long computing times will make radiosity an unlikely candidate for flight simulation.

Radiosity Approximations for Increased Performance

Because of the long computing times, even the mathematical purists have been driven to develop approximations and shortcuts for radiosity solutions. The key to using these *heuristic approaches* (approximation approaches that follow a rule versus the optimal solution) is that for a static scene with no highly reflective objects, we need only compute the diffuse contributions of the surfaces once. The contribution depends only on the geometry of the objects, not on the particular lighting within the scene. This contribution is expressed in terms of effective light intensity from the surfaces involved and so can be used for the diffuse contribution directly. This is ideal for a z-buffered ray tracing approach in that the diffuse contribution can be computed and stored at the same time as the z-buffering occurs. Once this diffuse intensity map is created, you can add new light sources to the scene with much less difficulty. Only the contributions due to this light source need be considered; all of the others have been accounted for. It is still time-consuming, but much less so than recomputing the entire scene.

Advantages and Disadvantages of Radiosity

The advantage of a radiosity solution is that it can make a scene appear much more like its real-life counterpart, providing more details in shadowed areas and correctly depicting the effects of indirect lighting. This is particularly useful to an architect who wants to know what type of lighting and what intensity to use in designing a new office building. A radiosity solution is flexible enough to let you add new light sources at will, such as a desk lamp, and literally being able to turn it on and off and see the effect. Shadowing effects are more accurate in a radiosity solution as well. The real advantage, however, is that it provides a test bed for fully understanding and testing our theories of how light propagates through a scene. The main problem using radiosity in real-time simulations is that the computation times are too long for a useful interactive simulation.

Conclusion

Well, you have made it to this point, the end of the technical section, and the very end of this book. Hopefully, you were surprised to find that you understood many of the technical concepts and that you learned much about flight, and simulation systems for flight. In any case, let us review conceptually the workings of the real-time simulation (graphics) system that we have developed.

First, refresh your memories about the technologies for our flight simulator visual systems. To help you understand and develop a visual system that will support the flight simulation illusion, a basic set of mathematical tools and processes were developed. The tool set discussed included geometry, matrix algebra, and trigonometry operations, and basic computer graphics. You learned about these things:

- The projection of polygons from a 3-D polygonal world onto a 2-D computer display.

- The sorting of polygons from farthest to nearest for order of display.

- The clipping of polygons that fall behind us, and the clipping of polygons that fall partially or totally off to the sides of the computer display.

- The shading and texturing of polygon to create a realistic appearance.

- And the removal of hidden polygons that exist on the unseen sides of objects.

So let us now journey once again into how all of the technologies work together to produce the effect.

Imagine that you are back in that airplane from Chapter 14. Imagine that you are flying in that airplane. You have a window at the front of the cockpit that allows you to see the world before you. You know that the world outside is made of three-dimensional objects like trees, mountains, buildings, but if you had never been outside to experience these objects up close, the two-dimensional image that you see through the window of your airplane would be all that you would know. Assume your computer screen to be the airplane window.

Imagine that the surfaces of all of those three-dimensional objects in your world are made up of tiny polygonal patches such as triangles and rectangles. That simple building in your view, for instance, could be made of four rectangles for walls, two rectangles for a roof, two triangles to fill in the ends of the roof, and assorted rectangles for windows and doors. The more polygons you use to construct your objects, the more detail your objects will have.

Try to visualize how your complex three-dimensional world might look if it were made only of triangles and rectangles—pretty choppy and without any interesting detail. Many simulators pride themselves by coloring, shading, and texturing those polygons. Whether rough, or smooth, or complex with texture, our objects and their interactions with light can be simulated by mathematical equations.

Let us examine where we are. We have a three-dimensional world whose objects are constructed from shaded and possibly textured polygons. We have a computer display that acts like a window into that

three-dimensional world. Like the airplane's cockpit window in relation to the real three-dimensional world of real objects, our computer display can assume any position and orientation in relation to our virtual three-dimensional world of polygonal objects. What you see through the cockpit window of your airplane is a projection of the three-dimensional world onto that two-dimensional cockpit window. By performing perspective projection onto the computer display of all of those three-dimensional polygons that make up objects in our virtual flight simulation world, we will see our virtual world through our window.

Imagine next that we can move our window around in three-dimensional space, just like the airplane cockpit window, repositioning it and reorienting it as time goes by. You might now say that we are flying.

A flight simulator functions in a nutshell like this: you orient and position the viewer (the person sitting in front of the computer display) relative to the screen and relative to the three-dimensional polygonal-object world. You project all of those polygons from three dimensions into two dimensions with geometric perspective and display them on the computer screen. You may also project any light points such as runway lights from the three-dimensional world onto the two-dimensional computer display. The computer takes input from your control devices (keyboard, mouse, joystick, yoke, pedals, wheel, and so on), and the computer reorients and repositions the viewer based on the status of those controls.

Repeating the above process, and given that you have mathematics that accurately physically model the way the viewer would move, bounce, and crash based on input from controls, then you have the beginnings of a flight simulator. Make the display system large enough for a pilot and co-pilot to feel like they are really looking out of a cockpit window, and you are closer to immersion. Add tactile feedback to the controls so that they feel real (that is, in older aircraft with mechanical linkages, you could feel some resistance in the controls when performing dynamic maneuvers), add sound (the change in hum of the engines when banking), and maybe add smell (the greatly undesired fire that resulted from one of your engines falling off in a Chicago-to-LA flight, where someone in Colorado Springs gets a new whopper turbine air conditioning system), and you have an immersion flight simulator.

Closing Comments

Well there you have it, flight simulation in a nutshell. By no means have we totally covered the technical and physiological aspects, psychological aspects, historical, and application aspects, or any other aspects of the field. We do hope that you see that the field is really a collection of many diverse technologies developed over quite a few years, and that many intelligent ways for humans to interact with computers for a variety of purposes have been developed as a result of the need for simulation.

As with all good things, this too must come to an end. We really hope that you enjoyed your flight, as well as working and playing with the software. As with most of these book projects with software, many seemingly endless hours and bottles of Jolt Cola went into its development, so now it is time for you (and us) to have fun with it all.

If you found the section on human perception particularly interesting, you can contact Vincent Mallette at the Georgia Institute of Technology, or Christopher D. Watkins at Algorithm, Inc. in Atlanta, Georgia. Vincent Mallette is an expert in the human visual system and human perception. If you found the sections on computer graphics interesting and you would like to know more about computer graphics, virtual reality, image processing, or other computer-related technologies, look for the following excellent books and organizations. *Virtual Reality ExCursions* will probably be of particular interest, as it augments the materials found in this book.

Books

- *Photorealism and Ray Tracing in C*—a most excellent general-to-technical graphics text including disks with a very useful photorealistic ray tracer and assorted fractal database generators (includes all source code with explanations and three-dimensional models used to generate color images in the book), by Christopher D. Watkins and Stephen B. Coy, M&T Books / San Mateo, CA (Henry Holt / New York).

■ *Programming in 3 Dimensions, ray tracing and animation*—a simple graphics text including a disk with a ray tracer, renderers, and an animator (includes all source code), by Christopher D. Watkins and Larry Sharp, M&T Books / San Mateo, CA (Henry Holt / New York).

■ *Advanced Graphics Programming in C and C++*—a simple graphics text including a disk with a ray tracer, height-field renderer, and shaded-polygon (reflections) renderer (includes all source code), by Roger T. Stevens and Christopher D. Watkins, M&T Books / San Mateo, CA (Henry Holt / New York).

■ *Flight Simulation*—an all-encompassing book on flight simulation by J. M. Rolfe and K. J. Staples, Cambridge: Cambridge University Press, 1986.

■ *Virtual Reality ExCursions*—a general to technical text including diskette for a 3-D real-time flat and textured polygon renderer, anaglyph glasses for interactive 3-D (stereo) viewing of some virtual worlds. Virtual Reality ExCursions augments the technical and general interest material found in this book (includes all source code with explanations), by Christopher D. Watkins and Stephen R. Marenka, Cambridge, MA: Academic Press, Inc.

■ *Modern Image Processing*—A simple general image processing text including diskette (includes all source code), by Christopher D. Watkins, Alberto Sadun, and Stephen R. Marenka, Cambridge, MA: Academic Press, Inc.

■ *Computer Graphics, a programming approach*—an excellent general graphics discussion, by Steven Harrington, New York; McGraw-Hill.

■ *Computer Graphics, principles and practice*—an excellent, more technical graphics text (a must-have), by James Foley, Reading, MA: Addison Wesley.

Soon-to-be Books

■ *Introduction to Photorealism and Ray Tracing*—a general graphics text for the beginner, including disks with a very sophisticated and easy-to-use and very useful photorealistic ray tracer, and assorted fractal database generators, and a 3-D Modeler that runs under Microsoft Windows. You might even be able to import some of your .DXF AutoCAD/Studio 3-D models (includes all executables and three-dimensional models used to generate color images in the book), by Christopher D. Watkins, Stephen R. Marenka and Vincent Mallette, M&T Books (Henry Holt / New York) (available spring 1995).

■ *The Internet Edge*—a general reader text discussing the Internet, how to get on, and actually do something useful quickly. Including diskette (and maybe CD) with IBM PC (and possibly Mac) shell software that runs under Microsoft Windows, and lists and look-up programs for internet information, "yellow-pages," etc., by Christopher D. Watkins and Stephen R. Marenka, Cambridge, MA: Academic Press, Inc.

Organizations

■ **Association of Computing Machinery** (ACM)11 West 42nd Street New York, NY 10036ACM/SIGGRAPH (**S**pecial **I**nterest **G**roup on computer **GRAPH**ics).

■ **IEEE** *Computer Graphics and Applications* (magazine) 10662 Los Vaqueros Circle, Los Alamitos, CA 90720.

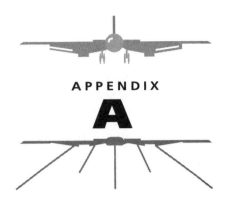

Bibliography

General References

Bartholomew, Wilmer. *Acoustics of Music.* Englewood Cliffs, NJ: Prentice-Hall, 1960.

Binder, R. C. *Fluid Mechanics.* 3rd ed. New York: Prentice-Hall, 1955.

Boothe, Ed. Personal communication with flight simulation consultant. June 1994.

Bracewell, Ronald N. "The Fourier Transform." *Scientific American.* June 1989.

Gibson, James J. *The Senses Considered as Perceptual Systems.* Boston: Houghton Mifflin Company, 1966.

Green, Roger G. and et al. *Human Factors for Pilots.* Avebury Technical, 1991.

Johansson, Gunnary. *Visual Motion Perception.* Scientific American. June 1975.

Josephy, Alvin M. Jr., ed. *The History of Flight.* American Heritage, 1962.

Journal of the Acoustical Society of America. Dec. 1964.

Kingston, Paul, Sherlock, Peter, and Martin, William. Personal communication with IVEX Corporation. June-July 1994.

Knudsen, Eric I. "The Hearing of the Barn Owl" *Scientific American.* Dec. 1981.

MacCaulay, David. *The Way Things* Work. Boston: Houghton Mifflin, 1988.

Mishkin, and Appenzeller. *Scientific American.* June 1987.

Morgan, Willard ed. *The Encyclopedia of Photography.* New York: Greystone Press, 1974.

National Geographic. Nov. 1992.

Parrish, Lex. *Space-Flight Simulation Technology.* Indianapolis: Howard W. Sams & Co., Inc., 1969.

Patronis, Dr. Eugene. Personal communication. Nov. 16, 1993.

Philosophical Transactions of the Royal Society of London. Vol. 3. 1668.

Physics Today. Dec. 1992.

Reader's Digest. March 1972.

Rolfe, J. M. and K. J. Staples. *Flight Simulation.* Cambridge: Cambridge University Press, 1986.

Rossotti, Hazel. Colour: *Why the World Isn't Grey.* Princeton, NJ: Princeton University Press, 1983.

Scientific American. Dec. 1981.

Scientific American. May 1970.

Sedeen, Margaret. "In Touch With The World." *The Incredible Machine.* Washington D.C.: National Geographic Society, 1986.

Sinclair, Michael. Personal communications. Jan. 1994.

Strother, G. K. *Physics, with Applications in Life Sciences.* Boston: Houghton Mifflin Company, 1977.

Von Fieandt, Kai. *The World of Perception.* Homewood, IL: Dorsey Press, 1966.

Watkins, Christopher D. and Stephen R. Marenka. *Virtual Reality ExCursions.* Cambridge, Mass.: Academic Press, Inc., 1994.

Wegener, Peter P. *What Makes Airplanes Fly?* New York: Springer-Verlag, 1991.

Wiener, Earl L., Barbara G. Kanki, and Robert L. Helmreich, eds. *Cockpit Resource Management.* Boston: Academic Press, 1993.

Willis, Roy, ed. *World Mythology.* New York: Henry Holt, 1993.

Technology References

Abrash, Michael. "Fast Convex Polygons." *Dr. Dobb's Journal.* Mar. 1991: 129.

Abrash, Michael. "The Polygon Primeval." *Dr. Dobb's Journal.* Feb. 1991: 153.

Arbib, Michael A., and Allen R. Hanson. *Vision, Brain, and Cooperative Computation.* Cambridge, Mass.: The MIT Press, 1987.

Arvo, James. *Graphics Gems II.* Academic Press. 1991.

Blanton, Keith. "Image Extrapolation for Flight Simulator Visual Systems." *AIAA Conference.* 1988.

Carpenter, L. "A New Hidden Surface Algorithm," *Proceedings of NW76,* ACM, Seattle, WA, 1976.

Catmull, E. "A Subdivision Algorithm for Computer Display of Curved Surfaces," University of Utah, Salt Lake City, December 1974.

Embree, Paul M. and Bruce Kimble. *C Language Algorithms for Digital Signal Processing.* Englewood Cliffs, N.J.: Prentice Hall, 1991.

Escher, M.C. *The World of M. C. Escher.* New York: H.N. Abrams, 1971.

Foley, James. Andries van Dam, Steven Feiner, and John Hughes. *Computer Graphics Principles and Practice.* Reading, Mass.: Addison-Wesley, 2nd ed., 1990.

Fuchs, H., Kadem, Z. "On Visible Surface Generation by a Priori Tree Structures," *Computer Graphics,* vol. 14, no. 3, pp. 124–133, 1980.

Glassner, Andrew S. *An Introduction to Ray Tracing.* Academic Press, 1989.

Glassner, Andrew S. *Graphics Gems.* Academic Press, 1990.

Harrington, Stephen. *Computer Graphics, A Programming Approach,* McGraw-Hill Book Company, New York, 1987.

Heckbert, P. S. "Survey of Texture Mapping," *IEEE Computer Graphics and Applications,* 6 (11), pp. 56-67, 1986.

Heckbert, P. S. *Graphics Gems IV.* Academic Press, 1994.

Kirk, David. *Graphics Gems III.* Academic Press, 1992.

Morley, T. D. and A. D. Andrew. *Linear Algebra Projects Using Mathematica.* McGraw-Hill, Inc., 1993.

Newell, M. E., Newell, R. G., Sancha, T. L. "A New Approach to the Shaded Picture Problem," *Proceedings of the ACM National Conference,* 1972.

Newman, W. M. and Sproull, R. F. *Principles of Interactive Computer Graphics,* McGraw-Hill, New York, 1981.

Pavlidis, Theo, *Algorithms for Graphics and Image Processing.* Rockville, MD.: Computer Science Press, 1982.

Peachy D. R. "Solid Texturing of Complex Surfaces," *Computer Graphics*, 19 (3), pp. 253--259, 1985.

Perlin, K. "An Image Synthesizer," *Computer Graphics*, 19 (3), pp. 287--296, 1985.

Press, William H., Brian P. Flannery, Saul A. Teukolsky, and William T. Vetterling. *Numerical Recipes in C: The Art of Scientific Computing.* Cambridge University Press, 1988.

Rigden, John, S. *Physics and the Sound of Music - 2nd Edition.* John Wiley & Sons, 1985.

Sutherland, I. E., Sproull, R. F., and Schumacker, R. "A Characterization of Ten Hidden-Surface Algorithms," Computing Surveys, 6 (1), pp. 1--55, 1974.

Watkins, Christopher D., and Stephen R. Marenka. *Introduction to Photorealism and Ray Tracing.* New York, New York: M&T Books, 1994.

Watkins, Christopher D., and Stephen R. Marenka. *Virtual Reality ExCursions.* Cambridge, Mass.: Academic Press, Inc., 1994.

Watkins, Christopher D., Alberto Sadun, and Stephen R. Marenka. *Modern Image Processing: Warping, Morphing and Classical Techniques.* Cambridge, Mass.: Academic Press, Inc., 1993.

Watkins, Christopher D., Stephen B. Coy, and Mark Finlay. *Photorealism and Ray Tracing in C.* New York, New York: M&T Books, 1992.

Watkins, Christopher D., and Larry E. Sharp. *Programming in 3 Dimensions: Ray Tracing and Animation.* New York, New York: Henry-Holt and M&T Publishing, Inc., 1992.

Watkins, Christopher D., and Roger T. Stevens. *Advanced Graphics Programming in C and C++.* New York, New York: M&T Books., 1991.

Watkins, Christopher D., and Roger T. Stevens. *Advanced Graphics Programming in Turbo Pascal.* New York, New York: Henry-Holt and M&T Publishing, Inc., 1990.

Watt, Alan. *Fundamentals of Three—Dimensional Computer Graphics.* Addison-Wesley, 1989.

Wolberg, George. *Digital Image Warping.* IEEE Computer Society Press Monograph, 1990.

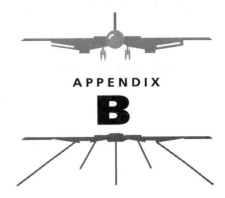

Terrain Generation and Other Issues

This appendix covers some additional issues that are quite important to modern flight simulators, but were not adequately covered earlier in this book—the issue of fractal terrain generation in particular. It also includes totally non-directly-related but interesting material.

Fractal Terrain Generation and A Fractal Sparkgap

Let's briefly take a look at how fractal geometry is used to create the wonderful terrain found in many flight simulation systems.

The Programs

*SPARKGAP resolution roughness soun*d generates a lightning-arc spark-gap effect using the basic algorithm for terrain generation. *Resolution* relates to the number of line segments used to approximate the arc (20.0), *roughness* sets the jaggedness of the arc (0.15), and *sound* turns on (1) and off (0) sound effects.

TERRAIN spread tilt seed creates a fractal terrain using recursive midpoint subdivision, and renders the terrain using the horizon rendering method, and the standard polygon rendering method. *Spread* smoothens a surface by setting for the surface normal calculation the radial number of averaged surrounding surface normals. A value of 0 means that only the one surface normal is computed. A value of 1 means that the one surface normal and the surrounding 8 surface normals are all averaged together to make one surface normal. A value of 2 means that 25 surface normals are averaged to yield the one. Keep this number small, as the time taken to compute the scene increases rapidly (by the square) with increasing spread. *Tilt* represents the angle for viewing. Values around 15 degrees will work well. (Spread and tilt only affect the horizon rendering.) *Seed* is the pseudo-random number generator seed. By changing this number, you will get your own private terrain scene. Since *seed* seeds the random number generator, you are practically guaranteed to generate the same terrain scenes with the same seeds, over and over again.

Some Thoughts

The term *fractal geometry* was coined by Benoit Mandelbrot to describe the attributes of certain natural phenomena such as coastlines and plantlife. A coastline, as seen at a microscopic level (surfaces of rocks), or at a macroscopic level (from an airplane), will tend to exhibit similar roughness and configuration. This is a kind of statistical self-similarity. Fractal geometry provides a mathematical description for this phenomenon in nature, and its tendency towards self-similarity.

Generating Terrain Data

In computer graphics, and especially "photorealistic" flight simulation equipment, fractal geometry has been used to create terrain models through use of the recursive subdivision of a line or polygon. Imagine that you have a line. Imagine that you bend the line near the center so that you now have two slightly differing length lines. Now bend each of those lines near their centers, and so on, and so on, until there is nothing else left to bend (given your limited non-magnified eyesight). Your original straight line is now a rough line (or more correctly a large collection of small lines). The roughness is based on how much you bent the line segments with each recursive bending pass. Your rough line might resemble a coastline or the edge of a rock. Carry this idea into three-dimensions. You have a planar surface such as a single page of paper. You offset the center of the page, so now you have four smaller "pages" or polygons.

Do the same center-offsetting for each of those four polygons. Then for each of the new resulting sets of polygons, on and on, until you can do no more. Your sheet of paper may now resemble a mountain, or some type of terrain. This process is called *recursive midpoint subdivision*, and if you add a little randomness to how you offset and bend things (in height offset, and in your choices of bending points), you technically have a *random fractal*. The randomness will help to add to the realism. Your random fractal exhibits two interesting qualities; it is self similar in that it has similar texture throughout, and it is no longer a two-dimensional sheet of paper, nor does it completely fill a three-dimensional volume. This is where the name fractal comes in; it has *fractal dimension*. It is more complex than a 2-D planar surface, but is not quite a solid 3-D object, so we say it has *fractional dimension*, that is, dimension somewhere in between 2-D and 3-D. For those now interested in generally how we render our fractal terrain, read on. For more details, also see the book *Advanced Graphics Programming in C and C++* by Roger T. Stevens and Christopher D. Watkins (New York: M&T Books).

Rendering Terrain

To begin our discussion on rendering terrain data, let's discuss the common format for such data. Our data is stored in a two-dimensional buffer called a height-field. There are *resolution* elements along each edge, *resolution* x *resolution* elements total. The height values stored in each of these element positions are scaled so as to fit the "unit" cube (that is, a *resolution* x *resolution* element two-dimensional array whose element values are *0* to *resolution-1*). The values found at the x-y array element locations are considered to be z values, or height values of the terrain at that x-y location.

Shading and Illumination

As you might imagine, we must generally simulate the way light reflects from objects in order to create scenes that look somewhat realistic. We call this a local lighting model. The surface normal is important for us in the computation of such a lighting (or illumination) model. Given a point

$$\mathbf{P} = (x_i, y_j, z_{i,j}),$$

the surface normal is given as

$$\mathbf{n} = ({}^{dx}/_r, {}^{dy}/_r, {}^{dz}/_r)$$

where

$$dx = z_{i,j} - z_{i+1,j}$$
$$dy = z_{i,j-1} - z_{i,j}$$
$$dz = 1 / (resolution-1)$$

and

$$r = \text{sqrt}(dx^2 + dy^2 + dz^2).$$

Such a technique for surface normal calculation works very well for smooth surfaces. For many fractal surfaces and terrains, you must make averages over several such approximations for nearby points.

Actual calculation of a reflected light ray is necessary. Given the surface normal **n** and the light direction vector **l**, you can compute the reflected light vector **r**.

$$\mathbf{r} = 2 \cos \theta \cdot \mathbf{n} - \mathbf{l}$$

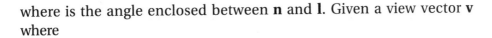

where is the angle enclosed between **n** and **l**. Given a view vector **v** where

$$\mathbf{v} = (\, 0, -\cos\phi, \sin\phi \,)$$

with ϕ representing the tilt of the terrain ($\phi=0$ as a side view, and $\phi = \pi/2$ as a top view), and given that α denotes the angle between the view vector **v** and the reflected vector **r**, we can develop a simple illumination model taking into account the diffuse and specular reflection of light as:

if $(\cos\,\theta < 0)$

    // we are on the back side of the object, so only add

    // the ambient light

    $I(\mathbf{P}) = I_a$

else

    $I(\mathbf{P}) = I_a + f_d \cos\theta + f_s\,(\cos\alpha\,)^b$

I_a denotes the ambient (from everywhere light, or inherent light) contribution of light. This is really a fudge factor regarding reflection, since we are not computing all light energies within the scene properly (called *radiosity* from heat-transfer systems). f_d and f_s are weight factors for diffuse and specular reflection. And b is an exponent that controls the shininess of the surface. Note that *diffuse reflection* is based entirely on the light source direction and surface normal here. This is like the way you might see a planet's moon from outer space, where the brightest part of the moon is the one closest to the sun, and there is a gradual (by cosine) decay in intensity until you hit the edge going to the other (dark) side of the moon (great album).

Specular reflection is based on the direction of the viewer, and the direction of the reflected light vector (which was based on the surface normal and light direction vector). It is seen as the bright spot of light on a surface that follows you as you walk by the surface. This is a direct reflection of the light source into your eye. The size of the specular reflection is determined by the specular exponent. The greater the exponent, the tighter the bright spot. The diffuse refection model is sometimes called the *Lambertian shading model,* and the complete model, encompassing the specular reflection and exponent is called the *Phong shading model.* The Phong shading model is used widely in computer graphics. See Chapter 21 for more details on techniques. Also see the book *Photorealism and Ray Tracing in C* (New York: M&T Books) by Christopher D. Watkins and Stephen B. Coy.

Rendering Techniques

We have two rendering techniques by which to process our height field, the first is called the *horizon rendering method,* and the second is the more applicable and common *polygon rendering method.*

As mentioned above, we have a height buffer of *resolution* elements in x, and *resolution* elements in y, with element values (heights) spanning from 0 to *resolution*-1. This is our unit cube. The surface that we plan to render lies in this unit cube.

For the horizon rendering method, we use parallel projection to get our surface from the unit cube to the screen. We do this such that one column of data elements is projected to one column of the screen. Given that we will view the surface at angle ϕ as described above, the projection from the three-dimensional unit cube to the two-dimensional screen is given by

$$(x, y, z) \longrightarrow (x, y\sin\phi + z \cos\phi).$$

As described in the illumination model, $\phi=0$ is a side view (as though you were looking at the terrain edge-wise), and $\phi=\pi/2$ is a top view (as though you were looking directly down onto the terrain).

For the horizon rendering method, slices of the surface that are parallel to the y-z plane are projected onto vertical lines of the screen (parallel to the y-axis of the screen). Thus we can render the lines one at a time and independently of each other. Define the integer part of the y-value of the projection of a point (x, y, z) in pixel units as

$$P(y, z) = (\texttt{AlgDefs\_int})[(resolution - 1) \times (y\sin\phi + z\cos\phi)].$$

Then rendering is simple. Project the data points for a given column, one-by-one, starting at the front and moving towards the back. A variable called *horizon* keeps track of the current maximum height for all of the projected y-values for the given column. If a point is projected below this horizon, you do not see it; else the surface normal and the intensity are computed and the intensity stored into the given screen pixel. The *horizon* variable is now updated with this new height. What happens when there is more that one pixel left out between the old and new horizons? Interpolation is what happens. If we compute the intensity at our new horizon, and interpolate intensities linearly between the new and old horizon intensities for the pixels between the new and old horizons, we perform Gouraud shading. If we interpolate surface normals and recompute intensities for the intermediate pixels, we perform *Phong shading*.

And finally, for the polygon rendering method, we use perspective projection to get our surface from the unit cube onto the screen. Here the same operations that got our flight simulator polygon vertices projected will project our terrain. Once projected, polygon filling routines will fill the polygons to make a solid surface.

References

Advanced Graphics Programming in C and C++ by Roger T. Stevens and Christopher D. Watkins (New York: M&T Books).

Photorealism and Ray Tracing in C (New York: M&T Books) by Christopher D. Watkins and Stephen B. Coy.

Virtual Reality ExCursions (Academic Press) by Christopher D. Watkins and Stephen R. Marenka.

The Science of Fractal Images by Peitgen and Saupe (Springer-Verlag).

Computing the Number Pi

The Program

PI x computes the number π to **x** number of decimal places.

Some Thoughts

π is important to us, as much of the software in the book requires π for proper calculation of lighting and viewing vectors, and for positioning and orienting objects. π relates the circumference of a circle to its radius. (C = 2πr). Thus, π is very valuable for determining the path that a point will move when an object or a viewer is rotated, for instance. Commonly the sine and cosine functions found in compilers will require their angle arguments to be in radian measure, which invokes π. Arctangent functions commonly return their values as radian measures. π radians is equivalent to our more familiar 180 degrees. Note that 2π radians is 360 degrees. Take a quick look at the circumference calculation again, and think about a circle having 360 degrees. π, which is equal to 3.14159, is an irrational number, thus it cannot be exactly represented by a quotient of integers (sorry...it doesn't equal 22/7). This means that π can only be approximated to a certain number of decimal places. Let's take a brief look at how the number π is approximated.

Archimedes (c.287-212 BC) gave the approximation of π to be:

$$3^1/_7 > \pi > 3^{10}/_{71}.$$

Around 200 AD the Chinese mathematician Liu Hui uses—what else—polygons, to calculate π as 3.14159. (Later, Hui solves equations with "Horner's" method, 1600 years before Horner.)

Viéta (1540–1603) gave the iterative computation formula for p to be:

$$2/\pi = \text{sqrt}(\tfrac{1}{2}) \times \text{sqrt}(\tfrac{1}{2} + \tfrac{1}{2}\,\text{sqrt}(\tfrac{1}{2})) \times \text{sqrt}(\tfrac{1}{2} + \tfrac{1}{2}\,\text{sqrt}(\tfrac{1}{2} + \tfrac{1}{2}\,\text{sqrt}(\tfrac{1}{2}))) \times \ldots$$

which Turnbull calls "the first actual formula for the time-honored number π."

Other interesting iterative (or recursive) formulas for the approximation of π are Lord Brouncker's

$$\pi/4 = 1 / (1 + 1^2 / (2 + 3^2 / (2 + 5^2 / (2 + ...))))$$

and Wallis'

$$\pi/4 = \frac{(2 \times 4 \times 4 \times 6 \times 6 \times 8 \times ...)}{(3 \times 3 \times 5 \times 5 \times 7 \times 7 \times ...)}$$

Of all of the formulas for computation of the number π, Liebniz's formulation was on the track for being the most useful:

$$\pi/4 = 1 - 1/3 + 1/5 - 1/7 + ...$$

This mathematical series comes from the series for $\tan^{-1}x$, where

$$\tan^{-1}x = x - x^3/3 + x^5/5 + x^7/7 + ... \text{ where } |x| <= 1.$$

If we put $x = 1$, $\tan^{-1}(1) = p/4$, we get Leibniz's formula:

$$p/4 = 1 - 1/3 + 1/5 - 1/7 + 1/9 - ... + (-1)^{(n-1)} / _{(2n-1)} + ...$$

Since this series converges quite slowly, it is not used to compute π in practice to many decimal places. Since the series $\tan^{-1}x$ converges most rapidly when x is near 0, people who use the series for $\tan^{-1}x$ to compute π use trigonometric identities so that x is near 0. See *Calculus and Analytic Geometry* by Thomas and Finney (6th edition) for an example. In recent times, Jean Guilloud and Martine Boyer quickly computed π using the arctangent series. Eugene Salamin's algorithm produces sequences that converge to π even more rapidly than the arctangent series. See "Computation of π using arithmetic-geometric mean," in *Mathematics of Computation*, 30, July, 1976, pp. 565-570 for an algorithm. In 1989, π was computed to over one billion places by a Japanese team using a Hitac computer; this certainly beats the value 4, which π was declared to be *by law* in 1897 by the General Assembly of Indiana (look it up—House Bill No. 246).

References

World of Mathematics, Vol 1 (New York : Simon and Schuster, 1956), p. 121, 138.

Calculus and Analytic Geometry, 6th edition (Addison Wesley Publishers, 1984, by Thomas and Finney).

Computing Prime Numbers

The Program

PRIMES x   computes all of the prime numbers less than a certain number **x.**

Some Thoughts

Prime numbers are simply those integer numbers that cannot be divided by some integer number other than 1 or itself, in order to obtain division without a remainder (i.e. a result that is an integer number, and not real or floating point). Prime numbers are in the news today because they are the basis of some encryption schemes used by government and industry.

The Julian Day and the Modified Julian Day and the Gregorian Date

The Programs

JD_DOY   converts the Julian Day to the Gregorian Date (day of the year).

MJD_DOY	converts the Modified Julian Day to the Gregorian Date (day of the year).
DOY_JD	converts the Gregorian Date (day of the year) to the Julian Day.
DOY_MJD	converts the Gregorian Date (day of the year) to the Modified Julian Day.

 The original algorithms for the programs and some of the general information were obtained from the U.S. Naval Observatory, to whom grateful acknowledgment is made.

Some Thoughts

The Modified Julian Day (MJD) is an abbreviated version of the old Julian Day (JD) dating method, which has been in use for centuries by astronomers, geophysicists, chronologers, and others who needed to have an unambiguous dating system based on continuing day counts.

The JD counts have very little to do with the Julian calendar, which was introduced by Julius Caesar in 46 BC and was nearly universal in Western Christendom until 1582. At that time, Pope Gregory XIII directed the use of an improved calendar, now known as the Gregorian calendar. The Julian Day system was devised in 1583 by J. J. Scaliger, a true Renaissance man and all-around genius. Scaliger called Jan. 1, 4713 BC Day 1, and numbered all days consecutively from there (for example, Jan. 1, 1990 is JD 2,447,527). Scaliger named his system "Julian"—not for the ancient Roman Julius Caesar or for the Julian Calendar—but for his father, Julius Scaliger, another genius, who introduced platinum into chemistry. The JD counts days within one Julian Period of exactly 7980 Julian years of 365.25 days; that is the weak connection to the Julian calendar.

Start of the JD count is 12 NOON 1 JAN -4713 (4712 BC, Julian Proleptic Calendar). This day count conforms with the astronomical convention of starting the day at noon, in contrast to the civil practice where-by the day starts with midnight (in popular use, the belief is widespread that the day ends with midnight but this is not the proper scientific use—astronomers don't want their observing "day" interrupted by a changeover at midnight).

The Julian Period is given by the time it takes from one coincidence to the next of a solar cycle (28), a lunar cycle (19), and the Roman indiction (a tax cycle of 15 years — Roman tax collectors had their own calendar). At any rate, this period is of interest only in regard to influencing Scaliger's adoption of the start, 4713 BC, at which time all cycles counted backwards were in coincidence. This has no real scientific importance —any remote date in the past could have been picked — but it pleased Scaliger's aesthetic sense and legitimized his choice of a "kickoff" date.

The Modified Julian Day, on the other hand, was introduced by space scientists in the late 50's of this century. It is defined as

$$MJD = JD - 2400000.5$$

The half day is subtracted so that the day starts at midnight in accordance with civil time reckoning. This MJD has been sanctioned by various international commissions such as IAU, CCIR, and others who recommend it as a decimal day count that is independent of the civil calendar in use. To give dates in this system is convenient in all cases where data is collected over long periods of time. Examples are double-star and variable-star observations, the computation of time differences over long periods of time such as in the reckoning of small-rate disagreements among atomic clocks.

The MJD is a convenient dating system with only 5 digits, sufficient for most modern purposes. It is easy to complete the days of the week because the same weekday is obtained for the same remainder of the MJD after division by 7. For example,

$$MJD\ 46324 = MON.,\ 16\ SEPT,\ 1985$$

Division of the MJD by 7 gives a remainder of 5. All Mondays have this same remainder of 5.

Note that:

For 1986 the MJD = 46430 + DOY

For 1987 the MJD = 46795 + DOY

For 1988 the MJD = 47160 + DOY

For 1989 the MJD = 47526 + DOY

For 1990 the MJD = 47891 + DOY

For 1991 the MJD = 48256 + DOY

For 1992 the MJD = 48621 + DOY

For 1993 the MJD = 48987 + DOY

For 1994 the MJD = 49352 + DOY

For 1995 the MJD = 49717 + DOY

where DOY is the *Day of the respective Year,* which is provided by the built-in calendars in many computers and some word processing packages; if all else fails, there is always *The Old Farmer's Almanac.*

The MJD (and even more so the JD) has to be distinguished well from this day of the year (DOY). This is also often but erroneously called Julian Date, when in fact it is merely a Gregorian Date expressed as number of days in the year. This is a grossly misleading practice that was introduced by some who did not learn the proper terminology. It creates a confusion that should not be taken lightly. Moreover, a continuation of the use of expressions "Julian" or "J" day in the sense of a Gregorian Date makes matters even worse. It inevitably leads to dangerous mistakes and even greater confusion.

The MJD has been officially recognized by the International Astronomical Union (IAU), and by the Consultative Committee for Radio (CCIR), the advisory committee to the International Telecommunications Union (ITU). The pertinent document is

CCIR RECOMMENDATION 457-1, Use of the Modified Julian Date BY THE STANDARD FREQUENCY AND TIME-SIGNAL SERVICES.

This document is contained in the CCIR "Green Book" Volume VII. Additional, extensive documentation regarding the JD is contained in the *Explanatory Supplement to the Astronomical Ephemeris and Nautical Almanac*, and in the yearbooks themselves, now called *The Astronomical Almanac*. The *Almanac for Computers* also provides information on such matters.

Our programs JD_DOY, MJD_DOY, DOY_JD, and DOY_MJD allow an easy conversion from MJD to DOY and vice versa.

 N O T E The MJD is always referred to as a time reckoned in Universal Time (UT). The same is not true for the DOY. This is usually meant in a local time sense, but in most data given at the many observatories, most refer the DOY to UT also, except where specifically noted. One could call it something like Universal Day of the Year to emphasize the point. However, this would introduce a completely new term, not authorized by any convention. Moreover, it is not really necessary in this case to adopt a special terminology because we are logically extending the standard practice of using the UT reference as we do when we give any date or hour.

NASA sometimes uses what they call the Truncated MJD or TJD. It is the MJD less the first digit. The date used in our example above (MJD 46324 = MON., 16 SEPT, 1985) would be 6324. However, that in this case the remainder for the days of the week comes out differently (3 for Mondays).

References and Literature

U.S. Naval Observatory bulletins and circulars

Gordon Moyer, "The Origin of the Julian Day System", *Sky and Telescope*, vol. 61, pp. 311-313 (April 1981). See also a subsequent letter by R.H. van Gent, *Sky and Telescope*, vol.62, p.16 (July 1981).

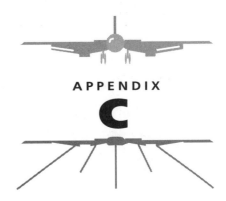

APPENDIX

C

FAA Rules, Regulatory Bodies and Simulator Companies

This appendix covers some of the rules and regulatoins involved in fligght simulation. Various requirements for different levels of acceptance for a simulator is given, as well as lists of regulatory bodies and simulator companies.

FAA Rules for Training Permissible in Visually Equipped Flight Simulator: Visual System Requirements

And now for lists of criteria for varying levels of training permissible for levels of acceptance.

Phase I—Recency of Experience, Night Takeoff and Landing, and Proficiency Checks

- Night Scenes

- Operational Landing Lights

- Visual response—300 ms max

- Tests for comparing response time with airplane data

- Minimum 45 deg. Field of View

- Automatic focusing

- Provide cues to assess sink rate and depth perception during landings

- Scene to instrument correlation

- Compatible with aerodynamic programming

- Adequate Runway Feature Resolution:

    - 5 Miles: Runway, Taxiway, Strobes, Approach Lights, Edge Lights, VASIs

    - 3 Miles: Runway Centerline Lights

    - 2 Miles: Threshold and Touchdown Zone Lights

    - Within Landing Lights: Threshold, Centerline, Touchdown Zone Markings

Phase II—Transition Training , Upgrade to Captain, and Phase I

- Dusk Scenes
- At least three specific airports with general terrain characteristics and significant landmarks
- System Response—150 ms max
- 75 deg. horiz. by 30 deg. vert. minimum continuous field of view per pilot seat
- Permissible display gaps are in airplane or as required by visual system hardware
- Radio aids oriented to airport runway layout
- Weather representations:
  - Variable cloud density
  - Partial obscuration of ground (scattered/broken) clouds
  - Gradual break out
  - Patchy fog
  - Fog effect on airport lighting
  - Category II and III conditions
- Capability for moving ground and air hazards
- Quick system readiness test procedure

Phase III—Initial Training and Phase II

- Daylight Scenes
- Full color presentation
- No display gaps

- Sufficient scene content to recognize a specific airport, the terrain and major surrounding landmarks and to accomplish a visual landing

- 4000 edges or 1000 surfaces for daylight and 4000 light points for night and dusk

- 6 foot-lamberts (fL) of light at the pilot's eye (highligh)

- Cockpit ambient lighting of 5 fL at knee height or 2 fL from pilot's face without visual display washout

- 3 arc-min resolution

- Landing illusions (over water, runway gradient, rising terrain)

- Thunderstorm precipitation

- Wet and snow-covered runways (Reflections and obscuring of runway lights)

- Realistic color and directionality of airport lighting

- Visual/weather radar correlation

- Display free of apparent quantization and other distracting visual effects

Some Regulatory Bodies

And now a list of some of the major regulatory bodies handling flight simulation. These groups are involved in defining and administering the rules and regulations set out for flight simulation and training devices.

International Civil Aviation Organization (ICAO)

Documents

Manual of Criteria for the Qualification of Flight Simulators, 1993.

International Air Transport Association (IATA)

European Joint Airworthiness Authority (JAA)

U.S. Federal Aviation Administration (FAA)

Documents

Advisory Circular 120-40B, *Airplane Simulator and Visual System Qualification.*

FAR 121-14H, *Aircraft Simulator and Visual Ssytem Evaluation and Approval.*

Address

National Simulator Program Manager (NSPM)

Department of Transportation

Federal Aviation Administration

800 Independence Avenue SW

Washington, DC 20591

United Kingdom Civil Aviation Authority (CAA)

Documents

CAP 453, *The Approval of Flight Simulators for the Training and Testing of Flight Crews in Civil Aviation.*

Address

Chief Inspector Flight Operations
Flight Operations Inspectorate
Civil Aviation Authority
Aviation House
129 Kingsway
London WC2B 6NN

Some Flight Simulation Companies

Atlantis Aerospace Corp.
1 Kenview Blvd.
Brampton, Ontario,
Canada LT6 5E6
905-792-1981

Binghamton Simulator Company Inc.
4 Chenango Street
Binghamton, NY 13901-2902
607-722-6504

Burket (subsidiary of Thomson CSF)
7041 E. 15th St.
P.O. Box 1677
Tulsa, OK 74101
918-831-2334

CAE Electronics
C.P. 1800 Saint-Laurant
Quebec, Canada H4L 4X4
514-341-6780

Evans and Sutherland
P.O. Box 8700
580 Arapeen Dr.
Salt Lake City, Utah 84108

FlightSafety International
Marine Air Terminal
LaGuardia Airport
Flushing, NY 11371
718-565-4126

Frasca International
906 East Airport Road
Urbana, IL 61801
217-344-9200

Gemini Technology Corporation
5 Jenner Street,
Suite 165 Irvine,
California 92718
(800) 827-1980, (714) 727-1980, Fax: (714) 727-3066

Image Data Corporation
600 South Lake Ave. Second Floor,
Pasadena, California, 91106
(818) 796-9155, Fax: (818) 796-8574

Ivex Corporation
4357 J Park Drive,
Norcross, Georgia 30093
(404) 564-1148, Fax: (404) 381-0622, Telex: 6503144415 MCIUW

Martin Marretta
6801 Rockledge Dr.
Bethesda, MD 20817
Reflectone
4906 Tampa West Boulevard
Tampa FL 33634
813-885-7481

Companies providing Low-End Simulators:

AST

ATC

Binghamton

CTA

ECC

ETC

Frasca

Simtec

TRO

WICAT

Companies providing High-End Simulators:

Atlantis

CAE Electronics

Contraves

CSC

FlightSafety

Loral Corporation/Quintron

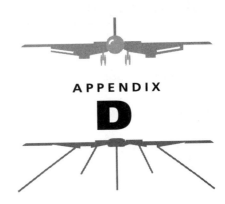

The C Programming Language

This appendix is intended both as an introduction to the C programming language and as a description of the kind of programming style that we adhere to in the programs accompanying this book. Some familiarity with programming is required.

Since the code was developed primarily by one person over a year or so, the style changes just a little from module to module. This is inevitable in any creative and time-consuming project. We wanted to develop certain programming practices to make the project go more smoothly. We do not intend to lecture you on what our idea of good programming style is. Rather, we merely want to give you the benefit of our experience of which techniques do and do not work.

Advantages of the C Language

The C language has become the language of choice for the development of most complex modern software, such as programs for interactive computer graphics and scientific simulations. Though classified as a high-level language, it allows the scientist and engineer to produce code whose efficiency approaches that of assembly language for real-time applications. It was initially available only on larger machines and certain operating systems, but is now available on just about every system around, including IBM compatibles.

The C language has many advantages over FORTRAN and Pascal. C's portability between machines of both the UNIX and MS-DOS platforms makes it quite appealing to those who have little choice of which machines to use. The C data structures are well-suited for graphics programming, due to their inherent modularity. Fast, efficient compilers, debuggers, and other tools are now available, which makes using C the attractive choice for large projects. The C language is most appropriate for the development of general library routines, which can be used as the building blocks for many graphics programs.

Naturally, the C code is much quicker and easier to develop than its equivalent assembly code. Without too much effort, the C code efficiency can approach that of assembly code. What may take days to program in assembly code can take as little as half an hour in C. The added performance that assembly might provide is not worth the effort in developing it. It is often the case (such as in using Borland C++) that C and assembly code can be mixed together in the same program. Such a hybrid can have a main program and human interface written in C, and other routines that are computationally intensive (such as mathematics and graphics modules) would be written in assembly. Now that we have established that C is the program language of choice for our purposes, let's see how it is used in the development of graphics applications.

The Main Element for Expressing an Algorithm

The main purpose of a programming language is to provide a means of expressing an algorithm that can then be executed by a computer. A programming language should have five basic elements in order to conform to this definition:

1. A methodology for organizing data (*data* refers to data types and variables).

2. A methodology for describing operations (these are *operators*).

3. A methodology for controlling operations based on previous operations (this is called *program control*).

4. A methodology for structuring the data and operations so that a sequence of program statements can be executed from any location within the program (these are *data structures* and *functions*).

5. A methodology for moving data between the program and the outside world (referred to as *I/O*—input/output).

How these goals are achieved in C makes up the remainder of this chapter. The following program is an example of some of the points mentioned.

Listing D.1 *A simple C program to add numbers*

```
main()
{
float    add_nums();           // declare functions
int      added,numbs_to_add;   // declare variables
int      index, i;
float    num_array[50];
```

```
float    total;

printf("\n\nNumber of numbers to add? ");
scanf("%d", &numbs_to_add);

printf("\n\nEnter numbers to add?\n ");
for(index=0; index<numbs_to_add; index++)
{
    i = scanf("%f", &num_array[index]);
    if (i != 1) break;
}

total = add_nums(num_array, numbs_to_add);

    printf("\n\nTotal is %f", total);
}



float add_nums(array, array_size)
float array[], int array_size
{
int i;
float sum=0.0;

    for(i=0; i<array_size; i++)
    sum = sum + array[i];
    return(sum);
}
```

Listing AD-1 is of a sample C program that sums numbers and contains each of the elements mentioned above. The first line is *main*(). This declares that a program which has no arguments will be defined after the left brace (the { found on the next line) and up to the line just before the next function called *add_nums*. The main program is the main control of the program. This is the first executed part of the program.

The next line declares the functions that are called throughout the main program. The function addnums will sum the elements of an array called array of length array_size and return this value. This corresponds to goal 1, providing a means to organize data—in this case, using the array data construct. The term // is used for comments at the end of a line (on many compilers). The /* and */ can be used to define multiple line comments on all compilers. Notice next that we declare variables such as "added" and "numbs_to_add."

Input is then taken regarding the number of numbers that you wish to add together (goal 5, interaction with the outside world). The program then prompts you to enter the actual numbers into an array for later addition. The function add_nums is then called to add the numbers found in the array and return the value to a variable called "total." The provision for functions and operators satisfies goal 4. Within addnums, a for loop is used to cycle through the array and add all of the elements together. This corresponds to goal 3, program execution control. The provision of operators like + and - satisfies goal 2. The result from add_nums() is subsequently displayed on the terminal.

Variable Types

Computer programs operate by the manipulation of information represented in some digital format. A variable in C is defined by a declaration of an alphanumeric group of characters which, for all references to that variable, will recall the number assigned to it. This variable name (*identifier*) must start with a letter or an underscore and cannot be the same as the standard or compiler-specific C key words. Note that C is a case-sensitive language—numbs_to_add is different from Numbs_To_Add and Numbs_to_add, for instance.

There are many different number types in C. Table AD-1 shows some of the standard types and how they are represented internally.

Table D.1 *Variables declarations in C*

Variable declaration	Number of bits	32-bit range
char	8	-128 -> 127
unsigned char	8	0 -> 255
short	16	-32768 - > 32767
unsigned short	16	0 -> 65535
int	32 (16)	-2.1e9 -> 2.1e9
unsigned int	32 (16)	0 -> 4.3e9
long	32	-2.1e9 -> 2.1e9
unsigned long	32	0 -> 4.3e9
float	32	-1e-38 -> 1e38
double	64	-1e-308 -> 1e308

Arrays

Most high-level languages allow for the definition of indexed lists, more commonly referred to as *arrays*. Arrays can also be multidimensional. Such multidimensional arrays are implemented in C as an array of arrays. An element of such an array can be accessed in the following way:

```
type name_of_array[size1][size2]...[sizeN]
```

This example shows an N-dimensional array of a generic type. The specific types available are those listed in Table AD-1 (such as *int* and *double*). In C the size for each dimension is held in brackets, whereas in many languages the sizes of each dimension are separated by commas.

Text data types such as char actually define 8-bit numbers that represent an alphanumeric character (ASCII). Strings in C are terminated with a NULL (ASCII 0) character. So a 35-character message will actually occupy 36 bytes (characters) of data. Some particularly useful characters are:

Table D.2

Character	Description
\\	Defines a backslash.
\'	Defines an apostrophe.
\"	Defines a quote.
\n	Defines a carriage return line feed.
\xhhh	Defines a hexadecimal ASCII character.

Operators

Here we are referring to the methods used to manipulate variables and actually produce some sort of useful result. The C language seems to have a nearly endless set of *operators* (mathematical functions) to perform both mathematical and logical operations. C++ compounds this tremendously by allowing you to define your own operators on your very own data types. Some of the more common types of operators are presented below.

- **Assignment operators** assign a value to a variable. The equal sign is the assignment operator.

- **Arithmetic** and **bitwise operators** are used to perform multiplication, division, addition, subtraction, and modulus (integer remainder after division). The modulus operator works only on integer-type variables, whereas all of the other operators will work with all variable types. In C, there are three unary arithmetic operators, the unary minus (-), an increment (++), and a decrement (– –). The increment and decrement are usually used with pointers (data addresses).

- **Binary bitwise operations** are performed on integer operands using the ampersand (&) for AND, the pipe (l) for OR, the caret (^) for bitwise exclusive OR (XOR), two less than symbols (<<) for the arithmetic shift left, and two greater symbols (>>) for the arithmetic shift right. The number of bits is the operand for the arithmetic shifts. The unary bitwise NOT operator will invert all of the bits in the operand. The symbol for this is the tilde (~).

Operators can be combined using the assignment operator and any of the arithmetic operators. A few examples are listed below.

```
a = a+b    a += b
a = a-b    a -= b
a = a*b    a *= b
a = a/b    a /= b
a = a%b    a %= b
a = a&b    a &= b
a = a|b    a |= b
a = a^b    a ^= b
a = a<<b   a <<= b
a = a>>b   a >>= b
```

For readability of code during development, many programmers do not use the combined operators. They can be very useful, though, if instead of the variable *a*, you have some kind of complicated pointer expression. In this way, you don't have to enter it on both sides of the expression, and the meaning is a little clearer. That is, you want to modify the value and store it back in the same location.

Logical operators are operators that yield an absolute, true, or false response. They are commonly used to control loops and to perform machine level coding. The double equal sign (==) operator is used to determine the equality of two arguments. Do not confuse this with the equal (=) assignment operator. The less-than sign (<) is the less than comparison operator. The less than or equal to sign (<=) is the less than or equal comparison operator. The greater than or equal to sign (>=) and greater than (>) logical operators are greater than or equal to, and greater than logical comparisons, respectively. The exclamation point and equal sign together (!=) is the not equal to logical operator. And the

last three logical operators are double ampersands (&&) for AND, double pipe (||) for OR, and the exclamation point (!) for NOT.

Our last glance at operators takes us into the subject of operator precedence (the order in which multiple operations will be performed in the absence of () to clarify it) and type conversion. Here is a list of operators in decreasing precedence:

Table D.3

Operator	Precedence
++ – –	Increment, decrement
-	Unary minus
* / %	Multiplication, division, modulus
+ -	Addition, subtraction
<< >>	Shift left, shift right
< <= >= >	Comparison with less than or greater than
== !=	Equal, not equal
& ^ |	Bitwise AND, XOR, OR
&& ||	Logical AND, OR

Conversion Operations

A few rules regarding C and the conversion of types must be taken to heart. First, if an operation involves two types, the one of higher rank takes precedence. The ranking from highest to lowest is *double, float, long, int, short,* and *char.* Unsigned outranks signed. For example, if you add a float and a double together, the float is promoted to type double and then added to the double variable. The result is then converted to the type of variable on the left-hand side of the assignment. In an assignment statement, the result is converted to the type of the variable being assigned.

The next discussion describes how to control the conditional execution or repetition of certain statements based on the results of certain expressions. We start with conditional execution. The If-Else statement is used to execute conditionally a series of statements based on the results of some expression. Its format is as follows:

```
if (integer_value)
{
    first set of statements
}
else
{
    second set of statements
}
```

If integer_value is nonzero, then the first set of statements are executed, else the second set of statements are executed. Note that compound statements can be created with the If-Else statement by use of brackets enclosing certain statements.

The switch statement is another useful statement when more than four alternatives are chosen for a situation. The statement reads as follows:

```
switch(integer_expression)
{
    case constant1:
            statements;
            break;

    case constant2:
            statements;
            break;

    case constant3:
            statements;
            break;
```

```
    case constant4:
            statements;
            break;

    default:
            statements;
}
```

C also supports an unusual kind of single-line conditional expression that lets you express a single If-Else statement in one line. The form for such an expression is:

```
expression1 ? expression2 : expression3.
```

If expression1 is nonzero, then the whole conditional expression has the value of expression2. If expression1 is zero, then the whole expression has the value of expression3. This type of expression should never be used directly in your code. However, it can be used to define a macro that will be very efficient to execute. For example, we can define a macro to find the maximum of two variables as :

```
#define MAX(a,b) ( (a) > (b) ? (a) : (b) )
```

C supports this type of expression because it can usually be implemented efficiently by the compiler. Since macros are usually in-line substitutions, the MAX function above will be performed efficiently.

Loops

The next basic program control construct is the *loop* (where a collection of instructions with the loop are repeated until some condition is met). C has three loop types: the while loop, the do-while loop, and the for loop. The while loop takes the form :

```
while(expression)
    statements;
```

The while loop will repeat the statements until the expression becomes zero. The decision to pass through the loop is made at the beginning, so we may never pass through it. The format for the do-while loop is as follows :

```
do
{
    statements;
} while(expression);
```

The do-while loop repeats the statements until the expression becomes zero. Note that the decision to pass through this loop is made at the end of the loop; therefore, we will always pass through this loop at least once. Finally, we have the for loop, which is a more general form of a FORTRAN do loop. The for loop looks as follows:

```
for(initial condition; test condition; modify)
    statements;
```

The for loop is commonly used for indexing arrays. It is an infinite loop if no bounds are set, that is, if you leave out the test condition all together. The initial condition is the initial value for a variable. The test condition may be any logical expression but is usually a comparison of the loop variable to some ending value like i < 10. The loop variable is usually altered by the modify expression, such as i++.

Control Statements

Now we jump into other program control issues. C provides three additional control statements: break, continue, and goto. Note that these statements can make a complex program difficult to follow but are often quite handy. As shown earlier, the break statement can be used to exit a switch statement or any other type of loop. The continue statement, on the other hand, tells the program to skip to end of the loop and proceed with the next iteration. Goto is just that, a statement that will carry you to any other place in the program, exiting out of any loop that you might be in at the time.

Functions

Now that we know a little more about variables, data types, and program control, let's move our focus to the all important *function* (a segment of code that will likely be called more than once if made from a collection of instructions). All C programs consist of one or more functions; even main() is considered a function. A function has a type, a name, a pair of parentheses containing an optional argument list, and a pair of braces containing an optional list of executable statements. The format is as follows:

```
type name(argument list)
    declarations for arguments in argument list
{
    body of function (statements)
}
```

The type is that of the value the function returns. C provides a special data type of *void* for functions that do not return a value. The types for the arguments in the argument list are located in the second line of the function. Within the function body, the return statement returns a number as the value of the function. Many of the recent batch of compilers allow the declarations for the arguments in the argument list to be included in the parentheses. This type of declaration corresponds to the ANSI standard version of C as well as to C++.

C makes extensive use of header files, traditionally having the extension of .h, to define data structures and to declare functions. The ANSI standard supports the use of function prototypes to define not only the return value of a function but also the data types of its arguments. Note that for C, function prototypes are optional, whereas C++ requires them. Function prototypes allow the compiler to do much more extensive error checking of your code at compile time. Calling a function with the wrong number, type of argument, or both is very common. If the function has a prototype, the compiler can check each of the calls to see that the correct number and type of variables are passed to the function. This can greatly reduce the number of mystifying bugs in a program. A typical prototype in a header file looks like:

```
extern void thefunction(int)
```

Macros

Macros (a way of redefining or representing functions and constants) and the C preprocessor make up some of the most appealing aspects of C. Because C can conditionally compile program segments, create aliases of any text in the program, and create user-defined macros, it is a very powerful language. "Very powerful," however, can also be translated as *very confusing*. One short example of a macro is one that finds the greater value of two numbers. When using a macro that has arguments, *always* put the arguments in parentheses as we did in the MAX macro above. This is to ensure that if an expression is passed to the macro, the expression is evaluated before the rest of the macro is processed. Without this convention, you can create some of the most irritating and subtle bugs imaginable.

Note that the use of macros can increase the performance of your compiled code, since the particular block of code that the macro represents will be inserted into your into your compiled code many times by the macro, saving time-costly address jumps.

Pointers

Pointers are variables that hold addresses of the data, rather than the data itself. Pointers are primarily used to access different data elements within an array, to allow for dynamic memory allocation, and to access different locations in a data structure. They are also used to pass structures as arguments. C uses the call-by-value convention for argument passing. This means that it passes a *copy* of the data to the function, not the data itself. If you want the function to be able to modify the actual variable, you must pass a pointer to that variable. If you want to pass some huge structure to a function, you pass the pointer; otherwise, the program will copy the entire structure each time the function is called. This would be most inefficient.

There are three pointer operators: *, &, and ->. The first is called the indirection operator. The indirection operator is used whenever the data stored at the address pointed to by a pointer is required (thus, indirect addressing). The second pointer operator fetches the address of the variable to which it is applied. For example, &a is the address of a. The third pointer operator is the member access operator. If s is a pointer to a structure, then s->member is the element member of that particular structure.

Memory Allocation

Unlike FORTRAN, C fully supports dynamic memory allocation. There are four standard functions used to manipulate memory in C. The first function is *malloc*. The malloc() function allocates a chunk of memory of whatever size (in bytes) that you pass to it. It returns a pointer to this newly allocated memory. The *calloc()* function does the same thing except that it sets all of the memory to 0 as well. The *free()* function returns the memory allocated by malloc() or calloc() back to the system, making it available for other uses. The *realloc()* function essentially performs a free() followed by another malloc(). It recognizes the case that you may want less memory than was already allocated, so it would give you back only the memory you already had. It is more efficient in some cases than using free() and malloc() separately.

Example uses of these functions are:

```
malloc
    int *pointer;       pointer = (int *)
malloc(sizeof(int));
calloc
    int *array;  array = (int *) calloc(100, sizeof(int));
```

Note the use of the *sizeof()* function. This function returns the size of data types in bytes. This makes your code system independent. For example, an *int* on a PC is usually 16 bits long, whereas on a workstation it may be 32 bits long.

One of the most useful features of C is the *structure* data type. Structures allow you to group together data types into a manageable packet. Unlike arrays, you may freely mix and match data types in whatever fashion you need. For example, you might want to define an image as:

```
struct texture_map_image
{
    int xres;
    int yres;
    int pixres;
}
```

Now let's declare a structure called *ourimage:*

```
struct texture_map_image ourimage;
```

The *ourimage* structure is now type *texture_map_image*. We can now initialize and access the data in the structure as follows:

```
ourimage.xres = 1280;
ourimage.yres = 1024;
ourimage.pixres = 32;
```

We can also declare a pointer to such a structure as:

```
struct texture_map_image *image_ptr;
image_ptr = &ourimage;
image_ptr->xres = 1280;
image_ptr->yres = 1024;
image_ptr->pixres = 32;
```

Now all of the data for an image can be passed around in one easy-to-use package, rather than as separate arrays with confusing and complicated indexes.

C provides the capability essentially to define your own data types via the *typedef* statement. Basically, you declare one name to be equivalent to some other name, usually a structure definition. You may then use this equivalent name just as any other data type declaration like *int* or *char*. For instance, if we want another way to express our texture_map_image structure template, we can create the TEXTURE_MAP_IMAGE type.

```
typedef    struct texture_map_image    TEXTURE_MAP_IMAGE;
```

This statement replaces all occurrences of TEXTURE_MAP_IMAGE with the struct texture_map_image definition. We can now declare our image to be :

```
TEXTURE_MAP_IMAGE        ourimage;
```

which looks much cleaner than

```
struct texture_map_image        ourimage;
```

The scanf and printf functions

Two of the fundamental I/O functions in the C programming language are *scanf* and *printf*. Scanf parses a line entered by the user and places this data into a variable (or variables), much like the FORTRAN read statement. *printf* displays variables on the console in a program-specified format using a format string. A *printf* statement might look something like this:

```
printf("\nImage X Resolution = %d", ImageResX);
```

And some of the format specifiers are the following:

```
%5d         signed integer with width 5
%16p        pointer value with width 16
%5.4f       floating point number with width 5 and 4
            places past the decimal point
%5.4e       floating point number in exponential format
            with width 5 and 4 places past the decimal
            point
```

```
%c              single character
%s              string
%8x             integer in hexadecimal format with width 8
```

A few of the special escape sequences in the format string are:

```
\\ print a single backslash
%% print a single percent sign
\n carriage return and line feed
```

The scanf function is very similar to the printf function. For example:

```
scanf("%d %f", integernumber, floatingpointnumber);
```

Input/Output Functions

There are many standard C disk I/O functions, so we'll just look at the basics. Most C file access is *sequential*. That is, the file is read until you reach the end of the file. A file may be read character-by-character using the functions *getc()* and *putc()*. The functions *fprintf()*, *fsanf()*, *fgets()*, *fputs()* allow you to treat a file as a buffered stream of text. To randomly access a binary file, use *fread()*, *fwrite()*, and *fseek()*. A conventional way of handling a file might look like this:

```
FILE *file_pointer;
file_pointer =
fopen("the_filename","the_filetype_string")
fclose(file_pointer);
```

First we must open a file called the_filename, using the options specified in "the_filetype_string." The available filetype strings are:

r	open file for reading
w	create new file or overwrite old file
a	append existing file or create new file

r+	open existing file for reading and writing
w+	create a new file for reading and writing
a+	append an existing file for reading and writing

Also, a t or a b can be appended to the strings listed above to select either ASCII file format or binary. You will find that most UNIX systems will not require this distinction, as MS-DOS-based PCs do.

C programming, like any other art form, requires a great deal of practice, patience, and understanding. Many subtle tricks and nuances must be seen and tried before they can be used effectively. While pointers allow great program flexibility, they may also cause no end of grief. Typical examples are use of uninitialized global pointers or freeing the wrong portion of memory. These kinds of problems are difficult to track down as well. So, be careful and let your experience be your guide.

We have tried to make the included code fairly modular and straightforward. Modular code means keeping such things as file I/O limited to one small set of routines. Try not to put disk I/O calls throughout your code. Instead, make one set of routines to read and write each file type you support. This is only one principle of modularity. There are many xothers that are beyond the scope of the present discussion. You may wish to examine the simulator code to see both where we have tried to modularize things and where we did not because of the type of information we're presenting in this context.

Software Conventions

The easiest way to convey the software conventions used is to show examples of *pseudocode (code used for explanations—but not compliable)*. For functions and variables, the name of the file where the function or variable is located becomes the first part of the function, and this is followed by an underscore:

```
AlgMath_RAND()
```

The remainder of its name follows the underscore. Global variables are indicated by a g preceding the first letter of the variable. Global variables and local variables are both lowercase, where local variables receive no special treatment or marking. Macros are always uppercase, and look like the following:

```
#define   DAMPING_FACTOR = 3;
#define   AlgDefs_ROUND(a)    (int)((a)+0.5)
```

Data types will always take the similar form:

```
AlgDefs_point_3D_type
```

Summary

We strongly recommend that you peruse some of the references in the bibliography for further information. In particular, Kernighan and Ritchie's *The C Programming Language* is the virtual bible of C programming style and convention. There is also a wealth of other books at your local technical bookstore that can assist you.

Index

359

Tex *
3DGT **
Object 3D ReAdMe
file

CMARs